DISASTER MANAGEMENT
THROUGH THE NEW MILLENNIUM

Edited by
Ayaz Ahmad

ANMOL PUBLICATIONS PVT. LTD.
NEW DELHI - 110002 (INDIA)

ANMOL PUBLICATIONS PVT. LTD.
Regd. Office: 4360/4, Ansari Road, Daryaganj,
New Delhi-110002 (India)
Tel.: 23278000, 23261597, 23286875, 23255577
Fax: 91-11-23280289
Email: anmolpub@gmail.com
Visit us at: www.anmolpublications.com

Branch Office: No. 1015, Ist Main Road, BSK IIIrd Stage
IIIrd Phase, IIIrd Block, Bangalore-560 085 (India)
Tel.: 080-41723429 • Fax: 080-26723604
Email: anmolpublicationsbangalore@gmail.com

Disaster Management: Through the New Millennium

First Edition, 2003

ISBN 81-261-1366-9

Reprint, 2010

PRINTED IN INDIA

Printed at Mehra Offset Press, Delhi.

Contents

Preface

The word disaster, according to Oxford dictionary means; great or sudden misfortune. In the light of these meanings, one concludes that the event, which may be termed as 'disaster' should be big in magnitude. Secondly, it comes without notice. In this manner, the massive scale and the suddenness, are two essential ingredients of the destructive happening, defined as disaster. Regretfully, these days disasters are very common far more in frequency and devastation, in comparison with the past few centuries.

Disasters are of two types; natural and man-made. Natural disasters are beyond human control. We can not stop them but, we can always take precautions, which may either evade such disasters or at least lessen their effects. Man-made disasters, on the other hand, are totally manageable. One can not control cyclones, floods and earthquakes, but, any effective government can always stop terrorism, rioting and vandalism. Stopping, controlling and managing disastrous situations is termed as disaster management. Incidentally, the Oxford dictionary provides another meaning of the word 'disaster', i.e., complete failure. It simply implies that in case an establishment does not succeed in controlling a disaster, then it eventually causes another disaster with far more dangerous effects and after-effects.

Disaster Management is now a discipline and a part of governance. But, it is the irony that this exercise is quite uncultivated and undeveloped in the developing world, including India, while disasters are more common there. Hence, a need for mastering this kind of management.

The Gujarat Earthquake has opened the eyes of the society and the rulers alike. With the result, there is a spurt in discussions, research and evolution of new ways and means to rein the menace, known as disaster.

This study is a modest effort in the same direction, for understanding the problems and the occurrences and also offering suggestions for seeking a remedy for the same. The whole issue has been approached and treated in a very systematic and scientific manner, keeping the practical aspects in mind.

Hopefully, this book, though not voluminous, yet comprehensive and exhaustive in its totality, would create an awareness among all concerned and prove to be a source of enrichment, for the general readers, which may eventually help them cope with similar situations in future. If that much is achieved, the editor would feel pride in rendering a service to the society in particular and to mankind in general.

Editor

ONE

INTRODUCTION

The term 'disaster' may be defined as an unexpected happening, causing a huge loss of life and property. Major disasters may be defined as those causing at least one of three consequences which are as follows: (i) Causing damage to more than 1 per cent of Gross National Product. (ii) Causing deaths of more than 100 persons at a time and place. (iii) Affecting more than 1 per cent of the total population in an area.

According to another estimate during 1950-2001 about 6 lakh deaths took place due to major disasters out of which 1 per cent were in developed countries and 99 per cent in developing countries. Before 1950 the situation was quite different and at that time 30 per cent of total deaths took place in developed countries and 70 per cent in developing countries. These figures indicate the gravity of the situation and seriousness of the problem.

All said and done, the point remains as to how to prevent, predict and mitigate major disasters? So far through scientific and technological development the prevention of earthquakes and cyclones, floods, droughts, fires, etc., may be possible and can be predicted to some extent.

There is no doubt that a proper planning and effective management can reduce the effects and hazards of disasters, like earthquakes, since it is not the earthquake itself but the defective buildings, which cause loss of life and property.

In development, an important issue which deserves consideration in the context of Disaster Management is the bottlenecks of the development processes of the planned development.

The concept of development is illusive. To some it may mean change; (but all changes are not necessarily development) to others it may be alleviation of poverty and well-being. Still to some others 'development' represents an increase in the capacities of a society to organise for its own objective and to carry out its programmes more effectively. Some hold the Marxian conception. Thus, many of us speak of development with reference to 'social', 'cultural', 'political' and 'economic' with the qualifying connotation or adjective or of a complex amalgam of all these. However, our reference is to the tribal society and with their problems, the resolution of which is so-called tribal development.

Development is an important phenomenon of the contemporary world and it is one of the study of which anthropologists have a very clear contribution to make. Understanding the phenomenon is important, not only because its potential for good or for ill is great, but because understanding can make a difference. It concerns what people do at least as much as what happens to them, choice and decision are prominent, and not only on the developer's side. The understanding in terms of which people act is, therefore, particularly significant here. It calls for what Malinowaski called 'practical' and which may be also called Applied and Action Anthropology. To some its scope is wide, so as to encompass all anthropological research which has been helpful to government while others take a more restricted view. To achieve sustained development in a country, its people have to benefit and also feel that they have benefited. Its leader and people have to establish appropriate roles and equitable relations that are personally rewarding and socially accepted. They have to rework the system of their society and culture to cope with the new conditions, reconciling disparate sectors, establishing revised channels for conflict expression and conflict resolution, making relevant knowledge available to all social strata, linking their society with world society.

All plans for development have greater chances for success if the relevant cultural and social factors are integrated into the planning. That integration, however, should not add yet another extraneous load on already overburdened planners. Social and cultural considerations must be so presented that they are plainly appropriate to the problems at hand and are clearly useful for makers of development decisions. There is no gain from deluging planners with data they cannot deploy, with recommendations too wordy to be carefully read or too abstruse to be readily understood. There is, however, great potential gain in broadening development policies so that they include significant forces that have hitherto been largely overlooked (Mandelbaum, 1981).

All the social and behavioural sciences can be tapped for this purpose. Anthropologists have special resources to offer (Mandelbaum, 1978). Their emphasis on a holistic view disposes them to take into account the social matrix in which particular problems are embedded. Their practice of fieldwork directs attention to development as perceived from within, how the people understand, accept or reject introduced innovations (C.F. Srinivas, 1977; Wallmen, 1977). Anthropologists are also inclined to relate what they learn in the microview to the macroview, to some general perspective on the human career (c.f. Patch and McMorrow, 1977).

Seen in the longest human perspective, development is part of a series of cultural thresholds crossed by humankind. At each successive crossing people gain greater control over their environment and enrich their material circumstances, as they did when some learnt to produce their food through agriculture and herding rather than to depend only on hunting and gathering. Soon after came the great social invention of civilization with its characteristic components of specialization of work, cities, state organization, writing very recently, as human history runs, some groups learnt how to command vast amounts of energy through mechanical and industrial means. And just a few generations later there came the upsurge in science, together with the highly effective, cumulative applications of science. In making a transition, a people share certain similar consequences with others who have done so, but different groups have crossed these cultural thresholds at different times, in quite different ways, impelled by differing reasons (Eisenstadt, 1977). From the vantage of this long view, current development efforts make up a movement to enable all peoples to benefit from the newly opened cultural potentials. But it is not enough to take over more efficient tools and agricultural procedures or to import tourists and export labour. That may result in some quick economic growth, but does not necessarily lead to lasting development, to being able to maintain a continuous flow of the material benefits, to achieving social and personal rewards made possible by new technology. If a people are to maintain higher productivity, they must also establish an appropriate social and cultural infrastructure for such development (Uphoff and Ilchman, 1972; Belshaw, 1972). That infrastructure includes adapted, revised institutions, associations, education, roles rewards, values. Social capital has to be built no less than physical capital (Mandelbaum, 1981).

There is no one road to development and certainly not the identical sequence traversed by countries now deemed to be developed. Whatever course is urged or coerced by planners and political leaders, each major group within a nation, eventually judges what the purpose of development is for them, and for whom the development bells toll. The outcome of any model of development depends ultimately on the effectiveness of their participation (De Kadt, 1974; Eisenstadt, 1977).

It is true that before other measures for development can be effective, certain basic conditions must prevail. People cannot do much construction for the future if many of them are struggling for more subsistence survival. Nor can development programmes take shape if a state is torn with turmoil, its land more the scene of battles than of building. But given such basic requirements, people do respond effectively to programmes for development if the programmes are presented in terms they can understand and accept. (Mandelbaum, 1981). When the people of a country become assured that their basic material needs are reasonably well available, then their aspirations for development are likely to turn to the quality of their lives. This concept includes a great many components that are not always mutually compatible or strictly logical. But a leading element is their shared idea that they are entitled to feel self-reliant, autonomous, worthy (or superior) as a people (Wallmans, 1977).

There is a growing number of people in many nations both in the more and in the less affluent, who realize that a satisfactory quality of life does not necessarily depend on over-increasing economic growth. Development, it is true, must first of all establish reliable provisions of the basic necessities for a physically secured life. But development processes do not stop there (Mandelbaum, 1981).

Anthropologists now have more opportunity than before to contribute to development. Their own ethical and procedural problems in the field have been sufficiently arised to permit such work to proceed at a fast pace. Planners and administrators are coming to realize that their previous models have slighted some critical elements, namely the cultures and societies of the people whom and on whom development plans were enacted (cf. World Bank, 1978: 33-42). Anthropologists not only view development problems from the perspective of the people, they also try to understand particular projects as parts of a larger system. And very frequently, it is the system of social relations and cultural understandings that is critical for the success or failure of projects. For, as, we now recognize, development is not only the adaptation of advanced technology and economic programming, nor is it just another term for change. Development consists of purposive efforts by a people, led by public figures and planners, to organize themselves in new technical, cultural, and social ways. These are ways that will enable them to achieve the style and quality of life which they aspire. When their aspirations shift, the direction of development efforts much shift accordingly. (Mandelbaum, 1981). Tribal development consists of deliberate efforts by the tribals along with the planners, anthropologists and the elite groups to orient them towards the new cultural and social ways of life and actions. More adoption of new cultural and social ways of life and actions by the tribals is no longer a tribal development. When the tribals feel that the quality of life to which they aspire is in fact achieved, we may have a claim for tribal development. It may sound a dream of a Utopian society and seem even "impossible" to some of us to attain the level. The truth lies in the finding out how to approach the basic problems of the tribals and which gaps have held up the developmental process. It necessarily calls for the strategies to improve the prevailing affairs. Over the years since planning began, we have been working out strategies to improve the socio-economic conditions of weaker sections and development for the vulnerable groups. The poor, weaker, peasantry and slum dwellers were the pet subject of discussion for planners, professors and politicians until very recently. Out of gross vacillation or the inability to deal effectively with their problems, the ethos of our national feelings seems to have shifted very recently towards, the dearest of our weaker section namely the 'Scheduled Tribes'.

India is one of the few nations of the world noted for its tribal concentration. According to the 1981 census, the tribals in India account for 7.18 per cent of the total population. About 80 per cent of them live in remote forest areas and hill tracks without any access to modern socio-economic inputs.

Although there are ethnographic variations in terms of their 'anthropological identity', most tribals share certain characteristics: nature of rurality, speciality of illiteracy, economic backwardness and social deprivation. Their standard of living, judged by the standard measures of income position, calorie-intake, nutritional norms, educational standards and 'Physical Quality Life Index' (PQLI), does not fit anywhere within the scope and ambit of the Planning Commission's stylized standards. The employment problem of these communities cannot be discussed in isolation, for most of them are unemployed and a very few are engaged in traditional occupations. Their earnings, apart from the monetary angle, do not even conform to the barest minimum necessary for their sustenance. The expert definitions of the 'poverty line' or 'poverty gap' for these groups have yet to be defined or redefined.

Although Articles 15(4), 46, 244 (i) and 339 of the Indian Constitution speak of special provisions meant for the administration and control of scheduled areas and tribals therein, for their welfare and protection, except for commissions and Reports, the executive power at the action level has done practically nothing to improve their socio-economic conditions. Of course, many heroic explanations have been advanced for their failures, but these do not seem to point out the culpability of tribal welfare departments and their protectors, just as the Harijans (The sons of God) referred to in the special provisions of our Constitution have become a 'sweet means' of exploitation for all who are concerned and connected with their welfare or ill-fare.

Even after three decades of independence, the tribals continue to remain aloof from the general prosperity of the nation and are still in the lowest strata of society. Their way of living is a challenge to modern civilization. They have been subjected to various types of exploitation for generations and their life is characterized by servitude, poverty and misery. Generally speaking, they are still under the clutches of their century old traditions and inimical customs. They are in the firm grip of a subsistence economy and indebtedness is the average hallmark of tribal existence in India.

The origin of the present day Integrated Tribal Development Projects (ITDP) can be traced back to 1950, when the Government of India initiated the National Extension Schemes (NES) in 1951, with the intension of intensifying the block level development activities to raise the general standard of living of the weaker sections. When the Block level activities became a blockade to the development of the weaker sections therein, a new scheme was reinstated in the name of the Tribal Development Block (TDB) in 1962. These blocks were able to initiate some efforts on the social welfare front of tribals. However, since these programmes were patterned after the development efforts attempted in the earlier periods, they turned out to be not in tune with the tribal context and culture. But, the experiment over a period often years or more proved that the emancipation of tribal communities was a complex process with serious socio-political and economic implications. The powerful feudal and vested economic interests, therefore, had to be fought against and new modes of role relations had to be established to ensure tribal claims.

These sporadic and isolated attempts could have only nominal impact on the welfare of the tribals. When it was found that the agencies created and appointed for tribal development were unqualified and ill-equipped to restrain the exploitation by powerful local forces, the Integrated Area Development Programme (IADP) was baptized in 1972 by the special convocation of the Tribal Development Department of the Ministry of Home Affairs with the consultation of various state level tribal development agencies. But, following the same line of experience as over the preceding years has proved that without developing the tribals therein cannot succeed. Yet, all of this seems to have got concealed in the new label of Sub-plan Scheme for Tribal Development (SSTD) in 1976 without defining the area coverage and plan objectives.

The new sub-plan under the main plan (of State and Union Government) started functioning in almost all states under the new name of Integrated Tribal Development Projects (ITDP) without 'project officials' to control, direct and manage the development activities of the various State and Union Government Departments. According to the new strategy, Area Sub-Plans comprising several projects are prepared for each such 'sub-plan area'. For each one of these projects, IADP focusing attention on the specific problems of the tribal people in that area has been formulated.

Consistent with the norms and directives of concerned departments, the Pilot Report, Preliminary Report, Primary Report, Pre-revised First Draft Report, Revised Confidential Report and Final Reports (strictly confidential and official) were prepared in all States. The State Planning Boards and Tribal Welfare Departments were entrusted with the task of preparing periodic reviews and studies on 'specific problem oriented tribal development issues'. Inspired by the heavy budget allocation for tribal development, the experts in the field were eager to conduct national and international seminars and conferences at the cost of the half appeased starving tribals.

'Action-oriented' researches were held under the expert guidance of eminent scholars in the field weeded to tribal life and dedicated to the welfare of the weaker sections of society. Resultantly, the volume of 'Reports' increased at an alarming pace along with the number of Institutes and 'Directors', Joint Directors,

Deputy Directors, Additional Directors, Assistant Directors, Acting Directors and Special Executive Directors. But at the end of it all, the truth is sad indeed for the only comment that can be made is: 'poor are my tribals, rich are their protectors'. This is a fact that, the more the plans, the more are the tribals moving from 'poverty to absolute pauperism'. What they needed is not expert seminars, comprehensive reports or directives from ministers and ministries, but a time bound solution to their century old socioeconomic problems with which they are struggling. Nevertheless, credit does go to the planners for what they have planned, rather than for what they have been able to do.

It is a fact that in all ages those who think must act for and govern those who toil for them. The people at the grassroots level must feel proud of their more fortunate countrymen whose vision and learning can be of benefit to the more unfortunate masses. But the most distressing fact of our present day nationalism is that, instead of the elite and educated community representing the 'brain and consciousness of a nation', as the legitimate spokesmen of the illiterate masses—their dream, the custodians of their interest we have become actually anxious to exploit whenever and wherever possible.

Now we are aliens within our own national boundaries, strangers to each other and even to our own people. The ideas and beliefs of the nation are not shared by the masses or the people at the lower rung of the ladder, but only by a small class of affluent few for whom there is nothing more appealing than acquisition at any cost. They are clear about their own ends but not the means, thus shattering the fond dreams of the destitute millions who recoil with horror and dismay at what is generated by the liberal leaders of our political economy.

We are taught to be obedient to the law of the land 'but not to be against the power of the few'. We are taught that 'the law will take care of us', but not 'who will take care of the law' the 'masses or the mightly few'. If the achievement of political freedom is a proven historical and necessary event, the achievement of economic freedom is the natural right of every human being, a matter of the utmost urgency.

The genuine question that arises now is: should the government of the country be left to the elected representatives of the minority (in the factual sense) of their own party without any ideology to represent the masses. Should it be reduced to the level of street demonstrations and conspiratorial meeting? Even then, the masses are supreme. They must be trusted to define their economic objectives and to work for their strategies of development. The theories and models must become relevant to their needs and not become objects for 'soap bubble oratory', we must test our development theories so that we do not degenerate into a twentieth century off-shoot of nineteenth century imperial legalits.

When social thinking is tardy and parochial, the power structure tends to keep an ambivalent attitude to institutional changes. This fact is evident in many fields of the development process in India. Thus, the social thinkers always become the worst enemies of a society which lives on the wages of exploitation. Pretence of action is worse than inaction. Inaction generates resistance and pretence distrust. Thus, there is a fundamental difference between organized resistance and organized distrust. Both lead to conflict. But the latter invariably introduces an element of perversity. When programmes of development are initiated without certain institutional changes, one of the inevitable outcomes to begin with, is the strengthening of already entrenched social interests. This is what is happening in the case of tribal development in India. It is a game without rules. The brave words of the Planning Commission, except for sentimental potentialities, have failed to come to grips with the entrenched interests of tribal planners and protectors.

The party in power was unable to create any new and more effective instrument for the implementation of its social and economic policies than 'the crushing bureaucratic machinery' which has proved unsuitable beyond all doubt. In this context, advocacy of radical policies at the highest level of plan action does not get translated into fact. In fact, as policy declarations become more radical, the gap between the preaching and the practice becomes strikingly evident. So it is wiser to retreat to realistic plans rather than radical phraseology to which partymen are heroically accustomed. Therefore, it is not surprising that the present mode of development which has been stimulated over the years can only meet with failure.

The positive discrimination policy of the state on behalf of the disadvantaged groups and weaker sections of the society is the most effective way to help the tribals and weaker sections enter the modern mainstream. However, the quasi-structural frame, when linked with abstract development theories with the inbuilt institutional flavour, can only thwart the various measures for poverty eradication. The feasibility of measures of development through the superimposition of democratic institutions on a non-egalitarian social structure, is questionable; it stems from cynical and quacks, really, who believe in the self-percolation effect of the benefits of development towards the lower strata of the society. Such practice based on abstract theories has proved that well intentioned state intervention often ends up in accomplishing the very opposite of the objectives laid out in the plans and proposals. Any number of solutions to the problem of economic development of weaker sections in areas perennially handicapped by basic infrastructural constraints, coupled with gross financial misuse, organizational impotence, incorrect priorities and faulty identification processes will only help to aggravate the socio-economic tension which prevails within the backward tribal regions. Finally, the eruption of violence and bloodshed, in whatever form that we see in India, is not an accident but the inevitable outcome of the development experience.

Over the last three decades now, we have been planning, doing research and making policies for positive state intervention towards the most obviously disadvantaged groups in the society. But, by and large, the sad truth prevails that, by now the lack of political will has been amply demonstrated and gaps exist between the policy and the legislations, between the law and its implementation. Perhaps, there is no sphere of government action in our country which has shown such a deep hiatus between precept and practice as in the domain of planning for the weaker sections and socially deprived groups.

Despite all our integrated plan programmes and concerted efforts, the tribals still remain mostly disintegrated within our society. Unfortunately, planners are yet to define how to integrate and what to integrate, and why at all to integrate, if integration is a self-permeating process of economic development. But, it provokes us to think that if disintegration is the basic concealed objective under the disguise of integrated development, then nothing could be better done.

To bring the tribals into the mainstream of modern life, still a large gap has to be made up. But it is a reality that the tribals are much more socio-economically isolated and even if development is ensured, they are often dragged into subproletarian servitude by the reactionary forces of a society which lives on the wages of exploitation. The statutory reservations, discriminations, special provisions, guarantee of minimum needs, etc., as a means of social change is, no doubt, a welcome approach. This will bring about change in educational programmes, occupational mobility, cultural conditioning, redistribution and would also raise the overall competitive level of disadvantaged groups in what they are able to attain by their own effort and means.

No doubt, schemes and special provisions are obviously a help towards this end, but in the absence of comprehensive remedial measures to check the Alteration processes of exploitative organs, they can only lead to social conflict and structural dislocation within already wounded social patterns. The reality is that the tribal plans look elegant and egalitarian, in appearance but the conspired practise makes the approach shabby and inegalitarian, as now the areas of elite catchment have widened to enlightened towns of 'integrated social groups'.

Most alarming of all, the special provisions have so far only ensured representation for the people who are in the power structure, who help to perpetuate the stratification in the social organizations. What is fundamentally wrong with the tribal development programme is a lack of awareness of the social dimensions, and the stunted vision on what needs to be done and how. So, the tribal development strategy calls for a change, and reshuffle in the administrative structure towards those on whose behalf it is supposed to function. Otherwise, the proposals can only buttress social fragmentation. So the existing measures to improve the socio-economic condition of tribals must dissolve into a cohesive whole of the society of which the whole is larger than the sum of its part. But the question is, how to dissolve and what are the norms of division. Even otherwise, the virtual exclusion of wider objectives and substitution of temporary devices is only a conditional measure which makes the returns negative through short-sighted and misconceived policies which are objectively questionable and practically refutable (Verghese, V. Alexander, 1983).

Sometimes, the uncertainty of consequences of change among the tribals also block the developmental processes meant for them. They would rather go through a life which is known or familiar, than make a change where the consequences are uncertain. Fear of failure in the new ventures or new roles may deter them from taking advantage of the whatever little new opportunities provided to them. However, it does not mean that they do not like to live and lead the changed way of life, but the element of fairness sometimes resists the development process. An attempt towards the solution of the issues of why to approach and what to approach, may facilitate the tribal development process.

Moreover, a study covering about eleven countries, revealed some interesting trends in the context of social structures. Those who held positions in the centre (the top) were 'open minded' but sceptical, they possessed all the intellectual means for reconsidering their strategy, but they were not willing to introduce or accept major changes especially if those endangered their position. On the other hand, it was found that those at the periphery (bottom) were dogmatic, less educated, dissatisfied with their situation but without the initiative to change it, often not even aware of their own interest but eagerly advocating changes which they assumed would imply a development for the better. The 'top' predicted developments and achievements for which they did not show enthusiasm whereas those at the `bottom' expressed their hopes for what they did not really believe would happen.

The 'top' who are close to the instruments of communication and decision making would be the ones to take initiatives, to plan and appear to be effectively in charge of what had to be done to meet the future. At the same time, those at the "bottom", convinced that their ideas would not be realised anyhow, would do little to promote them. What they did would matter little anyhow, so long as they did it only at the individual level. One of the major stumbling blocks in the way of united action by those at the bottom is that while they do have quite a bit of change-oriented, thinking, it is rarely that the same idea prevails throughout those who constitute the periphery.

These are some observations based on a study across eleven nations which hold true in most of the hierarchical structures. In this context, any socio-economic change planned for groups occupying positions which are economically, socially, or both, vulnerable should take into account their feelings, their attitudes and the role of the structures—social, cultural, political, administrative—in shaping and reinforcing them. Therefore, improvements sought to be brought about among disadvantaged groups of people should not only take measures to unsettle the existing social structure but also modify the attitudes reflecting the dictates of that social structure (Muthayya, B.C. 1983).

Lack of interest in the tribal development by the administrative and executive personnel have also held up the developmental processes to a great extent along with lack of proper training to the administrative personnels, meant to implement the ambitious tribal development. No doubt, statistics tell us an impressive story of tribal development. Thus, each five-year plan allocation in respect of their preceeding one reveals an increase in the outlay and the fifth plan allotment of a sum of Rs. 1182 crore marked a phenomenal increase from earlier plan outlays. But an increase in the allocation of the outlays is no longer, a real achievement in the field of tribal development. And it may be remarked in the words of Adelmann and Morris that "hundreds of millions of disparately poor throughout the world have been hurt rather than helped by economic development". We often identify the tribal development with that of the economic development. We often assume that without economic development, the real tribal development cannot be achieved. No doubt, we cannot expect too much of the success of developmental schemes of the tribals when the basic needs are not assured to them. But it happens so that in doing it, we overemphasize the economic development as if the tribal development is wedded to the economists and divorced from anthropologists. In absence of social and cultural heritage of the tribal population, the schemes result into failure. It is not seriously taken into account both by the public and bureaucracy because of the fact that government schemes need not always succeed.

Moreover, the developmental programmes meant for the tribals are uniformly planned not keeping in mind the fact that there is a differential development among the tribals themselves and consequently of their needs. It may be observed that there is a well-marked differential development among those tribes who have adopted or are practising Christianity and those who are non-Christian. It may be added here again that the tribals who are still primitive or have dwellings on the hill, forests, and are not much in contact with the forces and agents of change of the plains, still show a poor state of affairs in contrast to the tribes which are on plains and to those who are exposed to the forces of industrialization and urbanization. It is evident from these facts that the developmental plans for the tribals should have a wide range of variability and should be formulated accordingly. Thus, the uniformity in the frames of plans, being away from the needs of a particular tribal community and its differentiation from the needs of another particular tribal group has also resulted in their failure. What it requires is not a separate plan for each tribal group, a long agenda, but must be in conformity with the classificatory tribal communities.

When we look at the tribal development in the state of Bihar, we are soon confronted with the sad picture that emerges even after a concerted effort made in the last 30 years of planning. It is still an experiment in the field, the cause and effect relationship remains to be inhibitory and inferences are far ahead to be drawn.

Studies conducted recently to examine the tribal participation in the developmental schemes through the institution of Panchayati Raj in the four Blocks of Ranchi district, reveal an increased participation. The latter is of utmost importance for the successful implementation of the developmental schemes meant for them. The figure that we have well explains the developmental efforts of the tribals for whom the developmental schemes are meant, but the stray cases cannot take the place of generalizations. Moreover, the fruits of the project are taken by the non-tribals as the study reveals instead of the tribals.

Studies conducted on the Sauria Paharia of Bihar reveal a distressing picture. The tribe is facing extinction but no tangible solution has come up uptil now. The bureaucratic display of development achievement is a misnomer and bleak. There should be a close understanding between the implementing officials and the poor tribals in order to attain the goal of real development. There should be no gap between the officials and the tribals. Sometimes the tribal elite acts as a 'mediator' between the tribals and the officials, the bulk of the fruits of the schemes go in the share of the so-called elite group rather than those who really deserve it. Moreover, there should be a close understanding between the economists and anthropologists not at the planning level but also up to the evaluation stage. Such a wedding is not only inevitable but also realistic in the sense of improving in present state of affairs. A training to the officials for a fixed period is no longer a parameter to the fact that he/she has become competent enough to undertake the project and its success is imminent. A coach of class and an operation in the field are two distinct identities and cannot replace or clash but rather reinforce each other. The symbiosis can be of immense value for the effective launching of the schemes and its success is the objective before us to improve their lot.

The cooperative credit movement was started to get the farmers out of the clutches of the money lenders. Now the problem is how to get the cooperative movement out of the 'clutches' of the vested interests. It seems nobody has a solution to this.

Panchayati Raj was introduced with a view to increasing people's participation in development efforts. The basic idea was to get the development activities out of the 'clutches' of bureaucracy. Now, the problem is how to keep local bodies out of the 'clutches' of the local power-oriented politicians.

In short, the obvious conclusion is that the failure to improve the lot of the tribals in the tribal areas, so far, has been the result of a complex interplay of economic and political forces and many maladies in the administrative machinery. It seems the failure has been partly due to wrong policies and partly due to interest weakness in the political and economic institutions and administrative machinery, in addition to the faulty planning. All need careful investigations and corrections to realize the fruits of the tribal development in real sense. If we are really concerned for the development of the tribe then we have to think for their development in terms of their 'Felt' need and not in terms of their 'Assessed' need. What is being done till todate is that the needs are assessed by those who are strangers to them, which results into negative development. Data gathered from various departments of the State and central Government engaged in the development of tribes and reveal that approximately Rs. 3.75 lakh has been spent so far per square metre on their development. Density of population per square metre is two in tribal Bihar. Even if this amount would had been given as dole to each tribe, which comes to approximately Rs. 1.87 lakh it would have helped and reached each tribal.

An example of providing safe drinking water to Paharias without any cost but on which crores of rupees were spent and the result was zero, well explains the intentions and motive of the authorities involved. Providing drinking water through experiment did not involve any expenditure as it was made available with the indigeneous materials. Bamboo is available in abundance among Sauria Paharia. Inner portion of the bamboo is hollow. One piece of bamboo was jointed with another and in this way 20 to 30 bamboos, sometimes more than this helped in bringing safe drinking water to the doorstep from the natural spring. These bamboos are periodically changed in order to keep the water safe. Likewise use of milk was also introduced in the community. These examples demonstrate that if the 'Felt Need' of the community is designed and implemented through participatory development then the chances of 'positive development' in the community is higher.

These days a good number of national and regional seminars are organized for the development of various state including Bihar and a good number of recommendations are being made. But the pre-condition for any development is the human behaviour and its management which is missing the 'participatory development' or the 'empowered development' is a development from within the community for which understanding of human feeling is a must probably here anthropologist have a great role to play.

Thus it is evident from the foregoing discussions that the Anthropology of Disaster Management broadly discusses the Natural Disaster as well as the man made disaster. At the beginning of 21st century the anthropologists are more concerned with the man made disasters. Researches and development in science have minimized the occurrence of natural disasters but through planned development the occurrences of manmade disasters have maximized. Death of innocent people in explosions and bomb blasts, proxy wars, sex scandal of U.S.A. President, Bill Clinton, spread of HIV and AIDS, ethnic violence in Canada, etc. are a few glaring examples of manmade disasters. In course of time we learnt the art of controlling the natural disasters but we are yet to learn the management of disasters caused by man. Majority of disasters of 21st century will be due to human failure. The emotions, human feelings, fellow feelings, compassion, fear from God, etc., have evaporated and have been dried in human beings due to scientific and planned development. If anthropology has to survive it has to take care of such disasters and UNESCO has rightly declared the 21st Century as the century of Anthropology.

We must therefore stress at world level meetings of anthropologists that development is for mankind rather than mankind being there for development.

TWO

PROBLEMS AND ISSUES

R.K. Celly and T.N. Gupta in their article "Dimensions of Natural Disaster Management in India" in *Shelter* (Oct. 12,1999) observe that "a natural hazard is an event of nature, which causes sudden disruption to the normal life of a society and causes damage to life and property, to such an extent that normal, social and economic mechanisms available to the society are inadequate to restore normalcy". Viewed in this manner, a host of natural phenomena cause disasters to a society, whether they are related to an occurrence in micro-environment or not. In macro terms, the hazards, which cause widespread damage and disruption in India are floods, cyclones, earthquakes and landslides.

The past decade has witnessed an extraordinary increase in the number and extent of natural disasters. As Kofi Annan, Secretary General of the United Nations, points out, "The facts are startling. The costs of weather-related disasters in 1998 exceeded the costs of all such disasters in the decade of the 1980s. In the Caribbean, the hurricanes designated George and Mitch, killed more than 13,000 people, with Mitch being the deadliest Atlantic storm in 200 years. Major floods hit India, Nepal, Bangladesh and much of East Asia, with thousands killed. Two-thirds of Bangladesh was inundated for months, leaving millions homeless. There were three times as many great natural hazards in the 1990s as in the 1960s, while disaster costs increased more than nine-fold in the same period."

The humanitarian community does a remarkable job in responding to disasters. But the most important task in the medium and long-term is to strengthen and broaden programmes which reduce the number and cost of disasters in the first place. While we should continue to improve and strengthen our response capacity, we need to engage in working together to build a "global culture of prevention". This means greater efforts to reduce vulnerability to natural hazards in the first place.

As we enter the beginning of the new millennium, the International Decade for Natural Disaster Reduction (IDNDR) is proved to have contributed, with all its partners world-wide, to fostering a "global culture of prevention" for the 21st Century. To build on the progress achieved during the IDNDR, we have to act decisively, so that disaster reduction becomes an essential element of government policies. Recalling the Geneva Mandate adopted at the IDNDR Programme Forum, we have to adopt and implement policy measures at the international, regional, national and local levels aimed at reducing the vulnerability of our societies to natural disasters. These measures should have as main objectives the establishment of hazard resistant communities, the protection of people from the threat of disasters and the safeguarding of our natural and economic resources and of our social well-being.

K. Rajan, Adviser, Planning Commission, in his Article, "Natural Disaster Management in National Development—An Indian Perspective" outlines the following adversities, which befall people and the area.

- Loss of crops and availability of essentials like food and agricultural commodities;
- Loss of employment opportunities in the area where natural disaster occurs, particularly rural employment;
- Problems of health and diseases arising both from insufficient availability of the basic necessities causing malnourishment, hunger, etc., or lack of the availability of good and hygienic drinking water;
- Financial distress caused to the farming community and those dependent on land which affect their ability to withstand hard conditions immediately following the occurrence of the natural disaster but also importantly, their ability to recover well enough before the next cropping season and take full advantage of normal conditions which may prevail;

- Impact on industrial sector due to loss of production of raw materials, reduce generation of power, etc; and
- Lastly, the impact of the disaster on the cattle wealth.

V. Suresh has rightly summed up that Natural disasters, which damage national economies and produce hardships for large sections of the population, are one of the single largest concerns for most nations. Human settlements are frequently affected by natural disasters—earthquakes, floods, hurricanes, cyclones, landslides, sea erosions—which take a heavy toll on human lives, destroy buildings and infrastructure and have far reaching economic and social consequences for communities.

Ashok Pahwa, Secretary, Ministry of Urban Development has rightly said, "Natural hazards are not new to the earth system. Like natural resources, they have been, and are, a part of biosphere and eco-systems. It is the human interventions, its endeavours towards development, that these hazards turn into disasters, causing enormous devastation to the life and property of the nations .... The extent and frequency of damage, that is being caused by these extreme events, has raised concerns all over the world resulting into declaration of present decade (1999s) as international Decade for Natural Disaster Reduction."

Bhagat Singh, Additional Secretary, Ministry of Agriculture had suggested various ways to reduce its serious effects. While occurrence of these natural disasters cannot be prevented altogether, their adverse impact can be reduced substantially by undertaking various preparedness and mitigation measures by community involvement. Minimizing the loss of precious human life is the first priority in disaster management. Significant achievement has been made in designing of disaster resistant houses and inventing quality building materials to withstand the fury of natural disasters. It is gratifying to note that HUDCO has given a lead by taking a number of initiatives to propagate these designs as well as materials among the vulnerable community besides imparting training to the artisans and masons through their building centers.

Earthquakes, floods, draught, cyclones, accidents, AIDS are major types of disaster phenomenon occuring in the region. India is a large country and has had more than its share of major natural hazards like drought, floods, earthquakes and cyclones throughout its history of civilization. Naturally, the country developed its own practices and strategies for coping with the various natural calamities. Since independence in 1947, India has developed a nationwide relief administration where a lead role of the State Governments is envisaged.

American geo-physicist James, N. Brunes visited India in March 1997. He made a clear-cut observation that there was a high probability of a great earthquake of magnitude 8.5 on the Richter Scale in the northern Indian subcontinent any time within the next 100 years. He warned planners, engineers and contractors involved in the building of dams and houses in areas above the Gangetic plains in the north. He predicted that damage expected after such great earthquakes would be much more devastating than in normal cases.

Earthquakes, the very name of it, sends shock waves. Earthquakes cannot be predicted by any method available so far. On the one hand, we enjoy pleasures living on mother earth while on the other, we face its fury in the form of floods, fire, earthquakes, etc. Lyle Bavadam in *Frontline*, Feb. 13-16, 2001, (p. 14) quoting Dr. P.P. Patel, Professor and Head of the Department of Geology at M.S. University, Baroda, feels that earthquakes send a forewarning. When Dr. P.P. Patel, felt the tremors on the morning of January 26, his professional instincts told him that an earthquake with Bhuj, Bhavnagar or the Narmada Valley as the epicentre had occurred. An engineering, environmental and hydro-geologist, who has intimate knowledge of the Kutch region, Patel emphasised the fact that the earthquake could have been foreseen. "On December 27, there was an indication of heightened seismic activity. A minor earthquake measuring around 4 on the Richter scale occurred in Bhuj. It was ignored—it appeared as a small report in a Gujarati newspaper. Fearing renewed seismic activity, Patel organised a field workshop at the Bhuj Observatory in collaboration with the local administration and the Department of Science and Technology.

CHRONOLOGY OF EARTHQUAKES IN INDIA

Date	Place	Toll
1803	Garhwal	200 die
April 4, 1905	Kangra valley (Himachal Pradesh), 8.0 magnitude	20,000 die
July 8, 1918	Assam, 7.6 magnitude.	10,000 die
July 2, 1930	Dhubri (Assam), 7.1 magnitude.	—
January 15, 1934	Bihar and Indo-Nepal border, 8.3 magnitude.	—
June 26, 1941	Andaman islands, 8.1 magnitude.	532 die
October 23, 1943	Assam, 7.2 magnitude.	—
August 15, 1950	Assam, 8.5 magnitude.	—
July 21, 1956	Anjar (Gujarat), 7.0 magnitude	—
December 10, 1967	Koyna (Maharashtra), 6.5 magnitude.	—
January 19, 1975	Kinnaur (Himachal Pradesh), 6.2 magnitude.	—
August 21, 1988	Bihar and Indo-Nepal border, 6.5 magnitude.	1000 die
October 20, 1991	Uttarkashi (Uttar Pradesh), 6.6 magnitude.	1500 die
September 30,1993	Latur and Osmanabad (Maharashtra), 6.3 magnitude.	7928 die
May 22, 1997	Jabalpur (Madhya Pradesh), 6.0 magnitude.	40 die
March 29, 1999	Chamoli (Uttar Pradesh), 6.8 magnitude.	150 die

Source: Ministry of Agriculture, GOI, New Delhi.

GUJARAT TRAGEDY

When all over India, people were celebrating their Republic day, Gujarat experienced its worst natural calamity after independence. The earthquake which struck on 26th January 2001 at 8.46 hours measuring 6.9 on the Richter Scale, hit certain regions of Gujarat state, very hard. The tremor left behind huge devastation of life and property, both private and public and created utter panic, chaos and trauma among the people.

It has been 50 years since Gujarat witnessed an earthquake and therefore most of the people did not know what to do, except that those who could rush out of their houses in whatever state they were in. It was only after getting over from the terror and shock of the earthquake tremor that the people began to think about the situation of neighbours, other cities, and other areas of the state and the country. Gradually, the disaster sinked, the cries of the injured and bodies trapped inside the debris began to be heard by others.

It was a calamity of unprecedented magnitude which caused large-scale damage to houses over extensive areas in Gujarat and also resulted in the break-down of vital infrastructure.

Magnitude of Earthquake on 26.1.2001

* Severe earthquake of magnitude 6.9 on Richter scale occurred at 0846 hours.
* Epicenter 20 Kms. North-east of Bhuj.
* Impact felt in various parts of the county; Many parts of Gujarat severely affected.
* Colossal damage to life and property in Gujarat; Kutch district adversely affected. No reports on damage from other parts of the country.
* After shocks still being received; More than 400 already received.

Extent of Damage

* 7904 villages in 182 taluks in 21 districts affected.
* 7633 affected villages in Zones III to V (5690 in Zone III, 1062 in Zone IV and 881 in Zone V).

* 1.59 crore out of 3.77 crore population affected.
* More than 19800 deaths so far; about 18200 in Kutch district alone.

AFFECTED AREAS BY CALAMITIES

Districts	*Talukas*	No. *of Villages affected*	*No. of affected families*
Surendranagar	Chotila	112	4919
	Dhangadra	64	8043
	Lakhtar	43	2023
	Limbdi	60	715
	Malwad	67	8790
	Sayla	67	620
	Patdi	89	9198
	Vadhwan	35	11012
	Mudi	58	4593
	Chuda	38	520
Jamnagar	Bhanvad	7	432
	Jamjodhpur	15	
	Kalawad	5	1195
	Jamngar	13	2064
	Okhamandal	24	886
	Kalyanpur	12	327
Bharuch	Amod	22	84
	Vagra	56	653
	Jambusasr	71	6585
Rajkot	Malia	7	700

Source: Ministry of Agriculture, GOI, New Delhi.

* 1.66 lakhs injured (1.36 lakh in Kutch district); 20,717 seriously injured.
* 232 persons missing in Kutch; Cattle deaths— 20712.
* Houses destroyed—1.72 lakh (pucca), 1.67 lakh (kachcha) and 1.16 lakh (huts); Houses partially damaged—4.88 lakh (pucca), 3.45 lakh (kachcha) and 0.34 lakh (huts).
* Preliminary estimates of damage—Rs. 21,262 crore as indicated here.

	(Rs. in crore)
Personal properties	387.00
Household properties	11195.00
Public utilities	600.00
Public infrastructure and amenities	1080.00
Industrial establishment	5000.00
Commercial establishment	3000.00

Road Transport and Highways

Out of 650 kms of national highways damaged, 100 kms were severely damaged. Most of the minor/major bridges were damaged. Surajbari bridge was damaged and repaired on war-footing and restored. National highways were made traffic worthy.

Telecommunication

Telecommunication facilities were disrupted. Number of exchanges damaged was 147 and tôtal lines damaged were 82,000. Optical Fibre system from Bhuj-Bachau-Rajkot was damaged. Exchanges started choking due to heavy traffic. Estimated cost of damages was nearly Rs. 200 crores.

Railways

Costs	Track	25 crores
	Signal & Tele	15 crores
	Electrical	7 crores
	Misc.	3 crores
	Total	60 crores

* Heavy damage to station buildings, station cabins, residential quarters, bridges in the affected sections.
* Signalling equipments at 25 stations and control communications on Viramgram-Gandhidham section damaged.

Steps taken by Government of India

* National Crisis Management Committee (NCMC) under Cabinet Secretary and the Cabinet met immediately on 26.1.2001 for taking immediate measures.

* Krishi Control Room was activated and started functioning round the clock from 26.1.2001.
* Armed and Para-military Forces were deployed immediately on rescue and relief operations.
* 23,500 Army troops and 3,000 Para-military Force personnel were deployed.
* Air Force deployed 48 aircrafts including helicopters and carried over 950 sorties for evacuating injured persons and for carrying relief, teams, equipments/ material, etc.
* Navy made available 3 ships and 2 ships were converted into hospitals.
* Satellite phones, hotlines, HAM radios and mobile phones were pressed into services.
* Teams of doctors and medicine/equipments arranged and sent immediately.
* Empowered Group of Ministers (EGoM) under Home Minister was set up; 4 meetings of EGoM held within 15 days.
* EGoM and NCMC were regularly monitoring the situation.
* Prime Minister held meeting with Leaders of all parties/ groups on 3.2.2001.
* As a follow-up, 37-member National Committee on Disaster Management (NCDM) setup under Chairmanship of PM; 1st meeting of NCDM held on 18.2.2001.
* All Central Ministries/Departments and agencies were assisting in relief operations.
* Immediate assistance of Rs. 500 crore from NCCF was released by GOI on 30.1.2001.
* Railways have restored the damaged tracks in BG/MG sections.
* Telecom service was restored in all 147 exchanges by - 2.2.2001.
* Civil Aviation arranged free transportation of relief materials and arranged transportation facilities for relief materials from abroad.
* External Affairs made arrangements for issue of 15 days visa at entry point without delay, to the relief teams from foreign countries.

* Ministry of Finance (Deptt. of Expenditure) arranged relaxation of Overdraft Regulation Scheme.
* Rs. 10 crore was released from PM's National Relief Fund.
* Deptt. of Food & Public Distribution allotted 1 lakh tonnes of foodgrains and released in advance 10,000 MTs of levy sugar.
* Regular monitoring of medical facilities at DGHS Headquarters, New Delhi.
* Adequate quantities of diesel and kerosene allotted.
* Ministry of Power arranged 19 large DG sets for utilisation of GEB at Bhuj/Anjar.
* Powergrid/NTPC were engaged in repair/ recommissioning of 10 GEB major sub-stations.
* PEC sanctioned loan of Rs. 100 crore for rehabilitation/ reconstruction of transmission and distribution system; REC sanctioned loan of Rs. 100 crore to GEB.
* Ministry of Rural Development made additional allocation of Rs. 250 crore for constructing earthquake resistant houses for BPL families; assistance of Rs. 22,000 per dwelling unit was proposed for the affected districts.

Steps taken by Government of Gujarat

(a) Relief

* In death cases, payment of Rs. 1 lakh to adult and Rs, 60,000 to minor.
* Rs. 13.23 crore death compensation paid within one month.
* Cash dole paid—Rs. 50.43 crore to 7.55 lakh families.
* 45 damaged sub-stations and 255 damaged feeders fully energised/restored.
* Power supply restored in all 925 disrupted villages.
* Water supply restored in all 1340 affected villages through pipes (994), tankers (277) and other sources (69).
* Heavy equipments, namely cranes/JCBs, bulldozers/ excavators, loaders/dumpers/trucks, jeep/ambulances, gas cutters deployed in large numbers.
* All ration shops operational; Essential commodities (foodgrains, vegetables, edible oil, kerosene, diesel, petrol) supplied.

* Shelter material (tents—about 51,000 and tarpaulin/ GC sheets—2.84 lakhs) supplied.
* Grass supplied free of cost for 30 days @ 4 kg. per day per animal in affected areas.

(b) Rehabilitation and Reconstruction

* Senior Officers deployed to oversee relief and rehabilitation measures.
* New Department of Earthquake Relief set up.
* Gujarat Disaster Management Authority (GDMA) under Chief Minister set up to implement rehabilitation packages.
* 229 identified for relocation; package for 4 towns (Bhuj, Anjar, Bhachau and Rapar) being worked out.
* 4 packages of rehabilitation declared:
    (i) Relocation and reconstruction of completely destroyed villages,
    (ii) Assistance in severely affected areas in Zones IV and V for in-situ reconstruction,
    (iii) Scale of assistance for destroyed/partially destroyed houses in areas away from epicenter,
    (iv) Corporation/Area Development Authority (except Bhuj, Anjar, Bhachau and Rapar).
* There is no separate adoption policy and it is part of the rehabilitation/reconstruction package.
* Restoration at new sites with essential infrastructure.
* All damaged/destroyed huts to be replaced by dwelling units.
* Repair/reconstruction of required public infrastructure conforming to earthquake resistant standards by the State.
* Plan of Action for adoption of affected villages.

Industrial Package

* Comprehensive package for damaged industrial units announced on 25.2.2001.
* Benefits include royalty exemption, concession for construction materials.
* Package also includes concession for cottage industries.

Temporary Shelter

* Requirement of 3.27 lakh temporary shelters projected.
* About 2.75 lakh families covered.
* 48327 tents, 2.50 lakh tarpaulin and 2.06 lakh GC sheets distributed.

Assistance by other State Governments

* Contributed total financial assistance of Rs. 48.68 crore (Andhra Pradesh, Assam, Bihar, Chhattisgarh, Delhi, Daman & Diu, Himachal Pradesh, J & K, Karnataka, Kerala, Madhya Pradesh, Maharashtra, Manipur, Meghalaya, Rajasthan, Tamil Nadu, Tripura, Uttar Pradesh, West Bengal).
* Also provided assistance in kind — food, food materials, shelter material (tents, blankets, plastic sheets), medicine, medical teams, water, equipments, etc.
* Assisting in relief operation with men and material.
* Despatched several loads of relief material.
* Assisting in adoption of affected villages.

External Assistance

* International Community responded generously.
* More than 70 countries and 17 International organisations provided assistance to the State Government to the tune of Rs. 178 crores.
* Assistance provided includes:
    (i) Financial assistance.
    (ii) In kind in the form of food items, shelter material.
    (iii) Rescue teams with sniffer dogs.
    (iv) Medical facilities by setting up mobile hospitals with surgical facilities.
    (v) Messages expressing deep regrets on loss of lives.
* US $ 300 million announced by World Bank.
* US $ 350 million announced by Asian Development Bank.

DISASTER POTENTIAL OF INDIA

India covers an area of 32,87,263 sq. km. extending from snow covered Himalayan heights in the North to the tropical rain forest of the South. In the North, the territory is bounded by the Great Himalayas and stretches southwards tapering off into the Indian ocean between the Bay of Bengal and the Arabian Sea. The main land extends between latitude 8°4' and 37°6' North and longitudes 68°7' and 97°25' East, measuring about 32000 km from North to South and West to East. The vast land frontier of 15200 km and coastline of 7,500 km. also has group of islands located both in the Bay of Bengal and the Arabian Sea. Hardly any other country has such a large land mass with such a diverse range of geo-agro-climatic zones. The main land of India comprises of four regions, namely, the Great Mountain Zone, Plains of the Indus, Ganges and the Brahamaputra; the Desert Region, and the Southern Peninsula. The Himalayan range comprises three almost parallel ranges interspersed with large plateaus and valleys. The mountain wall extends over a distance of 24,000 km. with a varying width of 240 to 320 km. The plains about 24,000 km. long, are formed by basins of three distinct river systems, viz. the Indus, the Ganges and the Brahmaputra. The desert region is clearly delineated in two parts—Sindh Frontier while the little desert extends between Jaisalmer and Jodhpur upto Punjab. The desert region is inhabited by local communities which have developed their own coping and recovery mechanisms. Between the two deserts is a zone of absolutely sterile region, consisting of rocky land cut up by limestone ridges.

According to 1991 census, India had a population of 843.93 million with 195.02 million housing units. The literacy rate as per 1991 census was 52.2 per cent, 64 per cent for males and 39 per cent for females. To protect such a large population with low levels of education from the fury of natural hazards is not an easy task. However, local initiatives and the governments efforts combined over the years, have tried to reduce risks and build community capacity to deal with emergencies.

Natural Hazards and Disaster

Because of the large geographical size of the country, India often faces natural hazards like floods, cyclones and droughts occurring frequently in different parts of the country.

At times, some areas normally subjected to drought situation have got flooded in certain years. Hazards like earthquakes, hailstorms, avalanches, landslides, etc., occur quite suddenly, but they are restricted in their impact in terms of time. The extent of the impact of an earthquake depends on its magnitude, season and time of occurrence.

Indeed, as Kofi Annan stated at the Programme Forum of the International Decade for Natural Disaster Reduction (IDNDR), held in Geneva in July 1999. "The humanitarian community does a remarkable job in responding to disaster. But the most important task in the medium and long-term is to strengthen and broaden programmes which reduce the number and cost of disasters in the first place". While we should continue to improve and strengthen our response capacity, we need to engage in working together to build a "global culture of prevention." This means greater efforts to reduce vulnerability to natural hazards in the first place.

Let us discuss briefly about some different disasters.

1. Earthquake

Earthquakes are the most feared natural hazards, as they occur without any recognizable warning, are unpredictable in space and time and inflict heavy losses in less than a minute duration. A UNESCO study indicates that on an average 10,000 people die each year from earthquakes and losses amounting to billions of rupees.

Sanjay Narayan in his Editorial in *Business Today*, Feb. 21, 2001 says that, The cruellest truth about earthquakes is that while they last for mere seconds, the grim after-effects can go on for what can seem an eternity. Nearly two weeks after India's blackest Republic Day, when the quake wrecked havoc in Gujarat in all of 45 seconds, business and industry is still picking up the pieces in what is one of India's most industrialised and investment-friendly states. The true extent of the damage to business and industry in Gujarat will only unfold over the coming months, and the journey to rehabilitation will be a long and arduous one. But Gujarat is blessed with the indomitable spirit of entrepreneurship, something that its businessmen have amply demonstrated in India, as well as elsewhere in the world, notably in the US. It is this spirit that will undoubtedly help the state bounce back and claim its rightful place in the sun.

The Indian subcontinent in general and India in particular is the region facing the maximum number of natural disasters. The phenomenon of occurrences of an earthquake is also very common in this region due to the continuous movement of the Indian plate and its striking the Eurasian plate as well as the location of the youngest mountain chain in the form of the Himalayas. Thus, the earthquake is a regular feature of the subcontinent and may result in the severe damage of life and property.

The effective earthquake disaster management can be achieved through the adequate preparedness, effective emergency management and by rehabilitating the communities affected by disasters. The entire approach of the earthquake management should be interlinked by connecting various phases of management and administration with each other. The preparedness phase should be linked to the rehabilitation of the community while we should start the preparation to face the next earthquake in the rehabilitation/reconstruction stage itself.

Special precautions are needed for quake-prone zones. Devices are provided to help buildings survive earthquakes. One is a damper unit which is similar to a car shock-absorber. Another is to isolate the building from the ground with thick rubber pads.

Countries having quake-prone zones have uniform building codes updated annually and published worldwide every three years. Such codes focus mainly on the safety of the building occupants and emphasize on factors such as resistance to fire and structural failure. The higher the seismic activity the tougher the building regulations. In seismic belts regular official guidelines are issued for protection against earthquakes. Some governments have even lowered the property taxes and insurance premiums in quake-prone areas. Incentives are also given to upgrade old buildings.

With the increasing frequency of earthquakes we have to learn lessons from the countries which have taken such precautions. In India, people care less about the structure of the building and spend much more on decoration. both exterior and interior.

2. Floods

Floods are not a new phenomenon in India. Severe floods occur almost every year in one part of the country or the other, causing loss of life, large scale damage to property and untold misery to millions of people. Besides, extensive destruction of forests, reclamation of more and more lands even within the riverine areas, have caused changes in the river regime over the years. All these have led to increased flood damage to various flood control measures undertaken in the country.

About 40 m hectare of land area in the country is flood prone, where floods are annual phenomena and emerge as the most destructive natural hazard. It is evident from the available data that the frequency and intensity of floods is increasing regularly. As per the Central Water Commission data, the average annual losses due to flood damages amount to Rs. 938.56 crores.

Even though the problem of floods has been receiving increasing attention and in spite of substantial investments in this sector during the last few decades, it is observed that the flood damage in the country has continuously been showing a rising trend. It was in this context that the National Flood Commission was set up in July, 1976 by the Government of India to examine and advise on various aspects relating to floods. In its report submitted in 1981, *inter-alia,* laid great stress on proper flood plain management without diluting the importance of structural measures for specific situation. Subsequently, the specific problems of Ganga and Brahmaputra basins were also studied by high level committee of experts.

Flood Forecasting and Warning System

Flood forecasting and flood warning system in a scientific way was commenced in the year 1958 by Central Water

Commission (CWC). At present, the flood forecasting and warning network of CWC covers 62 major interstate river subcatchments which include 132 water level forecasting stations and 25 inflow forecasting stations for important reservoirs. Hydrological and hydrometerological data from nearly 700 stations in these rivers are being collected and analysed, and flood forecasts and warning messages are issued, generally 24 hours to 48 hours in advance. In case of very large incoming floods, advisory forecasts i.e. 72 hours in advance or more are also issued which predicts the incoming floods at the downstream locations. Coordination between neighbouring districts, states and countries is being promoted to reduce loss of livelihood and life.

3. Cyclones

The most destructive of weather systems, severe Tropical Cyclones (TC), brings worst disasters when it strikes coast in the preferred locations of the earth. Tropical cyclones are intense low-pressure areas with fierce winds blowing in an anti-clockwise manner in the Northern Hemisphere extending on an average 500 to 1000 km laterally (over the Indian seas) and surface to 14.16 km vertically. They are classified according to wind speed in their circulation. The associated winds often exceeding 200 kmps, rainfall exceeding 50 to 100 cm in 24 hours and worst of all, very high storm tide (storm surge combined with astronomical tide) often exceeding 5-6 metres brings disaster over the coastal areas in the wake of a cyclone. In extreme cases, wind speed of 320 kmph gusting to 360 kmph, rainfall 120 cm in 24 hours and storm surge of 13-14 metres have been recorded in association with tropical cyclones. Out of these three destructive elements viz. strong winds, heavy rainfall and storm tide, the storm tide is responsible for 90 percent of the loss of life in the case of cyclone disasters.

The India Meterological Department (IMD) has a well established organizational set up for observing, detecting, tracking and forecasting cyclones and issuing cyclone warnings whenever a cyclonic storm develops in the Bay of Bengal and the Arabian Sea. It is tracked with the help of INSAT satellite, powerful cyclone detection radars with a range of 400 km. installed at Calcutta, Paradip, Visakhapatnam, Manchilipatnam, Madras, Karaikal on the east cost; and Goa, Cochin, Bombay and Bhuj along the west coast. The present cyclone surveillance system in the country is such that no cyclone in the region can escape detection any time in its life cycle.

Cyclone warnings are provided through six cyclone warning centers located at Calcutta, Bhubaneswar, Vishakhapatanam, Chennai, Mumbai and Ahmedabad. These centers have distinct responsibilities area-wise covering both the east and west coasts of India and the oceanic areas of the Bay of Bengal and the Arabian Sea, including Andaman and Nicobar Islands and Lakshadweep. The cyclone warning bulletins are issued to All India Radio and Doordarshan for broadcasting/telecasting them in different languages on all India basis. The cyclone warning division at Headquarter office, New Delhi also provides warning information to the Control Room and Crisis Management group set up in the Ministry of Agriculture, Government of India which is finally responsible for coordination with various Central Government agencies. Cyclone Warning Division at New Delhi also caters to the needs of international responsibilities such as issue of cyclone advisories to the neighbouring countries.

4. Drought

Drought is a slow onset of natural hazard and it offers time and opportunity to mitigate its impact. The droughts can be grouped on the basis of physical characteristics and their impact on socio-economic system, both in time and space:

* *Meteorological drought:* A situation arising from inadequate and mal-distribution of rainfall;
* *Hydrological drought:* Conditions denote reduced stream flow and inadequate filling of reservoirs, tanks or drying up of water in the surface water storage structures;
* *Soil moisture drought:* Inadequate soil moisture particularly in rainfed areas which may not support crop growth;

* *Agricultural drought:* Characterised by low soil moisture levels and shortage of water resulting in crop failures;
* *Socio-economic drought:* The reduction of availability of food and income loss on account of crop failures endangering food and social security of the people in the affected areas;
* *Famine:* When large scale collapse of access to food occurs which without intervention, can lead to mass starvation; and
* *Ecological drought:* When the productivity of a natural eco-system fails significantly as a consequence of distress induced environmental damage.

The Rajya Sabha was informed on 14.3.2001 by Minister of Agriculture about prevailing drought conditions in different states in India.

1. India is prone to a number of natural disasters like cyclones, droughts, earthquakes and floods. Due to the locational and geographical features, most of the States are affected by more than one natural disaster every year. About 68% of the country's total area is prone to drought. Approximately in 62% of cropped area, farming is entirely dependent on rainfall.
2. As reported by the India Meteorological Department (IMD), 28 out of 35 meteorological sub-divisions covering 65% districts and 70% area of the country received normal to excess rainfall. On the whole, 82 districts received excess rainfall, 190 normal rainfall, 135 districts got scanty rainfall and 8 received deficient rainfall during the South-West monsoon 2000. The rainfall during the post-monsoon period has also been deficient in the affected areas.
3. As reported by the Central Water Commission (CWC) in the Ministry of Water Resources which monitors the reservoir position, the total live storage in 70 important reservoirs in the country on 9th March, 2001 was 39.82 TMC (30 per cent of the storage capacity at full reservoir level) against 57.59 TMC (44 per cent of the storage capacity at full reservoir level) last year. The ground water table has also depleted considerably.

4. As a result, drought-like situation of varying magnitude is prevailing in parts of the States of Chhattisgarh, Gujarat, Himachal Pradesh, Madhya Pradesh, Maharashtra, Orissa and Rajasthan. Gujarat and Rajasthan faced severe drought situation during 1999-2000 also.
5. In Chhattisgarh, 10500 villages in 12 out of 16 districts are under drought, affecting a population of 94.91 lakh, 32.40 lakh cattle and cropped area of 11.37 lakh hectares. In Gujarat, 12240 villages in 22 out of 25 districts are reeling under drought affecting a population of 291 lakh and cropped area of 13.50 lakh hectares. In Himachal Pradesh also all the 12 districts are now facing drought-like situation affecting 46.64 lakh population and cropped area of 88,000 hectares. In case of Madhya Pradesh 22072 villages in 32 out of 45 districts are under drought affecting a population of 101.57 lakh, 85.78 lakh cattle and cropped area in 38.23 lakh hectares. As per reports from Maharashtra, 20700 villages in 23 out of 36 districts may face a drought situation affecting a population of 284 lakh and 2.58 lakh cattle population and the cropped area of 45,000 hectares. The situation in Orissa also indicates that 15,000 villages in 26 out of 30 districts are in the grip of drought affecting 119.50 lakh population, 35.88 lakh cattle and 56.00 lakh hectare cropped area. The drought in Rajasthan is in the third year in succession severely affecting 30,583 villages in 31 out of 32 districts affecting 330.41 lakh population, 400 lakh cattle and 89.47 lakh hectares cropped area.
6. The Central Government is constantly monitoring the drought situation in consultation with the concerned State Governments. A Group of Ministers (GOM) under the Chairmanship of the Finance Minister has been set up for providing policy directions and support. The Management Group at official level under the Cabinet Secretary has also been set up for regular monitoring and coordination. A number of meetings have been held also with the State Governments to review the situation and taking appropriate measures for mitigating the drought situation.

7. Central share of Calamity Relief has been released to the States to undertake necessary steps in advance. 25% advance release of CRF has also been made in case of Rajasthan and Orissa. In response to the request for additional Central assistance received from the affected States, Central Teams were sent and an assistance from the National Calamity Contingency Fund (NCCF) amounting to Rs. 48.68 crore to Chhattisgarh, Rs. 85 crore to Gujarat, Rs. 35 crore to Madhya Pradesh, Rs. 35 crore to Orissa and Rs. 85 crore to Rajasthan has been released. The Memorandum from the Government of Himachal Pradesh for additional Central assistance was recently received and a Central team is shortly visiting the affected areas in the State for an on-the-spot assessment of the situation. No Memorandum has so far been received from the Government of Maharashtra for additional Central assistance.
8. The other steps taken by the Central Government include advance circulation of the Drought Contingency Action Plan, allocation at BPL rates of 60,300 MTs of foodgrains to Orissa, 2,52,500 MTs wheat to Rajasthan and 96,600 MTs of rice to Chhattisgarh, allocation of 5.00 lakh tonnes of foodgrains free of cost under Food for Work Programme (Chhattisgarh 1.60 lakh MT, Gujarat 90,000 MT, Himachal Pradesh 5,000 MT, Madhya Pradesh 35,000 MT, Maharashtra 10,000 MT, Orissa 1.00 lakh MT and Rajasthan 1.00 lakh MT), release of 1.70 lakh MT feed category of foodgrains as cattle feed, issue of orders to ban movement of fodder outside the State on requests received, free transportation of drinking water and fodder by the Railways to the affected areas, relaxation of norms by the Department of Drinking Water Supply with regard to release of funds under scheme implemented by them to facilitate completion of projects in time and handing over of 620 exploratory tube-wells and offer of another 890 tube-wells for drinking water purposes etc.
9. The State Governments have also initiated necessary measures for mitigating the effect of drought. The steps by State Government include finalisation of Contingency Action

Plans, initiating employment generation programmes, preparation of Rail movement plans for water and fodder, opening of fodder depots and cattle camps, arrangements of drinking water including supplies through tankers, implementation of Food-for-Work Programme, identification of drinking water source in each affected village and care of women and child and other vulnerable sections. The State Governments are also associating non-governmental organisations and voluntary agencies in their relief efforts.

10. The Central government is in constant touch with all the drought affected States and providing all necessary assistance to help them in tackling the situation arising out of the drought. The Central Government and the State Governments are aware of the seriousness of the problem which is likely to arise in the coming summer months and are concerned about it. I may assure that all necessary measures will be taken in providing relief and succour to the people affected by the drought and the resources at the command of the Government will be available for providing relief to the people. I am confident that the State Governments which are primarily responsible for the Ground level relief will keep their administrative machinery geared up to respond effectively to the situation.

In order to find solutions, many conferences and symposia are arranged and literature published. Some of these are:

1. Symposium on Preparedness Mitigation and Management of Natural disasters, organised by Central Water Commission, New Delhi, August 2-4, 1989.
2. 9th Symposium on Earthquake Engineering, organised by DEQ-UOR and ISET, November, 1990.
3. National Policy Analysis—Workshop on Natural Disaster Reduction, organised by Administrative Staff College of India, Hyderabad, December 16-20, 1991.
4. Workshop on Uttarkashi Earthquake, organised by DEQ-UOR, December, 1991.
5. World Congress on Natural Hazard reduction, organised by

The Institution of Engineers (India), New Delhi, January 10-14, 1992.

6. 4th Session of the Scientific and Technical Committee of IDNDR, organised by Ministry of Agriculture, Government of India, February 1-5, 1993. New Delhi.
7. National Seminar on Hydrological Hazards— Prevention and Mitigation, organised by DEQ-UOR, March, 1993.
8. Workshop on Natural Disaster Reduction in the South Asia Region, New Delhi, March 30-April 2, 1994.
9. 10th Symposium of Earthquake engineering, organised by DEQ-UOR and ISET, November 1994.
10. Seminar on comprehensive Flood Loss Prevention and Management organised by ESCAP hosted by Govt. of India, 28-29 September, 1994, New Delhi.
11. International Conference on Wind Engineering, organised by Indian Society for Wing Engineering, Roorkee, at New Delhi, January 9-13, 1995.
12. IDNDR-Day celebrations on given theme on regular basis since 1995, on Second Wednesday of October every year, organised by NCDM.
13. Workshop on Himalayan Eco-Development and Natural Disaster Reduction, organised by NCDM, New Delhi, November, 1995.
14. International Seminar on Mathematical Modelling of Atmospheric and Oceanic Processes, organised by Department of Mathematics, Berhampur University, Berhampur, December 18-21, 1995.
15. International Conference on Disasters and Mitigation, organised by Anna University, Chennai, January 19-22, 1996.
16. Workshop on Safety from Forest Five: Courses and Remedies, organised by Uttar Pradesh Academy of Administration, Nainital and Forest Panchayat Training Institute, April 16-17, 1996.
17. PIARCG2 Group Seminar, Natural Disaster Reduction for Roads, organised by Central Road Research Institute, New Delhi, January 29-31, 1997.
18. International Seminar on Coping with Natural Disasters:

Aspects of Risks, Crisis and Development, organised by Natural Disasters Management Cell, Agri-Economic Research Centre, Visva Bharati, Shantiniketan, February 28-March 2, 1997.

19. Workshop on Earthquake Disaster Mitigation, organised by DEQ-UOR, October, 1997.
20. Seminar on Natural Hazards in Urban Habitat, organised by Central Building Research Institute, Roorkee at New Delhi, November 10-11, 1997.
21. International Symposium on Asian Monsoon and Pollution over the Monsoon Environment, organised by Indian Meteorological Society, New Delhi, December 2-5, 1997.
22. Third Annual Convention of Indian Building Congress on Built Environment & Natural Hazards, New Delhi, February 7-8, 1998.
23. International Conference on Disaster Management, organised by Tezpur University, Guwahati, Assam, April 23-26, 1998.
24. Workshop on Geohazard & Related Societal Issues, organised by Indian Society of Engineering Geology, Lucknow, November 26, 1998.
25. 11th Symposium on Earthquake Engineering, organised by DEQ-UOR and ISET, December, 1998.
26. Policy Forum on Future of Mitigation of South Asian Disasters, organised by Disaster Management Institute and Duryog Nivaran, New Delhi, February 5-6, 1999.
27. National Symposium on tropical Meteorology, organised by Indian Meteorological Society, Regional Meteorological Centre, Chennai, February 16-19, 1999.
28. National Advisory Group Meeting on Managing and Measuring the Vulnerability, organised by Disaster Management Institute, New Delhi, June 12, 1999.

The purpose of Disaster Management is to mitigate sufferings as well as find their causes and solutions. International Decade For Natural Disaster Reduction (IDNDR) has set the following objectives and goals in this direction.

When the UN General Assembly adopted resolution 44/

236 in 1989 and formally decided on the IDNDR, the following objectives and goals were established:

1. The Objective of the decade is to reduce through concerted international action, especially in developing countries, the loss of life, property damage and social and economic disruption caused by natural disasters, such as earthquakes, windstorms, floods, landslides, volcanic eruptions, wildfire, grasshopper and locust infestations, drought and desertification and other calamities of natural origin.
2. The goals of the Decade are:
   (a) To improve the capacity of each country to mitigate the effects of natural disasters expeditiously and effectively, paying special attention to assisting developing countries in the assessment of disasters damage potential and in the establishment of early warning systems and disaster-resistant structures when and where needed;
   (b) To devise appropriate guidelines and strategies for applying existing scientific and technical knowledge, taking into account the cultural and economic diversity among nations;
   (c) To foster scientific and engineering endeavors aimed at closing critical gaps in knowledge in order to reduce loss of life and property;
   (d) To disseminate existing and new technical information related to measures for the assessment, prediction and mitigation of natural disasters; and
   (e) To develop measures for the assessment, prediction, prevention and mitigation of natural disasters through programmes of technical assistance and technology transfer, demonstration projects, and education and training, tailored to specific disasters and locations, and to evaluate the effectiveness of those programmes.

CONCLUSION

V. Suresh and Taranjot K. Gadhok in their article "Disaster to Development", (*Shelter,* Oct. 13,1999) rightly suggest that it is high time that the thinking process is brought to a turn around from "actions to preaction". It requires strong political will to put knowledge base to work, to use the forces of legislation, education, public awareness and policy making on development and relief to make disaster reduction measures part of our everyday consciousness and planning activities.

Whenever disasters strike, they do not discriminate or differentiate between men and nations, poor or rich, young or old. They do not negotiate or listen and they do not wait, they simply come, kill and destroy, irrepairable losses which are irrecoverable. And when these hazards strike, it is the communities who are first to react, it is the communities irrespective of their profession, status, cast or culture who need to react. Therefore, it is important that capacities of communities are built to observe, understand and prepare themselves for worst impact. It is important to allow transparency of actions of the nodal agencies working towards mitigation measures to encourage communities to get involved, so that at the time of occurrence of disasters, they do not wait for help they can stand on their own feet and mobilize self-help, before rescue and relief reaches them. This may require coordination with NGOs, which are trained to handle such situation.

In the rapidly changing scenario, the real wealth will lie in knowledge, innovation and speedy action. It would mean discarding the bureaucratic apparels and getting into the space suit of the 21st century. The road ahead is bumpy, but exciting being totally in an uncharted territory. It is up to us to use our intellectual prowess and negotiate the road with bold imagination, and deep urge to succeed.

THREE

CHALLENGES AHEAD

Earthquakes and other disasters are a phenomenon which cannot be stopped altogether, but advance planning can mitigate sufferings. What precautions are necessary, is a difficult question which needs research, analysis and documentation. We must initiate action on it to avoid miseries and sorrows, which can be prevented. *Indian Express* Editorial (January 29, 2001) rightly suggests that the Republic Day earthquake does raise numerous questions about the quality of the country's development and disaster preparedness, about the nature of its urban planning, about the character of its housing construction, questions that don't have easy answers. For the moment, however, there is no getting away from the fact that earthquakes will continue to be part of our lives, perched as we are on a vast land plate floating on an ocean of molten rock: according to informed estimates, 57 per cent of the country is prone to earthquakes. The tremors of the earthquake were felt as far away as Tamil Nadu and Delhi. Incidentally, Kutch was hit by an earthquake in 1819 and the Sindree fort that once guarded its coastline there had collapsed under its assault. Yet, we seem to have learnt almost nothing from the past. While it is true that earthquakes cannot be predicted, the fact remains that while the 1993 Latur earthquake left over 10,000 dead, the one that had visited Los Angles some 22 years earlier was far more severe but killed just 55. One of the reasons for the heavy death tolls in India is its high population density. But it is also true that the country has not internalized any of the lessons it has learnt from encounters with death on a mass scale. Let us discuss the challenges which are responsible for heavy losses during disaster.

1. Lack of Efficient Organizational set up

To deal with all issues arising out of Earthquake in the short-term and long-term perspectives besides the Nodal Agency in the government of India, the state government should constitute a high powered committee to take quick and reliable decisions as well as review their implementation. Since the local administration is aware of the locale and its issues, therefore, their interest is vital to mitigate sufferings in the short-and long-term. *Indian Express* (February 7, 2001) has reported the constitution of such an authority by Gujarat Government only after the occurrence of the earthquake.

The state government has set up a Gujarat Earthquake Management Authority headed by Chief Minister Keshubhai Patel. It has also decided to create a separate Department of Earthquake Relief for better monitoring and implementation of rehabilitation, reconstruction and relief works in the quake-ravaged parts of the state.

The decisions were taken at a Cabinet meeting held on Tuesday for the first time since the killer earthquake struck parts of the state on January 26. "We could not convene a Cabinet meeting immediately after the quake, since all the ministers were engaged in rescue/relief operations in the affected areas", the Chief Minister reasoned at the post-Cabinet news conference.

Keshubhai Patel and the Gujarat Earthquake Management Authority would co-ordinate and supervise the rehabilitation and reconstruction works to be carried out by various agencies in the quake-hit areas. The authority would also have a Secretary-level official as its chief executive.

The decision to create a separate Department of Earthquake Relief in the General Administration Department (GAD) in the Secretariat, as has been done by the Andhra Pradesh and Maharashtra governments, is aimed at relieving the existing State Relief Commissioner of additional burden of dealing with relief-related works during natural calamities. The government would soon appoint a Secretary to head the new department, Patel said.

The CM said a district-level administrative unit would be set up in each of the 16 worst-hit taluka places where an additional district collector and additional district development officer would be appointed to ensure effective and speedy implementation of relief and rehabilitation of works. The talukas include Bhuj, Bhachau, Rapar, Anjar, Gandhidham, Jodiya, Morbi, Maliya-Miyana, Wankaner, Santalpur, Ahmedabad city, Daskroi, Halvad, Dhangadhra, Patadi and Dasada.

On the relaxation of relief norms, he said the government has accepted the Opposition parties' suggestion to raise the ceiling of three persons a family to five persons of a family to provide cash doles of Rs. 15 to each of the quake victims for a month. The revised ceiling will be in force from February 10. Cash assistance has been raised from Rs. 650 to Rs. 1,200 for the victims to purchase household articles.

There has been great delay on the part of authorities in taking decisions after a fortnight of the occurrence of earthquake. This speaks of callous attitude and absence of responsiveness. Decisions taken in time would have saved thousands of lives and smoothen the lives of those who survived the tragedy. We discuss here the comments of some eminent persons in this regard.

Bharat Desai and Anil Pathak in their article "Quake throws government out of gear" are also critical of the role of State Government and feel that chaos rules the corridors of the Gujarat government. The way things are moving, the state may soon match the Orissa government in misadministration.

First hand reports suggest that law and order has completely broken down in Kutch, though a large contingent of police officials have now been despatched. "Marauding gangs are moving around, looting people at gun point", the official said. "Food material is reaching only Bhuj town, that also the main camps situated close to the main road. Other relief camps are not getting anything, consequently able bodied men from these interior camps are waiting on the main road and pouncing on trucks coming with relief material," says a social worker who has just returned from the city.

The Hindu Editorial, February 2001, "Handling a Disaster" rightly comments about organisational deficiencies in the system. The quake was not the first time that we have seen that the response to a natural calamity of each level of the Government has been initially agonisingly slow and then chaotic. In spite of the fact that disasters blight the country with such regularity, affecting on an average some 50 million Indians and killing 5,000, the Government remains poorly prepared to cope with either rescue, relief or rehabilitation. There are already crisis management groups from the district upwards, with the apex being occupied by a committee headed by no less an official than the Cabinet Secretary. As a string of recent events has shown, all these committees either exist only on paper or are totally ineffectual in their responses. What is needed therefore is not yet another committee but Government machinery which is trained to see disaster management as a routine part of administration and a force of personnel skilled in the more critical aspects of rescue and relief which could be mobilised immediately and which would be backed up with adequate equipment for medical, power, telecom and temporary housing operations

Although the Orissa cyclone of 1999 revealed the structural flaws in the ability of the State and Central Governments to cope with a calamity, the Centre preferred, ostrich-like, to assume that all was well in disaster management. Relief may be a State subject but the severity of major disasters stretches the capacity of all Governments and therefore calls for *a* national response—in a quick, efficient and large-scale manner.

Kutch is not the only place where confusion abounds. Ahmedabad is no exception. Even five days after the quake, residents of the high rise apartments were still sleeping in cars and tents. A massive exodus began on the evening of January 31, following rumours about a supposed astrological prediction that another quake in the state is imminent.

Gujarat CM, Keshubhai Patel admitted that there was lack of coordination between government agencies and NGOs in handling relief and rescue operations. "I am camping here to supervise the entire operation and will not leave before ensuring there is coordination."

It is hoped that the Government under the leadership of the Chief Minister would accelerate the tempo of relief and rehabilitation so that the people return to normal life as early as possible. The Chief Minister and his colleagues have realized their mistake resulting in chaos. It should not remain merely on paper.

Hari Jai Singh has rightly mentioned in his article "Nation in Dire Distress" in the *Tribune*, dated February 2, 2001 that the time has come for the country to think on new lines in a positive manner. It is gratifying to note that the response from the world community to the Gujarat disaster is tremendous. The people have cut across the barriers of caste, community, creed, region and religion to offer a helping hand. This display of oneness is what has to be seen as a symbol of India's new liberal nationalism with a human face.

There are, however, no short cuts to the challenge of managing the country professionally and efficiently. Prime Minister Atal Behari Vajpayee should think on modern professional lines and lead the nation in the 21st century with the sole resolve of "less rhetoric and hypocrisy and more action"—the action which has to be for the good and welfare of the people and not for filling the pockets of operators, manipulators and power brokers. In every walk of national life, we ought to be professional and business like in our thinking and working. The miseries of the people who suffer in Gujarat could have been minimized to a large extent if we had taken preventive steps and worked out a viable disaster management plan.

Such a plan should automatically get into action in any crisis situation. In the final analysis, a preventive action plan will not require massive funds which are spent for relief and rehabilitation operations after a disaster strikes. The important thing is to think about the directions we ought to take. If our direction and goals are chosen strategically and pursued relentlessly, we may see the impossible to begin to look possible.

He further states in his article "Faulty System and Poor Response : Technology as a Tool For Disaster Management" in the *Daily Tribune* (February 9, 2001) that despite numerous natural calamities in the past, a viable disaster management system is missing. There is no point in boasting about our information technology revolution. We have hardly used IT power for the service of the people. It needs to be realized that information technology has made today's statecraft and politico-economic management virtually outdated. It is, therefore, necessary to shed the old mindset. It is not the people but the system, the persons at the helm and the poor standard of governance which have invariably failed the nation. This has once again been proved by the way the people, here and abroad, have responded to one of the biggest disasters ever to hit the country in the wake of the devastating earthquake in Gujarat.

However, nothing can work unless the government moves in the right direction and reforms itself by evolving community-based participatory structures and subjects itself to strict accountability. It also must overcome its various disabilities, particularly the lack of skills through networking. In this lies the seeds of hope for tomorrow.

Prof. V.K. Dhar, Associate Professor, NIUA, New Delhi remarked (*Economic Times*, February 6, 2001) that there is no doubt that public confidence gets shaken up by the manner in which relief measures are being handled or have, been handled in the past. In a condition of virtual collapse, the need is for a systematic organizational set up which has a range of capabilities needed to bring succour and order in state. Unarguably, it is the Defence Services particularly the Army which is well equipped with the range of skills; they are trained to be self-reliant in the battle zone which is not much different from the disaster zone. An effort should be made to constitute Disaster Rescue and Relief Committee which may include defence secretary and senior army officials, while the rehabilitation and reconstruction work may be left for civilian organization which may include central and state government officials and NGOs who are trained and experienced to tackle the after effects of such disasters. Alternatively, each NGO may be made responsible for a group of 500 affected persons for their relief and rehabilitation.

Tom Alcedo, Director, CARE India (*Economic Times*,

February 6, 2001), has suggested that Mitigation and Preparedness Measures (DMP) are actions, which are taken before a disaster. DMP is analogous to preventative health care. While most efforts and resources are directed towards post-disaster relief, as we are now seeing in Gujarat, there is often little interest or political will to take measures to prepare for such a disaster that hasn't happened yet. Yet, failure to address this can result in enormous losses of life, property and livelihood. Disaster mitigation involves implementing long-term risk reduction measures.

As was debated and agreed upon during the Disaster and Risk Reduction Forum in Geneva in July 1999, at the end of the International Decade for Natural Disaster Reduction (IDNDR), while natural disasters are inevitable and the elimination of all risks is impossible, there are many technical measures, traditional practices, and public experience that can reduce the extent or severity of economic and social disasters. Hazards and emergency requirements are a part of living with nature, but human behaviour can be changed. In the words of UN Secretary General: "We must above all, shift from a culture of reaction to a culture of prevention. Prevention is not only more humane than cure; it is also much cheaper ... Above all let us remember that disaster prevention, is a moral imperative, no less than reducing the risks of war."

Dr. G.S. Benipal, Civil Engineer, HT, Delhi (*Economic Times*, February 6, 2001) feels that Scientific understanding of such phenomena and development of technical experts for dealing with them is absolutely necessary for ensuring some safety from calamities. Relevant knowledge is available with the engineers to design safe buildings and other structures, if the severity of the phenomena occurring during the structure's life time is known. The uncertainty associated with these design techniques can be reduced through scientific research.

According to Dimock and Dimock, "Organisation is the systematic bringing together of inter-dependent parts to form a unified whole through which authority, co-ordination and control may be exercised to achieve a given purpose. . .

Organisation is both structure and human relations." We must build such organisation for disaster management.

2. Lack of Effective Administration to deal with Earthquake issues from all Angles

Public Administration is the heart of development. Any systematic effort towards earthquake management must be preceded by, or coupled with efforts, to make more effective the functioning of governmental machinery. Administration is essential both for developed and developing countries. No system of Government can survive without a good system of administration. It can be found in the poetic couplet: "For forms of government, let fools contest, whatever administered best, is the best". Dr. Rajendra Prasad said at the concluding session of the Constituent Assembly: "Whatever the constitution may or may not provide, the welfare of the country will depend upon the way in which the country is administered. That will depend upon the men who administer it. It requires men of strong character, men of vision, men who will not sacrifice the interests of the country at large for the sake of smaller groups and areas, and who rise above the prejudices which are born of these differences".

"Good Public Administration" writes Leif H. Share, Director, the Government Institution of Organisation and Management, Oslo, Norway, "could serve as a major instrument for promoting economic and social development and for introducing needed advances in science and technology, but major reforms in the organizations and operations of government and in the knowledge, skills and attitudes of public employees at all levels were often necessary for it to do so; deficiencies in administration had been a major reason for past failures in the implementation of national development plans." The failures of earthquake management in Gujarat confirms our views about the need of effective and efficient administration.

S.R. Chirmade in his article, "Administrative Preconditions for Nation Building" in *IJPA*, April and June

1988, has rightly said that "the worldwide commitment of new nations and low-income countries to achieve, virtually within a short span of time, higher levels of economic and social development has given a new dimension to traditional concepts of public administration. The formulations and implementation of strategies and programmes for the modernization of a nation, without doubt, present the greatest single challenge to public administration. Public administration is the process by which objectives are defined, plans and policies formulated, institutions created and managed, human energies mobilized, resources utilized and changes effected."

Public administration, through social and economic changes, has to attempt societal transformation either through direct involvement or through the regulation of other instruments of development. So public administration has to serve the process of the transformation of the society in both developed and developing countries. No attention was paid to administration of earthquake in Gujarat resulting into loss of thousands of lives.

Bhaskar Ghose in his article "The Final Countdown" in *Hindustan Times* dated February 8,2001 suggests that we cannot stop such disasters. What is needed to learn from failures and make the administrative system perfect for future to take care of all mistakes and faults in advance. He has pointed out that we will continue to live in the shadow of peril, and we will never know when it will come, whether it will come at all, and if it does, what shape it will take. But life must continue; shops must open and do business, offices must engage in whatever activity they are there to do, trains must run, power units must function (in the manner in which they're used to). In short, it has to be business as usual. Even in Gujarat, when the dead have been cremated or buried, when they have come to some kind of terms with grief and devastation, the business of living will continue. What we would call everyday living will, of necessity, be resumed, as time passes.

It is time for a system to be put in place which, firstly and most importantly, is under the direct control of one person, is capable of quick ordered reaction to a calamity, has access to information on the location of material and equipment, is able to mobilise personnel, and which is, by law, the overriding authority in a crisis, with the legal backing to issue instructions to all agencies of Government, civic bodies, and of private agencies which have to be carried out immediately. Its relations with the armed forces will need to be worked out in clear, unambiguous terms.

Disasters will occur; we don't need astrologers poring over their grubby rolls of papers and manuals to tell us that. We have to live with them and carry on living. As someone said, "If it be now, 'tis not to come; if it be not to come, it will be now; if it be not now, yet it will come: the readiness is all".

Amit Sengupta in his article "Dumbstruck by Devastation", in *Hindustan Times* (February 8, 2001) painfully remarks that: While the bureaucracy in Bhuj and Gandhinagar —and let us not forget New Delhi—twiddles its thumbs, making false claims and utterly hollow promises. Reality tells a dark tale of a democracy where the political class has proved its cold insensitivity and professional inefficiency even in the face of such a disaster. There is a lesson for the people of India after this catastrophe: the hallucinatory patriotic euphoria of India being a nuclear power and a potential superpower in the new millennium is a lot of hogwash. When it comes to the mighty Indian State, it is nothing but a clueless paper tiger, a dumb, monolith. It is nowhere in sight when it comes to coping with mass tragedy as we now see in the dead cities and villages of Kutch.

For citizens, in this ravaged society, the Government does not exist. These comments by those who have actually seen the events happening cause pain and agony in everybody's mind and raise many questions. What have we achieved after more than 50 years of independence? Our own elected government is making a fool of the people. They have different priorities except the people who are suffering in misery in this dark time of their life.

There will always be damage, deaths, grief and terror. That no one can prevent. But it can be minimized, to the extent that an effective government can, with a system that responds quickly, have access to what is needed, get it there, mobilize personnel and—very importantly—make as much information available as possible.

3. Apathy on the part of top Bureaucracy and Key Political Elite

Public Administration and citizens are intimately related to each other as the existence of one without the other is not possible in a civilized society. The harmonious relationship depends upon the sincerity, earnestness and cooperation between the two. To quote Robson, "The achievement of good relations between the government and the public is a matter which does not by any means depend solely on the conduct of civil servants and politicians. It depends equally upon the attitude of citizens, groups, corporations, associations of all kinds and, indeed, of all unofficial bodies to public authorities. If we want public servants to behave well towards us, we must behave well towards them. Moreover well... If politicians and civil servants are held in the low esteem, if their work is derived, if abuse and invective is poured on them continuously, if loose and unsubstantial allegations are made about their incompetence, dishonesty, laziness and indifference to the public interests, it is unlikely that officials will develop or display qualities of integrity, industry and public spirit"

Good citizen administration relationship would:

(a) Encourage people's participation—a *sine qua non* for development and modernization.

(b) Kindle the potential energy of the citizens into kinetic energy to accelerate development.

(c) Supplement the efforts of the Government in the conduct of its affairs.

(d) Strengthen the values of democracy in the minds and spirit of the people.

(e) Enlist respect in the constitution which is rooted in people's sovereignty.

(f) Develop bonds of friendship and goodwill between citizens and administration, and *vice versa*.

(g) Avoid social unrest, tensions, violence and other social upheavals which have become the order of the day.

Administration is never something apart from people and their needs; rather it is the means by which these needs are met and the administrator who thinks of his organization as something apart from the community will fail to recognize significant problems of the citizens and the administration will not be in a position to deliver the goods.

ARC has also observed in this very connection : "If, in the prosperity of the people, lies the strength of a government, it is in their contentment that lies the security and stability of democracy."

However in Gujarat, during earthquake and after that, we find that Politico-administrative leadership never realized their obligations to the people. They remained dumb spectators worrying only about their family and near and dear ones. They forgot their duties. Let us mention the comments of some eminent persons.

Inder Malhotra is very critical of Indian bureaucracy and Political Elite in handling Gujarat Earthquake situation. In his article, "Nightmare of Gujarat's mega-quake" in *The Tribune,* dated February 1, 2001 he clearly stated that Official media informed the country, in a tone that had a touch of crowing about it, that the Cabinet Crisis Management Committee (CMC) —consisting of top bureaucrats and technocrats—at 3 p.m. Instead of being pleased about it, all concerned ought to be ashamed. The worthy members of the committee ought to have quietly left the parade and buckled down to their primary responsibility without losing a single second. The deplorable delay on their part only underscores that no lessons were learnt from the similar dithering at the time of the hijacking of the IC-814 about thirteen months ago.

Then also it had taken several hours for the CMC to assemble. To compound this failing, official spokespersons trotted out the excuse that "it took time" to inform all the members of the committee who were busy in various parts of the city. In heaven's name what are the cellular phones that the taxpayer provides to every official above a certain rank meant for ? Indeed, why should it be necessary to summon the CMC members at all? At the first hint of a major crisis like the one that has overtaken the country they must automatically head for the pre-arranged spot, usually the Cabinet Secretary's office. This happens, as a matter of course, in all countries where governance hasn't deteriorated to the extent it has here. Reaction time in New Delhi to the super-cyclone in Orissa was equally long. It chills the blood to contemplate what might happen if there is similar lackadaisical approach to, God forbid, a nuclear threat to this country.

Bureaucratic file push cannot be permitted to become a substitute for work on the ground. Above all, no one should forget that the Oriya victims of the cyclone and even the sufferers from Bhopal gas tragedy of 1984 have not yet been fully compensated or rehabilitated. This shameful history must not be allowed to repeat itself now or ever again.

Even the *Tribune* editorial was very critical. To quote: "The first who should be rapped on the knuckles are the members of the Central Crisis Management Committee, comprising top bureaucrats, who got together at 3 p.m. for discussing the calamity which befell Gujarat minutes before the President arrived at Rajpath for taking the salute at the Republic Day parade. It is a matter of great shame even for central leadership who continued enjoying the Republic Day and did not bother to take stock of the Gujarat situation. Republic Day celebrations after the Gujarat News clearly prove that the Republic is for the political elite and not for the people. This has made our preamble a hollow enunciation.

4. Lack of Effective Leadership and Communication to deal with Disaster Issues

The success or failure of an organization depends, to a great extent, upon the administrative capability and motivation of its top leadership. Administrative capability is an important means of converting or processing programme inputs into outputs such as goods and services. It has been mentioned by V.L. Gabriel that: "what makes the leadership variable so crucial in the implementation process is its dynamic, not passive, quality, i.e. its capability to act and react on these critical inputs. It is this administrative and transferring quality of leadership that could significantly determine the administrative capability of implementing organization."

Leadership and Crisis Management

Crises are becoming a regular phenomenon at various levels. The leaders must learn to deal effectively with these crises to keep the administration on an even keel. Crises are going to increase in future, as external and internal environments are under constant turbulence. There is a need to devise methods to deal with these crises in a planned and effective way. Crisis mangement system should be built in the administration of every organization.

Anurag Goel suggests that leaders must know methods to deal with a critical issue or situation, which has become essential in the recent times. To quote him. The requisites of crisis management can be summed up as under:

(i) Identify the problems that could lead to a crisis and learn when and how to intervene most effectively,
(ii) Know how to carry out the difficult planning and coordination activities associated with preparing for, and managing crisis,
(iii) Develop special negotiating and communication skills required to reduce conflict or ensure cooperation in a crisis situation,
(iv) Develop special knowledge and expertise in the field.

Crisis handling is both an art as well as a science. It needs advance planning. Not to do it is to invite troubles and cannot be handled in a normal way. What is the result? Chaos and anarchy. We must not allow such a situation to occur.

Shivraj Patil, Former Speaker of Lok Sabha, has rightly suggested in his article, "Learn from Latur, re-create Gujarat", in *The Hindustan Times,* dated February 4, 2001 that the key to success is a combination of Leadership, planning and coordination. The key to success was a combination of leadership, planning and coordination. In a situation like Gujarat, a lot depends on the quality of leadership—both at the political level and the administrative level.

The head of the government should be available 24 hours for snap decisions. Sharad Pawar (Chief Minister of Maharashtra at the time of Latur quake) and his team of ministers and official provided exemplary leadership in the management of the Latur crisis.

Our experience in Latur is that there was never a dearth of relief materials or money. In fact, the entire world appeared to be eager to provide a helping hand. The World Bank sanctioned loans for reconstruction of Latur village within 24 hours of Finance Minister Manmohan Singh seeking help.

The state government can and should coordinate the flow of assistance that is pouring in, and is likely to come in bigger volumes. The responsible officers and ministers, preferably the Chief Minister himself should be available for three weeks in the vicinity of the affected areas to give guidance and sanction funds, and allow actions, which are needed.

In the task of helping the victims, the state Government can obtain cooperation of the Union government, the other state governments, the governments of other countries, international organizations, voluntary organizations, public and private industry, associations of doctors and engineers, traders and industrialists.

In every effort that went into constructing Latur, some things were absolutely critical such as leadership, planning and the willingness to cooperate and coordinate the activities and the will power of the people who suffered the most. Let us hope that the same elements go into rebuilding Gujarat's quake ravaged cities and towns.

Finally, it must be remembered that the only thing that is not possible is the revival of the dead. True, there is no way you can compensate the loss of one's loved ones. But, short of that, you can re-create everything else—in a beautiful manner. Let's do it in Gujarat. Let me quote Sosiah Gilbert Holland who through this couplet mention the required moral ingredients of top men:

God, Give us men!

God, Give us men, A time like this demands
Strong minds, great hearts, true faith and ready hands,
Men whom the lust of office does not sell,
Men whom the spoils of office cannot buy,
Men who possess opinions and a will,
Men who have honour, Men who will not lie.

5. Lack of Coordination among All Agencies Engaged in Earthquake Relief

In Gujarat, NGOs are doing useful work, but there is a lot of duplication, overlapping and wastage. There is no coordination even with the Government agencies.

NGOs are the most effective means of achieving an efficient communication link between the Disaster Management agencies and affected community. There are different types of NGOs working at advocacy level as well as grassroots level; in typical disaster situations, they can be of help in preparedness, relief and rescue, rehabilitation and reconstruction and also in monitoring and feedback. Properly put to use, NGOs can be the key to a successful and participatory approach to disaster management.

According to Mooney, coordination is the first principle of organization and includes within itself all other principles, which are subordinate to it and through which it operates.

Coordination is the process of bringing activities or groups of activities into proper relation with each other to make sure that everything that needs to be achieved is achieved and that no two people are trying to do the same job.

Coordination is the means of distributing authority, providing channels of communication, and arranging the work so that:

The right things are done	(What)
In the right place	(Where)
At the right time	(When)
In the right way	(How)
By the right people	(by Whom)

When an activity is coordinated, everything works well. A coordinated activity is orderly, harmonious, efficient, and successful.

According to Terry, coordination is the adjustment of the parts of each other and of the movement and operation of parts in time so that each can make its maximum contribution to the product of the whole.

According to J.C. Charlsworth, "Coordination is the integration of the several parts into an orderly whole to achieve the purpose of the undertaking."

Coordination implies the prevention of both duplication and overlapping so as to avoid administrative wastes of efforts, manpower and resources and to pool resources and experiences in dealing with problems and in achieving common objectives. Coordination—which is a means to an end and not an end in itself—must be considered in relation to its practical purposes which is to facilitate better performance and greater administrative efficiency in the system. To ensure efficient and economical functioning of an organization, coordination is not only desirable but even essential. For the same reason, inter-organisation coordination is advisable, especially when the activities of the various organizations concerned are of a complementary nature.

Stressing the need for coordination, the UN Secretary-General stated at the 41st Session of the ECOSOC held in Geneva:

> "Apart from the continuing need to avoid overlapping and inconsistencies, coordination is more and more conceived in a positive and dynamic sense and aimed at providing an agreed direction and a framework for action and at ensuring not only that activities dovetail into one another but there is a full measure of forethought and harmony in the carrying out of our responsibilities. Among all administrative activities, coordination is the most fascinating and, sometimes, the most delicate intellectual exercise. No organization can attain its goals without adequate coordination among its units and their functionaries .... Coordination is, indeed, the administrative manifestation of creativity, may be with an all-pervading effect on the organization as a whole .... It aims at an interlinking

between one experience and another with an emerging synthesis."

Coordination is distinct from the hierarchical process of authority, command and control. Unless coordination procedures are observed, satisfactory programming and implementation are impossible. Coordination may be achieved through collaboration in working for the same cause, or cooperation in the sharing of a joint task by two or more parties, often it includes both modes of action.

Coordination may lead to one organization performing services or attacking a problem on behalf of all organizations in the system. It may also lead one or more parties, on the basis of information and consultation, to refrain entirely from participation in a given activity so as to avoid duplication of efforts. Coordination in such circumstances is accomplished by separation of functions rather than by a decision to work in concert.

However, Gujarat administration did not bother for this fundamental principle of administration as already explained. Gujarat administration, on *ad hoc* basis, has been making the problems of earthquake complicated, complex and beyond control. Administration was working in isolated way without proper co-ordination. Let us explain with the comments of people who visited the area.

Ajit Seth in his Article 'Trauma in Gujarat" *(Economic Times,* January 30, 2001) rightly suggests the need of coordination among NGO's to tackle the problems of earthquake.

In this context, the role of NGOs deserves mention. No doubt these organizations often perform a yeoman's service. But past experience in the wake of other earthquake calamities shows that NGOs and individual volunteers in their anxiety and even zeal often bountifully give away relief material at sites nearest to the road. This leads to inequitable distribution. The moral: coordinate and guide the efforts of different voluntary agencies and individuals.

Coordination within and among various agencies/ departments of the state/central governments is, of course, paramount. No doubt, this is being done. But let us remember that in the confusion and chaos which follows such devastation, it is not unknown for such coordination to collapse, particularly at the district level. This sometimes can even lead to an erosion of the hierarchical structure which is most effective for decision-making under such disaster conditions.

Attention is required to be paid to the dissemination of correct information through regular media briefings, specially in the first few weeks. The media, which plays a crucial role in the wake of such an event, would also do well to appreciate the unenviable circumstance in which an army of officials, jawans and private citizens are together struggling to get a job done. If reporters are informed with empathy and understanding, it would be better for all concerned.

Irrelevant and harsh though it may appear to say so at this 'early' stage, when rescue operations are still on, there is need for following a streamlined accounting procedure for the distribution of relief. After all, there is life even after the disaster. Only we are too close to events to notice now. Sharad Pawar has rightly said that coordination should now be the key word in Gujarat (*Hindustan Times,* January 3, 2001).

A.K. Misra in his article "incorrigible" in *The Tribune,* (5.2.2001) observes that : Though people from the length and breadth of India even abroad are opening their hearts out and relief is pouring into Gujarat by rail, road and air at a frantic pace, a leisurely ambience prevails at the railway goods office in Ahmedabad.

In fact, the outpour seems to far outstrip the administrative ability of both the State and Central Governments. There is no nominee or liaison officer from the State government at either the Ahmedabad Railway Station or the air cargo terminal at the city airport. This correspondent spent a good deal of two hours at the cargo complex for two days every morning as flights came in and similarly over four hours at the railway station. Both places presented a scene of callousness, even criminal callousness. Half the compound at the air cargo terminal was full of packets and parcels.

Such a state of affairs of wastage of valuable resources is a poor reflection on Gujarat administration. This is because that Gujarat Government lacked advance planning and coordination mechanism, resulting into collapse of the entire administrative system.

Coordination is becoming complex, as the quantitative operations of the organizations are increasing at a very fast rate, without making changes in the administration structure and procedures responsible for coordination. Therefore, there is a need of advance planning and decision-making to achieve effective coordination. There is also need to create administrative structures like Cabinet Secretariat, Staff Agency, etc., to help in coordination. It is a continuous process. Coordination is not a simple process but is directly linked with the total management. Until and unless all the principles of the organization like planning, objectives, span of control, unity of command, authority and responsibility, etc., are not well defined, co-ordination becomes impossible and impracticable. A good organization leads to prompt and good coordination and *vice-versa.*

6. Lack of Positive Interest among University, Research Institutions and UN System in Dissemination of Disaster Management Knowledge Based on Research, Practical Experience and Observations

UGC can start disaster management courses and research in allied departments of the universities on a priority basis. Such experiences can be pooled and shared. J.C. Pant in his keynote address at the opening session of the Workshop on Disaster Prevention, held at NIRD, Hyderabad on 19th-20th December, 2000 remarked: Coming back to the main theme of disaster management, I would like to highlight the role of the elite and intellectual segments of our society. Every disaster is a unique event and every kind of data emerging out of it needs to be meticulously recorded for posterity. The scientific community, the technologists, the social scientists and other branches of knowledge need to be mobilized at short notice to record data and carry out necessary studies whenever a disaster strikes. This gives rise to a need for laying out a structure for initiating the learning exercise, at short notice, which can be used to collect data whenever a disaster strikes, in order to generate knowledge which may prevent future disasters as well as prepare people to face them in a better manner whenever they recur. This learning process has to be traced backward to know about the causes of various kinds of disasters, which is only possible through a process of networking of such knowledge as is available throughout the world today. We have decided to broadly network knowledge in three groups:

(i) Knowledge relating to natural disasters;
(ii) Knowledge relating to non-natural disasters; and
(iii) Knowledge relating to biological disasters.

This will also involve identifying centers of excellence in different fields of knowledge and technology which would need to collaborate to develop the required networks of knowledge. A small task force of eminent persons in the field of science and technology is working in this area and we hope to give concrete shape to this concept in the near future. This would help the country to prevent and reduce the occurrence of disasters and mitigate their impact whenever they strike. This exercise of harnessing science and technology in aid of disaster management promises to be an exciting venture which would hopefully usher in a comparatively safer world in the near future.

The whole process of preparation of disaster management plans initiated by the High Powered Committee is laying special emphasis on taking timely preventive measures by incorporating them into the very development planning system. This, in a manner of speaking, is promising to generate a nation-building exercise, which will involve the poorest of the poor in their own development. This will also need the willing co-operation of the elite of our society, working in close collaboration with people's organizations at all levels to plan for safe and better future.

There is an urgent need to integrate the school, college and university systems with disaster preparedness and response mechanism as they are a major seismic casualty of a super disaster, and have a major stake in preventing them, and also in mitigating their impact. Involvement of students and youth in disaster preparedness would also orient them for discharging their social responsibility towards the vulnerable sections of society in the long-run. The voluntary agencies need to come forward in a big way to mobilize students to prepare people to cope with disasters, as well as for organizing rescue and relief in a crisis. In a disaster situation it is the poorest sections of society which suffer most, and it is these sections of our population which have little access to the fruits of development due to illiteracy. The nation-wide network of NGOs has taken upon itself the task of integrating the people's movement for literacy, being implemented through the National Literacy Mission, with their own movement VASUDEVA for preparing people to cope with disasters. The Zilla Saksharta Samiti, i.e. the district level committee for promotion of literacy all over the country is being geared to prepare people to cope with disasters with particular reference to need for watchfulness in protecting the human rights of the poorest.

Universities, colleges and schools possess vast potentiality and with some training to students, a lot of rehabilitation work can be done after an earthquake with the help of students. National service scheme and NCC students can be used for such work. They would do such work with great pleasure.

7. No Attempt by Government and Urban Authorities to make Safe Buildings to withstand the Effects of Earthquake

Structures of houses are not safe to withstand the effects of earthquake. Besides, construction is violating all rules and regulations as in Delhi, Bombay, Shimla, etc. Ravi Kumar in *Hindustan Times* (January 31, 2001) has rightly analysed this problem and suggested :

This phenomena is global and many countries including Japan are coping with it by implementing new technologies to counter the quake. They have conceived quake-resistant analysis and are fully equipped to handle a crisis. Alternative designs of structures have also been applied at the ground level. In fact, quake-resistant structure is just about five to ten per cent costlier than the unsafe structures, which are routinely built in urban areas.

All over Indian cities and towns, every resident should wake up and check out if he or she is living in a safe building or not. In the wake of the Gujarat tragedy, both the Government and the civil society would do well to build quake-resistant structures and see to it that everyone follows the norm. Builders and consultants should be put under legal and ethical scrutiny. This is one way mass tragedies can be avoided.

Same view has been expressed in the *Hindustan Times* in Editorial (January 30, 2001). The Gujarat earthquake has seen financial aid flowing in—with the Ministry of Finance offering a blank cheque. This money has to be utilized not in quick-fix efforts, but in establishing a reliable disaster planning mechanism. Highest priority must be given to maintaining a grading system to assess how well communities actually enforce the construction codes. The criteria drawn up by the Indian Bureau of Standards for building houses in quake-prone areas must be taken much more seriously than what has been done so far. Predicting earthquakes is still an exercise in trial and error. The best one can do is be prepared for the worst. There is no harm 'overdoing' safety measures, especially when one can be sure that Gujarat hasn't seen the last of major earthquakes.

Arun Bapat in his article "Earthquakes don't kill, buildings do" in the *Indian Express* dated 6th February, 2001 observed that the probable reasons for failures of structures are improper design and not following the recommendations of the code. A small country like El Salvador has witnessed and suffered heavily in the earthquakes in 1986 and this year due to improper design. The worst example of the heavy destruction of high-rise buildings could be seen from the 1985 Mexican earthquake. The epicenter of this earthquake was about 300 kilometres away from the Mexico City, but it had to see the collapse of high-rise buildings only. The small houses did not suffer any damage. These examples will help in understanding the significance of a seismic design of structures, especially tall buildings.

Mandera Singh in his article "War against devastation", in *Hindustan Times* (February 19, 2001) suggests that if there are lessons to be learnt from Gujarat, then the first one is that ordinary

Indians are capable of rising to the occasion and putting in their bit. Imagine the difference that prior training would have made. The second lesson is that levels of seismic activity do not determine the levels of destruction. It is in fact the efficiency of the living space to absorb the quake that decides the scale of damage.

An earthquake of a similar intensity on the Richter Scale would not have caused an equivalent amount of damage in California for the simple reasons that all construction has to be "temblor-resistant". That lesson is beyond the purview of the armed forces. And if those responsible for implementing the building laws had been doing their work, Gujarat may not have suffered to the degree that it did on Republic Day.

Arbindra Ghose in his article "Quake codes against houses of Cards" in *Pioneer* (February 6, 2001) observes that unfortunately, the tendency now appears to be the use of inferior materials and neglect of municipal bye-laws and building codes set by the BIS. Once the rescue and relief work is over, one would expect the Gujarat Government to investigate the causes of collapse of the newer high-rise buildings in Ahmedabad and Rajkot. The persons found guilty and in collusion with builders should be given exemplary punishments. In future, building byelaws should be followed meticulously.

8. Lack of Utilizations of Multilateral Technical Assistance Available through UN System

In the post-war period, a very significant development has been the establishment of a pivotal international organization concerned with the problems of world peace and human welfare. This organization is commonly known as United Nations. Since its birth, it has been playing an increasingly vital role in easing the world tension and conflicts, which can erupt into a world conflagration as well as in alleviating the widespread hunger, poverty, ignorance, want, disease and allied problems. This organization has been supplemented by the establishment of closely allied specialized agencies, which deal with each of these stupendous problems more specifically.

When the UN Charter was being framed, attention was

initially focused on the problems of peace and security in the world. But at the instance of the USA, at the Yalta Conference, it was decided to create an Economic and Social Council as an integral pat of the new international organization (UN) to deal with the rapidly emerging economic and social problems. The ECOSOC is to study the problems of human and social well-being as well as to formulate appropriate policies and direct their implementation in this connection. The UN system is thus founded upon the sound idea that no peace can be stable unless it is based upon nations whose citizens are substantially free from distress, deprivation and frustration. The realization that removal of poverty and improvement of economic conditions all around would be potent factors for peace prompted the expansion of the UN system. The United Nations Development System comprises the UN itself, five regional Economic Commissions and 11 other major programmes and organs. Besides, there are 17 separate inter-governmental specialized agencies.

The UN System has its branches in India at Delhi as well as in the fields. All the specialized agencies and Organs of UN are contributing to the welfare of earthquake victims, not only for a short duration, but also in rehabilitating the affected persons. Each agency is contributing in its way. Let us mention the plan of UN system which is quite useful and based on expertise and resources as reported in *Times of India* (7th February, 2001). The UN has galvanised all its forces into action in a massive rehabilitation effort for the victims of the Gujarat earthquake. The total cost for this ambitious coordinated bid will come to a staggering US $ 50 million.

The UN is adopting a multipronged, coordinated effort to bring quick relief to the affected areas. The aim now is to reach the most vulnerable segments of the population, especially women and children.

Luckily, the UN has a wide network of agencies working in various fields all over the country. Each UN agency also has links with non-governmental organizations with a grassroot presence in many areas.

While mapping out its rehabilitation plans, the UN has taken care to focus on promoting gender equality and strengthening decentralization. Its action plan will focus on health, food and nutrition, education and child protection, shelter and survival, water and sanitation.

The good news is that the UN is not taking an *ad hoc* approach to rehabilitation, but is keen to continue through to the longer recovery process and reduce future vulnerability.

"The UN will involve the local population in their own rehabilitation and will promote self-help approaches, so that they are better able to respond to and recover from natural calamities that affect them."

The WHO will work closely with UNICEF and UNFPA to ensure disease surveillance and early warning systems for epidemics. It will work to ensure increased emergency health and medical care to the affected families, help to restore basic health services and undertake immunization, diarrhoea control and care for pregnant women. It will provide diet supplements like Vitamin A to women and children.

UNICEF will provide temporary school facilities. Textbooks and teaching supplies will be given. The UN will help provide training in trauma, counselling to teachers and social service workers.

UNDP will focus on the homeless and assist with shelter material as well as family survival kits to 50,000 families. Roaming teams will advise families rebuilding their homes on using earthquake resistant material. The programme will continue for a period of eight months.

However, Government of India, Gujarat Government and NGOs must utilize this multilateral technical assistance carefully as it is very scarce and given on the basis of dignity and not as a charity.

9. Lack of Action in Right Earnest: Mere Paper Planning to Impress the Press and People

Poornima Joshi in an article "Gujarat : Time for Stocktaking" dated February 11, 2001 in *The Hindustan Times* has rightly said that right through the crisis, the administration was conspicuously absent, abdicating its responsibilities to the Army and the army of volunteers descending upon Gujarat from all over the country and the world. While the Army and international rescuers looked for survivors in the debris, defence doctors tended to those injured and food and other relief materials were arranged and distributed by volunteers. Or, people managed on their own.

In fact, the administration failed to even help these agencies help it. Aircrafts bringing in relief supplies and voluntary groups eager to help were turned away as the officials of many affected areas just could not find ways to utilise their services.

L. Mansingh, the chief coordinator of relief operation in Kutch, had turned this failure into a virtue insisting "we are perfectly capable of taking care". He went a step further criticising the volunteers saying, "their presence is adding to the chaos." Brave, but unkind, words those.

He needs to do a reality check. A group of Central Industrial Security Force (CISF) officers complained bitterly about how relief material is not getting distributed. "My men are getting frustrated. They have been unloading tents from hundreds of trucks for the last one week, but there is nobody to distribute them. We are not here just to load and unload material. There can be better ways to utilise the forces. Either you do it yourself, or let us do it for you," an officer said angrily.

Sumer Kaul in his article "The good, bad and ugly Gujarat brings out the best—and the worst—in us" in *The Tribune*, dated February 12, 2001 remarked that to predict, let alone prevent earthquakes is not possible. What is possible is to avoid or at least minimise destruction of life and property in such calamities. Is there any serious thinking whatsoever on these lines? No evidence of that even two weeks after the disaster. Instead, we have an entirely monetary view of the tragedy, a petty accountant's view. Ordaining an income-tax surcharge and warning of a harsh budget, etc., are all very well, but is raising money all there is to responding to such a crisis?

This cultivated panic on the part of the Centre does not impress; in any case these measures will neither cover nor compensate for governmental and administrative failures, especially in the critical first few days after the calamity. Where, for instance, was the need for money in putting up tarpaulin sheets or big tents which lay around unused for days because the hapless villagers did not know how to put them up? Or in safeguarding medical consignments and reaching them to the needy rather than letting them rot on the roadside. There was no dearth of volunteers and NGOs, the only thing lacking was management—and, sadly, even concern—and that can't be bought with tax surcharges.

These Movers and Shakers (People's representatives and High Bureaucracy) of modern India themselves remain unmoved and unshaken—as much by the Gujarat tragedy as by any other human suffering in this country, and that is the underlying tragedy of the Republic of India.

10. No Sincere Efforts and Attention to Post Recovery of Earthquake Victims

Words written or spoken are of no use unless put to action. Robert Chambers has rightly observed, " It is action that matters ... But knowing does not guarantee a change of feeling; and a change of feeling does not guarantee a change of behaviour. So we come to the final, paradoxical, reversal; to start by acting . . . Not everything can or should be foreseen. It is often best to star?, to do something, and to learn from doing."

Ashok Ashta (*Hindustan Times*, February 2, 2001) draws from the experience of Earthquake in Japan (Kobe). To quote him: "The Great Hanshin Earthquake struck at 5.46 a.m. in January 17, 1995, a Tuesday morning after a three day weekend. It registered 7.2 on the Richter Scale—a first in Japan since records were maintained. Over 6,000 people died."

There can be said to be three main factors in Kobe's recovery. First, the incessant coverage provided by mass media that moved ordinary citizens into action. Next was the nationwide effort of the people to support their fellow citizens in distress. This was followed by the no-nonsense action plan based on utilitarian principles by the awakened Japanese Government, which concentrated on the core issue of shelter.

Whether an adequate disaster management apparatus is now in place is unanswerable at this time. Manuals already existed before 1995, but were of little use when calamity struck because practice is very different from theory. Only time will tell. What is clear is that the traditional Japanese management technique of 'slow decision', 'quick action' is not suitable for disaster management, where quick decisions are imperative to reduce loss of life.

As an epilogue, I would like to add that post-trauma stress remains a problem for many survivors even six years later. They are yet to forget the days of horrifying loss that surrounded them. However, even in the pain they suffer, many find time to thank God, for had the earthquake struck at a later hour, when the kitchen breakfast fires were on and the early commuters already packed in trains goings to work, the damage might have been exponentially worse. Perhaps, it is this tenacity of character that allows them to cope even today.

V. Suresh in his article in *Shelter* has suggested that the Action Plan which included following initiatives as in Chamoli/ Rudraprayaga:

1. Zonation of affected areas and estimates of total loss of buildings.
2. Technical guidelines for the Field Assessment of Damage by Revenue and Technical officials and trained volunteers.
3. Guidelines for identification of settlement and infrastructure and infrastructure vulnerable to landslide and rockfall risk.
4. Development of a Technology package for repair and reconstruction of damaged buildings and specifications and cost estimates of the same.
5. Technical Manuals for repairs, reconstruction of buildings.
6. Community-based rehabilitation and disaster mitigation measures and the role of NGOs and the community.
7. Preparation of financing plan based on the above

reconstruction action plan, for presentation to Financing institutions.

Indian Express editorial, 'After Shock—Band aids don't work when dealing with earthquakes' has stated that— But first we have to get the priorities right. If thinking has clarity, follow-up action will be focused and commensurately effective. For the moment, there are only three big 'R's on the national radar screen; rescue, relief and rehabilitation. This phase should receive all that we have got, from rescue teams and bulldozers to generators and mobile surgical units. And not just in the places where the TV cameras go, but in regions where they don't where there is no one to see ordinary people struggling to cope with devastation in terrifying oblivion. Help has already begun to pour in, both at the national and international level, but it would be of little use to anyone if the various state and central agencies involved in managing the disaster don't come together and coordinate operations in a planned and rational fashion. You cannot have a band-aid response to a reversal of these proportions. Today the country has one big advantage that it did not when the Uttarkashi earthquake struck in 1991 or when Latur happened in 1993—it has made a quantum leap in information technology and this, hopefully, should make all the difference to the efficiency of relief operations.

Wresting from the Delhi Government the initiative to incorporate earthquake-resistant provisions in building bylaws, the Urban Development Ministry has gone ahead to notify the draft amendment for the purpose. After waiting for the one-month statutory period to receive public objections and recommendations of local bodies, these amendments can be brought into force.

Besides making it compulsory for all new constructions to strictly follow the quake-safety standards set by the Bureau of Indian Standards (BIS) or the National Building Code, the proposed rules also seek to fix responsibility on the owner and architect of a building for its structural safety.

Urban Development Minister Jagmohan deplored the fact that neither the Delhi Government, nor the governments of other states and union territories had made the crucial changes in the building laws despite the fact that the ministry had recommended these a year-and-a-half ago.

The Gujarat experience has shown that the extent of disaster in terms of human lives and property loss could have been minimised if such safety features had been inbuilt into the houses and other buildings that collapse like a pack of cards.

11. Need to keep up the Morale of the Community so that they can take care of themselves

The will power of the community is the backbone to sustain any calamity like earthquake. Will power gives extra-energy to the community as well to the administrator. *The Times of India News Service* (February 7, 2001) indicates that the district collector of Kutch, Anil Mukim, is equally impressed by the spirit of the Gujarati people. I know that if such a thing had happened anywhere else, there would have been complete chaos. . . People would have been after each other's blood . . . but out here, we are flooded with all the help we can get. There is some inner strength in the people which is so reassuring. Rajeev Topno, the district development officer of Kutch, says: "Even though in the first few days the government machinery was buckling under pressure, it was heartening to note that the community at large had not collapsed. Kutch has shown a tremendous fighting spirit, which is a triumph in adversity."

The administration, through its sincere efforts, has to ensure that the morale of the community is not dampened. There is a need of constant counselling, guidance and advice. The strengthening of democracy in its social and economic aspect has to be attained through the participation on the part of the people.

We have to have a three pronged attacked to contain the ill-effects of earthquake. Hardarshan S. Walia in his article "Bhuj Quake from a geologists Perspective" in *The Tribune*, dated March 8, 2001 suggested the following :

(a) During an earthquake :

(i) If you are indoor: Follow the rule of DUCH (Duck, Cover and Hold under a strong piece of furniture). If there is no furniture, stand under a doorway. If you are in a highrise building and away from a furniture, move against an interior wall and protect your head with your arms. Don't use electrical, gas equipment.

(ii) If you are outdoor:
Move away as far as possible from the building, tall structure, power lines, etc.

(iii) If you are driving:
Slow down, move to clear area (if possible) stop and stay inside until shaking stops.

(b) After Earthquake:

(i) Wear Safety gears (specially heavy shoes):

(ii) Check for hazards (fire, gas, electric water, spills, etc.) shut off all the valves,

(iii) Provide first aid.

(c) Before Earthquake:

(i) Plan earthquake preparedness with family, neighbours, and friends (Talk about a meeting place to reunite and assign an out of town phone number of a relative to inform status),

(ii) Keep emergency supplies in a plastic container (example: canned food, water blanket, first aid kit, flashlight with extra batteries and bulbs, fire extinguisher, portable radio, etc.).

(iii) Know where gas, electricity, water main shut-off valves are.

(iv) Fasten structures inside the house that may fall during earthquake (e.g. refrigerator, furniture, bookshelves, etc.)

(d) Build earthquake resistant structures:
One cannot construct a dwelling completely earthquake proof but it can be made earthquake resistant. Also an older building can be retrofitted to resist an earthquake. Process is followed in two Steps :

(i) Know the hazard map of the area: Obtain a hazard map from the Regional Geological survey office. A hazard map shows geologic problems, soil and bedrock conditions which will determine the behaviour of building during shaking,

(ii) Incorporate earthquake resistant design.

Action Plan

(a) Initiate earthquake awareness.
(b) Build earthquake-resistant structures in seismic zone area.
(c) Force builders to adopt earthquake resistance code for structures.
(d) Strengthen the existing structures.
(e) Ask lawmakers to develop a strong programme of earthquake disaster preparation, mitigation, and management programmes.

A.S. Arya in his article "Action Plan For Earthquake Disaster Mitigation" rightly suggests the following steps to mitigate the effects of earthquake.

Preventive Phase Before Disaster

This phase should involve the following actions:

(i) Preparation of earthquake catalogues and epicenter and geologic-tectonic maps;
(ii) Analysis of seismic risk and seismic zoning for general purposes;
(iii) Development of anti-seismic codes of design and construction of various structures;
(iv) Education and training of engineers and architects in earthquake engineering principles and use of codes;
(v) Promulgation of laws and bye-laws for providing earthquake resistance features in all new construction according to the codes;
(vi) Development of methods for seismic strengthening of existing structures, particularly in the structures considered critical for the community;
(vii) Development of simple methods for upgrading the seismic resistance of traditional non-engineered construction and their dissemination to the common builders and owners by mass communication techniques, demonstrations, extension work, etc.
(viii) Earthquake insurance for the buildings and structures to reduce the economic impact on individuals; and

(ix) Installation of seismological observations for monitoring seismic activity with a density of instruments capable of recording and locating all earthquakes bigger than a selected magnitude.

Emergency Phase just after Occurrence of Disaster

This phase will include the following actions:

(i) Maintenance of law and order;
(ii) Evacuation of people;
(iii) Recovery of dead bodies and their disposal;
(iv) Medical care for the injured;
(v) Supply of food and water and restoration of water supply lines;
(vi) Temporary shelters like tents, metal sheds;
(vii) Restoring lines of communication and information;
(viii) Restoring transport routes;
(ix) Quick assessment of damage and demarcation of damage areas according to grade of damage;
(x) Cordoning off severely damaged structures liable to collapse during aftershocks;
(xi) Temporary shoring of certain precariously standing buildings to avoid collapse and damage to other adjoining buildings;
(xii) Immediate actions to prevent certain chain-reactions from developing; such as release of water from the reservoir behind a damaged dam to avoid flooding of the areas if the dam fail, emptying of containers of toxic or inflammable liquids and gases, treatment of environment for preventing spread of diseases, etc.;
(xiii) Collection of scientific data from field observations as well as from instrumentation specially deployed in the affected area to monitor the aftershocks; and
(xiv) Preparation of proposals about the reconstruction requirements and strategy to be adopted and whether reconstruction opportunity could also be utilized for affecting socio-economic development of the damaged area.

An effort needs to be made in the emergency phase, to involve the affected people to the maximum extent so as to create a feeling of self-reliance. They need to be encouraged to start following economic pursuits as quickly as possible so that the period of relief is minimized.

Consolidation and Reconstruction Phase

The phase will involve the following actions:

(i) Detailed survey of buildings for assessment of damage and decision regarding repair, restoration and strengthening or demolition;

(ii) Repair, restoration and seismic strengthening or demolition;

(iii) Selection of sites for new settlements;

(iv) Adoption of strategy for new construction, such as, through contractors, through self-help construction or core houses only, or supply of construction materials only, etc.;

(v) Execution of the reconstruction programme;

(vi) Preview of existing seismic zoning maps and risk maps;

(vii) Review of the seismic codes and norms of construction;

(viii) Training of personnel, engineers, architects, builders and artisans; and

(ix) Statistical studies regarding the earthquake.

Relief at a Glance

* Quick administrative response from Centre and State levels.
* Visit of Prime Minister and Cabinet Ministers to support relief efforts.
* Immediate deployment of Defence and Para-Military forces.
* Spontaneous public response with overwhelming generosity in terms of relief assistance.
* Rapid transportation of Relief materials, food items, medical supplies/equipments.
* Rs. 500 crore assistance announced by the PM, besides financial aid from many government and non-governmental organizations.

* Overwhelming international response with personnel and material.

There is a need to develop holistic approach and need of integration of disaster management plan with normal plans. A good administration in normal times can easily take care of disaster management as well. We must introduce administrative reforms which can keep the administration efficient.

Administrative improvement means the act or the process of improving the administration. As stated in a United Nations Report: "Management improvement comprised the planning, implementation and evaluation of various measures conducive to the increase of organizational effectiveness and efficiency."

Simple commitment by management is not enough. The improvement process must become basic and continuous. There is no magic approach or solution to be gleaned from either a textbook or a consultant, although either of these can help management discover an effective programme for carrying out its required responsibility.

The Indian Express editorial: "The Ugly and the Beautiful" over the private initiatives in relief and rehabilitation (January 31, 2001) stresses that the magnitude of the death and destruction of quivering of the earth caused, it is neither desirable nor feasible to leave the work of relief and rehabilitation entirely to the government. The situation calls for better private initiatives. It would be pertinent to recall how long before the term privatization came into common parlance, the great Bihar Earthquake of 1934 brought the entire state under the banner of a relief committee headed by Dr. Rajendra Prasad. It not only coordinated all the relief and rehabilitation work but also published a 400-page report listing every cash contribution received from the public. The report bore the signature of J.C. Mumarappa, a chartered accountant and disciple of Mahatma Gandhi, and it is even to day cited as an epitome of transparency. Such relief bodies need to be replicated by the dozen to meet the challenge in Gujarat.

Karuna M. Johan in his article "Gujarati Samaj cautions

donors" rightly pointed that the Shree Delhi Gujarati Samaj has appealed to residents of the Capital to be careful while donating money for quake relief programme. The 104 year old Gujarati Samaj that acts as an umberalla organization for all major Gujarati associations in the city has warned that the tragedy in Gujarat is being used by unscrupulous people for one-upmanship.

A number of temporary 'collection centres' have sprung up in residential and commercial areas across the city. Many stop passers-by and ask them to 'donate' money for Gujarat. However, the Shree Delhi Gujarati Samaj warns that many of these centers may not be genuine.

According to Gujarati Samaj President Prafull Joshi, the umberalla association has already received some complaints from harassed donors. "We appeal to the people to donate money only to authorized agencies", he said. The Samaj, he added will issue valid receipts against any donations.

Ela R. Bhatt in his article "Reconstructing Gujarat" in *The Hindu,* dated February, 2001 rightly thinks that Gujarat will have to be rebuilt. But in whose image and on whose ideas ? Given the scale of death and destruction, the answer is obvious: Gujarat will have to be reconstructed in the image of its common people. And who can be a better guide in this endeavour than Gandhiji, whose name Gujarat proudly uses. Let us not forget that his vision of a free India was abolition of poverty, misery and fear. How do we translate Gandhiji's concepts into practical lessons for reconstruction of destroyed villages and towns today? Three major principles can be recalled here. First is the centrality of rural India and the balanced rural-urban growth. Second is the removal of economic poverty and third the principle of trusteeship.

We need a holistic approach. Water, health, food, shelter, livelihood, child care are all closely integrated in human life that has clearly come out of the current relief work being done in Kutch. The earthquake has also showed us the strong spirit of voluntary work, of helping others, of community ties in Gujarat. Let us build on our community spirit to make these dreams into reality.

CONCLUSION

There is a Need of Transparency, Good governance, accountability and responsiveness. It has been reported in the press, TV. and other platforms that disaster management programmes have become haven of unscrupulous people. Money is collected and used for personal purpose. Therefore, there is a need for good account keeping, good governance and responsive administration to keep rogues out of this noble cause. Only the people with faith in ethics should be associated with such work. It is a challenging task, which requires hardwork, sincerity, loyalty and spirit of service. They should believe in social service.

FOUR

NATURAL DISASTERS

The unique geoclimatic conditions of the Indian sub-continent make this region among the most vulnerable to natural disasters in the world. Disasters occur with amazing frequency and while the community at large has adapted itself to these regular occurrences, the economic and social costs continue to mount year after year.

The Indian subcontinent is highly vulnerable to drought, floods, cyclones and earthquakes, though landslides, avalanches and bush fires frequently occur in the Himalayan region of northern India. Of the 31 States/Union territories in the country, 22 are disaster-prone.

Floods and Earthquakes

Among all the disasters that occur in the country, river floods are the most frequent and often the most devastating. The cause for floods is chiefly the peculiarities of rainfall in the country. Out of the total annual rainfall in the country, 75 per cent is concentrated over a short monsoon season of three to four months. As a result, there is a very heavy discharge from the rivers during this period causing widespread floods. As much as 40 million hectares of land in the country has been identified as flood-prone. An average of 18.6 million hectares of land is flooded annually. Floods are caused mainly in the Ganga-Brahmaputra-Meghna basin which carry 60 per cent of the nation's total river flow.

Earthquakes are considered to be one of the most dangerous and destructive natural hazards. The impact of this phenomena is sudden with little or no warning, making it just impossible to predict or make preparations against damages and collapses of buildings and other man-made structures. About 50-60 per cent of total area of the country is vulnerable to seismic activity of varying intensities. Most of the vulnerable areas are generally located in Himalayan and sub-Himalayan regions, and in Andaman and Niccbar Islands.

Droughts and Cyclones

Drought is a perennial feature in some states of India. Sixteen per cent of the country's total area is drought-prone and approximately 50 million people are annually affected by droughts. In fact, drought is a significant environmental problem too as it is caused by a less than average rainfall over a long period of time. In India, about 68 per cent of total sown area of the country is drought-prone. Most of the drought-prone areas identified by Government of India lie in the arid, semi-arid and sub-humid areas of the country.

India has a very long coastline of 5700 kms which is exposed to tropical cyclones arising in the Bay of Bengal and Arabian Sea. The Indian Ocean is one of the six major cyclone-prone regions of the world. In India, cyclones occur usually between April and May, and also between October and December. The eastern coastline is more prone to cyclones as about 80 per cent of total cyclones generated in the region hit there.

Natural Disaster Management at International Level

The United Nations Initiative

Natural Disasters are a global phenomenon and strike regardless of any national boundaries or socio-economic status of the region. This has led to a strong international fraternity defined at the highest level by several UN bodies. Interestingly, the United Nations declared the decade from 1990 till 2000 as the International Decade for Natural Disaster Reduction (IDNDR). The objective of the IDNDR is to reduce through concerted international action, especially in the developing countries, the loss of life, property damage and social and economic disruption caused by natural disasters.

As per the plan of the IDNDR, by the year 2000 all countries should have (1) comprehensive national assessments of risks from natural hazards, with these assessments taken into account on development plans; (2) mitigation plans at national and/or local levels, involving long-term prevention and preparedness and community awareness; and (3) ready access to global, regional, national and local warning systems and broad dissemination of warnings.

The last major conference of the IDNDR programme was held in Yokohama in May 1994, where a plan of action for disaster reduction, called the 'Yokohama Strategy' was evolved. The Yokohama strategy gave guidelines for natural disaster prevention, preparedness and mitigation. India was an active participant in the said conference and in the formulation of the guidelines. By doing so, it has recognized the need for further improvements in its disaster management mechanism and to develop a strong political will by way of a sound national policy in this regard.

Natural Disaster Management in India

India is a parliamentary democracy with a federal structure. An integrated disaster management mechanism exists within government framework. The essential responsibility of disaster management lies with the State Government where the disaster has occurred. However, in the event of disasters which spread over several states and assume uncontrolable proportions, the Central Government may be required to supplement appropriate measures in the fields of rescue, relief and preparedness. At the Central level, the National Crisis Management Committee (NCMC) oversees all disaster related efforts. The NCMC comprises the nodal ministry and other support ministries. For natural disasters, the nodal ministry is ministry of agriculture.

In the past, the government response to natural disasters has improved in terms of its effectiveness. This is chiefly due to the emergence of well-organized administrative machinery, presence of Relief Manuals at district level, predetermined allocation of duties and recognized public-private partnerships. However, absence of an integrated policy at national level has led to overlooking of some of the vital aspects of disaster management. As such, presence of a policy helps clearly define the government's basic approaches on a continuing basis. It provides for an appropriate legislation and associated regulations in this regard, besides providing an overall national competence and self-reliance vis-a-vis international initiatives.

Administrative Structure at Central Level

In the federal set-up of India, the responsibility to formulate the Government's response to a natural calamity is essentially that of the concerned State Government. However, the Central Government, with its resources, physical and financial, does provide the needed help and assistance to buttress relief efforts in the wake of major natural disasters. The dimensions of the response at the level of Central Government are determined in accordance with the existing policy of financing the relief expenditure and keeping in view the factors, like: (1) the gravity of a natural calamity; (2) the scale of the relief operation necessary, (3) the requirements of Central assistance for augmenting the financial resources at the disposal of the State Government.

Agriculture Ministry—The Nodal Agency

The Department of Agriculture and Co-operation (DAC), in the Agriculture Ministry, is the nodal department for all matters concerning natural disasters relief at the Centre. The National Contingency Action Plan (CAP) facilitates launching of relief and rescue operations without delay. The CAP identifies initiatives required to be taken by various Central Ministries, and Public departments in the wake of natural calamities, sets down procedures and determines the focal points in the administrative machinery.

In the DAC, the Relief Commissioner functions as the nodal officer to coordinate relief operations for all natural disasters. The Central Relief Commissioner receives information relating to forecast of the natural calamity from the Director General, Indian Meteorological Department from the Central Water Commission on a continuing basis. Agriculture Department monitors the developments taking place and provides the necessary inputs through the Agriculture Secretary to the Agriculture Minister, Prime Minister and the Cabinet.

Committees at National Level

Working of various other committees at the national level for disaster management is discussed in the following paras.

Cabinet Committee

The cabinet may set up a committee for effective implementation of relief measures in the wake of natural disaster. The secretary in the ministry of agriculture acts as the Secretary of this committee. In the absence of such a committee, all matters related to the relief shall be reported to the cabinet secretary.

National Crisis Management Committee (NCMC)

Under the chairmanship of cabinet secretary, the NCMC has been constituted in the cabinet secretariat. The other members of this committee include the secretary to prime minister, secretaries of ministry of home affairs, defence, research and analysis wing and agriculture and co-operation along with Director, Intelligence Bureau and an officer of cabinet secretariat. The NCMC gives direction to the crises management group as and when deemed necessary.

Crisis *Management Group (CMG)*

A group under the chairmanship of the Central Relief Commissioner, comprising senior officers drawn from various ministries and other concerned departments, reviews every year contingency plan formulated by central ministries/ departments. It reviews various measures required for dealing with a natural disaster, and coordinates activities of the central ministries and the State governments pertaining to disaster preparedness and relief and obtains information from nodal officers on measures relating to the above. The joint secretary (NDM) and Additional Central Relief Commissioner is the convenor of CMG. The CMG meets every six months.

Financial Arrangements

The centre plays a major role as far as mobilization of financial resources are concerned. The policy and arrangement for financing state governments to provide relief and rehabilitation measures in areas affected by natural calamities are governed by the recommendations of the finance commissions on the subject made from time to time. The scheme in force for the period 1995-2000 is based on the recommendations of the Tenth Finance Commission. Under the present scheme, a Calamity Relief Fund (CRF) has been constituted for each state with contribution from the Central and State Governments to undertake relief and rehabilitation measures. The annual allocations of the CRF to the various states are based on their trend of expenditure on natural calamities during the past ten years. The central share of CRF is released to the state governments in four equal quarterly instalments. As recommended by the Tenth Finance Commission, a committee of experts and representatives of the states has drawn up a list of items, expenditure on which alone will be chargeable to the CRF. A state level committee headed by the chief secretary decides the norms of assistance under each of the approved schemes. The norms so fixed could be modified by the Ministry of Agriculture, if these are significantly out of line.

In addition to the CRF, a National Fund for Calamity Relief (NFCR) has also been constituted to deal with calamities of rare severity. NFCR is available with the Government of India with an allocation of Rs 700 crore for the period 1995-2000. The fund is managed by the National Calamity Relief Committee, which is a sub-committee of the National Development Council, headed by the union agriculture minister. In normal circumstances, the state governments are required to undertake relief and rehabilitation measures utilizing the annual CRF allocations. They can, however, seek additional assistance from the NFCR in the event of calamity of rare severity.

Administrative Structure at State Level

As pointed out earlier, the central government only supplements the efforts of the state governments. The state governments are autonomous in organizing relief operations in the event of natural disaster and also long-term preparedness/ rehabilitation measures.

The states have Relief Commissioners, who are in charge of the relief measures in the wake of natural disasters in their respective states. In the absence of the Relief Commissioner, the Chief Secretary or an officer nominated by him is in overall charge of the relief operations in the concerned State.

The Chief Secretary is the head of the State Administration. The state headquarters have, in addition, a number of Secretaries who head the various departments handling specific subjects under the overall supervision and coordination of the Chief Secretary. At the level of the state government, natural disasters are usually the responsibility of the revenue department or the relief department. While important policy decisions are taken at the state headquarters by the cabinet of the state headed by the chief minister, day-to-day decisions involving policy matters are taken or exercised by the secretary in the department.

States Crisis Management Group

There is a State Crisis Management Group (SCMG) under the chairmanship of Chief Secretary/Relief Commissioner. This group comprises senior officers from the departments of revenue/relief, home, civil supplies, power, irrigation, water supply, panchayat (local self—government), agriculture, forests, rural development, health planning, public works and finance.

The SCMG is required to take into consideration the infrastructure and guidance received, from time to time, from Government of India and formulate action plans for dealing with different natural disasters.

It is also the duty of the Relief Commission of the state to establish an emergency operation centre as soon as a disaster situation develops. Besides having all updated information on forecasting and warning of disaster, the Centre would also be the contact point for the various concerned agencies.

Administrative Structure at District Level

States are further divided into districts, each headed by the District Collector (also known as the District Magistrate or Deputy Commissioner), who is the focal point at the district level for directing, supervising and monitoring relief measures for disaster and for preparation of district level plans.

The Collector exercises coordinating and supervisory powers over functionaries of all the departments at the district level. During actual operations for disaster mitigation or relief, the powers of the Collector are considerably enhanced, generally, by standing instructions or orders on the subject, or by specific Governments order, if so required. Sometimes, the administrative culture of the concerned state permits, although informally, the Collector to exercise higher powers in emergency situations and the decisions are later ratified by the competent authority.

A district is sub-divided into sub-divisions and *tehsils* or *talukas*. The head of a sub-division is called the Sub-Division Officer (SDO) while the head of a *tehsil* is generally known as the *tehsildar (talukdar* or *mamlatdar* in some states). Contact with the individual villages is through the village officer or *patwari* who has one or more villages in his charge. When a disaster is apprehended, the entire machinery of the district, including officers of technical and other departments, swings into action and maintains almost continuous contact with each village in the disaster threatened area. In the case of extensive disasters, like drought, contact is maintained over a short cycle of a few days.

The various measures undertaken by the district administration area are discussed in the following paras.

Contingency Plans

At the district level, the disaster relief plans are prepared which provide for specific tasks and agencies for their implementation in respect of areas in relation to different types of disasters.

A contingency plan for the district for different disasters is drawn up by the Collector/Deputy Commissioner and approved by the state government. The Collector/Deputy Commissioner also coordinates and secures the input from the local defence forces unit in preparation of the contingency plans. These contingency plans lay down specific action points, key personnel and contact points relating to all aspects.

District Relief Committee

The relief measures are reviewed by the district level relief committee consisting of official and non-official members, including local legislators and members of parliament.

District Control Room

In the wake of natural disasters, a control room is set up in the district for day-to-day monitoring of the rescue and relief operations on a continuing basis.

Coordination

The Collector/Deputy Commissioner maintains close liaison with the central government authorities in the districts, namely, army, air force and navy, ministry of water resources, etc., who supplement the effort of the district administration in the rescue and relief operation.

The Collector/Deputy Commissioner also coordinates all voluntary efforts by mobilizing the non-government organisations capable of working in such situations.

The entire hierarchy, right from the central government (the department of agriculture and co-operation in the ministry of agriculture and irrigation) to the district level, and even the sub-divisional/*tehsil* level, is connected with a telecommunication system. The normal mode of telecommunications is over land telephone and telegraphy, but in times of stress and if there is breakdown of the overland system, radio communication is resorted to. The wireless network is generally run and maintained by the police organisation in the country.

Besides the district officials, a host of other bodies too supplement their efforts in disaster situation—particularly the armed forces and the non-government voluntary organisations.

The Role of the Armed Forces

The armed forces of the country have played a vital role during disaster emergencies, providing prompt relief to the victims even in the most inaccessible and remote areas of the country. The organizational strength of the armed forces with their disciplined and systematized approach, and with their skills in technical and human resource management make them indispensable for such emergency situations.

Besides, when disasters are spread over large areas, it is usually beyond the capability of the administration to organize the relief activities, the armed forces are then called in to organize the relief measures.

Related to the efforts of the armed forces, are the civil defence and home guard organizations. These organizations are voluntary in nature and character and come in handy during emergency situations like natural disasters. A network of these is now found all over the country. Their aim—while not actually taking part in actual combat operations, like in army—is firstly to save lives, to minimize damage to property, and to maintain continuity of production. Thus, while disaster situations often lead to chaotic conditions where rescue and relief work is severely affected, these organizations are able to coordinate and support efforts in a disciplined manner, so that both the army and the district officials are able to carry out their respective activities efficiently.

The Role of Non-Government Voluntary Organizations

Emerging trends in managing natural disaster, have highlighted the role of Non-Governmental Organizations (NGOs) as one of the most effective alternative means of achieving an efficient communication link between the disaster management agencies and the affected community. Many different types of NGOs are already working at advocacy level as well as grassroots level. In typical disaster situations, they can be of help in preparedness, relief and rescue, rehabilitation and reconstruction, and also in monitoring and feedback.

The role of NGOs is a potential key element in disaster management. The NGOs operating at grassroots level, can provide a suitable alternative as they have an edge over governmental agencies for invoking community involvement. This is chiefly because, the NGO sector has strong linkages with the community base, and can exhibit great flexibility in procedural matters vis-a-vis the government.

Based on the identified types of NGOs and their capabilities, organized action of NGOs can be very useful in following activities in different stages of disaster management.

ORGANIZED ACTIVITIES OF NGOS AT DIFFERENT STAGES OF DISASTER MANAGEMENT

Stage	*Activity*
Pre-Disaster	Awareness and information campaigns; Training of local volunteers; Advocacy and planning
During Disaster	Immediate rescue and first-aid, including psychological aid, supply of food, water, medicines, and other immediate need materials; Ensuring sanitation and hygiene; and Damage assessment
Post-Disaster	Technical and material aid in reconstruction and Assistance in seeking financial aid Monitoring

In the recent past, NGO sector has played a major role in strengthening the community to face the disasters. The trend is based on a long-term experience of the need of maximum self-reliance at the lowest level.

The Role of the Community

It has now been revealed that the community as an institution in itself is emerging as the most powerful in the entire mechanism of disaster administration. In the event of actual disasters, the community, if well aware of the preventive actions it is required to take, can substantially reduce the disaster damage. Awareness and training of the community is particularly useful in areas which are prone to frequent disasters.

It is quite heartening to note the laudable effort made in certain areas where communities have formed their own organizations which take right initiative in such situations. One such community based organization is the Village Task Force formed in villages of Andhra Pradesh by the Church Auxiliary for Social Action (CASA). The Village Task Force has been trained in emergency evacuation and relief within the village. It is elected by the people themselves and during disasters it serves as the nodal body at village level which has to mobilize resources for the community and disseminates necessary information passed on by outside agencies.

While the community as an effective institution, is yet to take shape in this country mainly due to low literacy levels and widespread poverty, considerable efforts are being made to form and strengthen community-based organizations at grassroots levels.

Research and Training Institutions

With an increase in the perception towards spreading a culture of prevention in the disaster management scenario, considerable emphasis is now being placed on research and development activities, in addition to capacity building of all personnel concerned with disaster management. In India, a number of research institutes are conducting active research in the field of disaster management. Valuable inputs in technical, social, economic as well as management areas of the field are being looked into.

Research activities are being coordinated by different ministries depending on the type and level of research. An important role is played by the universities too in this sector who, besides running programmes on disaster management, also serve as think-tanks for the government. Institutes spread geographically across the country have developed specializations in terms of particular regions where most of their research is concentrated and also in terms of particular disasters. Notable universities are the University of Roorkee, the Indian Institutes of Technology, and the Anna University.

The Department of Science (Ministry of Science and Technology), Government of India coordinates activities through a network of scientific institutes, for example, the Central Building Research Institute at Roorkee. The Ministry of Urban Development carries out research through Building Materials and Technology Promotion Council on subjects, such as appropriate building materials for disaster-prone areas. These institutes, besides providing technical assistance to implementing and engineering organizations also trains field level officers and other concerned role players.

The Ministry of Agriculture and Cooperation too has set up a National Centre for Disaster Management at IIPA to look after administrative training activities in the field of disaster management.

The National Centre for Disaster Management

The centre was established by Ministry of Agriculture in March, 1995 at the Indian Institute of Public Administration, New Delhi. The NCDM, besides gearing up the national, state and district level administrations to tackle natural disasters, also coordinates various research and training programmes and builds a data-base on natural disasters.

Conclusion

In disaster situations, a quick rescue and relief mission is inevitable. However, considerable damage can be minimised if adequate preparedness levels are achieved. Indeed, it has been noticed in the past, that as and when attention has been paid to adequate preparedness measures, the loss to life and property has been considerably reduced.

Preparedness measures, such as training of role players, including the community, development of advanced forecasting systems, effective communications, and above all, a sound national policy and a well-networked institutional structure involving government organizations, academic and research institutions, the armed forces and NGOs would greatly contribute to the overall disaster management of the region. Later, it would lead to the much needed change in the overall orientation from rescue and relief to preparedness.

NATIONAL CALAMITY MANAGEMENT ACT

An Act to ensure the efficiency and effective management of natural and other calamities, to achieve a greater coordination and responsiveness in respect of prevention and mitigation of disaster arising out of such calamities and to provide for better relief and rehabilitation of the victims of such disasters and for matters connected therewith or incidental thereto.

Be it enacted by the Parliament in the 51st year of the Republic of India as follows:

CHAPTER I

Preliminary

1. Short Title, Extent and Commencement

(i) The Act may be called the "National Calamity Management Act, 2000".

(ii) It extends to the whole of India,

(iii) It shall come into force on such date as the Government of India may, by notification in the official Gazette, appoint in this behalf.

2. Definitions

(i) "Act" means the National Calamity Management Act, 2000.

(ii) "CRC" means the Central Relief Commissioner, the officer not below the rank of an Additional Secretary to the Government of India so designated by the Government of India and includes an Additional Central Relief Commissioner, officer not below the rank of a Joint Secretary to the Government of India, so designated by the Government of India.

(iii) "Calamity" means a catastrophe or a mishap, a grave occurrence which causes loss of life, human suffering, damage to and destruction of property and/or degradation of environment and/or which disrupts the normal functioning of the people/ communities and it includes the calamities specified in Schedule I.

(iv) "DC" means the Director General of the National Centre for Calamity Management, the officer not below the rank of Joint Secretary to the Government of India appointed as the Administrative Head of the National Centre for Calamity Management (NCCM).

(v) District Relief Commissioner (DRC) means the District Magistrate and includes any officer so designated by the State Government.

(vi) The "Government" means the Government of India.

(vii) "Management of Calamities" includes measures relating to prevention, reduction, mitigation, response, providing rescue, relief and/or rehabilitation.

(viii) NCCF means National Calamity Contingency Fund constituted for the purpose of carrying out objectives of this Act.

(ix) NCCM means the National Centre for Calamity Management constituted by Government of India,

(x) "Notification" means a notification published in the official gazette.

(xi) "Prescribed" means prescribed by the Rules made under the Act.

(xii) "Public servant" shall have the same meaning assigned to that term in Section 21 of the Indian Penal Code.

(xiii) "SRC" means the State Relief Commissioner, the officer not below the rank of Secretary to the State Government so designated by the State Government.

(xiv) STAC means the "Scientific and Technical Advisory Committee" constituted by the Government of India.

(xv) The "State Government" means the Government of a State or a Union territory.

CHAPTER II

Authorities: Their Powers and Functions

3. Principal Authorities for Calamity Management

The principal authorities for purpose of carrying out the objects of this Act and operationalising its provisions shall be as specified below:

(i) The Government of India represented by Ministry of Agriculture.

(ii) The State Government and authorities under the State Government including State Relief Commissioner, District Relief Commissioner, etc.

(iii) National Centre for Calamity Management to be constituted by the Government of India.

(iv) Scientific and Technical Advisory Committee to be constituted by Government of India in consultation with the National Centre for Calamity Management.

(v) An officer not below the rank of the Additional Secretary to the Government of India to be appointed as the Central Relief Commissioner and who shall be incharge of calamity management.

(vi) An Additional Central Relief Commissioner to be appointed by the Central Government who would be not below the rank of the Joint Secretary to the Government of India to aid and assist the Central Relief Commissioner and he would have the same powers and functions as that of the Central Relief Commissioner.

4. Powers and Functions of the Government of India

(i) Subject to the provisions of this Act, the Government of India shall have the power to take all such measures as it deems fit and expedient for the purpose of preventing and managing calamities including those specified in Schedule-1,

(ii) The Government of India shall constitute a National Centre for Calamity Management (NCCM) for the purpose of efficient and effective management of all kinds of disasters arising out of calamities.

(iii) The Government of India shall appoint the Director General of the National Centre for Calamity Management (NCCM) who would be the officer not below the rank of Joint Secretary to the Government of India. The Government of India may also appoint such other officer or officers for effectively discharging the powers conferred and the duties entrusted to the NCCM.

(iv) The Government of India shall constitute a Scientific and Technical Advisory Committee in consultation with the National Centre for Calamity Management for the purpose of advising the National Centre for Calamity Management in all matters relating to calamity management

(v) The Government of India shall appoint one Central Relief Commissioner who would be the officer not below the rank of the Additional Secretary to the Government of India and may also appoint the Additional Central Relief Commissioner who would be not below the rank of the Joint Secretary to the Government of India.

(vi) It shall be the duty of the Government of India to render all necessary help and assistance to the State Government as requested and deemed appropriate for effective management of the calamities and for prevention and mitigation of the disasters arising out of such calamities and to provide for required relief and rehabilitation to the victims of such calamities or for matters related therewith or incidental thereto.

(vii) Notwithstanding anything contained in any other law but subject to the provisions of this Act, the Government of India may in exercise of its powers and performance of its functions under this Act, issue directions in writing to any person, officer, or authority including State Government in appropriate cases and such person, officer, or authority shall be bound to comply with such directions.

5. Powers and Functions of the State Government

(i) Subject to the provision of this Act and subject to the general control and supervision by the Government of India the State Government shall have the power to take all such measures, as it deems necessary or expedient for the purpose of preventing and managing calamities.

(ii) In particular and without prejudice to the generality of the provisions of sub-section (i), such measures may include measures with respect to all or any of the following matters, namely:

(a) co-ordination of actions taken by officers, officials and other authorities and Non-Governmental Organisations (NGOs) under this Act or Rules made thereunder or under any other law for the time being in force which is relatable to the objects of this Act.

(b) Planning and execution of a Statewide programme for management of disasters caused by calamities.

(c) Laying down procedures and safeguards for management of calamities.

(d) Collection and dissemination of information in respect of matters relating to calamities including propagation of vital information affecting the public.

(e) Preparation of manuals, codes, or guidelines relating to management of calamities and updating thereof from time to time.

(iii) The State Government may constitute a Standing Technical Committee for the purpose of facilitating procurement related to calamity management and assuring the quality of material, equipments and services to be procured in connection therewith.

(iv) The State Government shall appoint a State Relief Commissioner who shall be an officer not below the rank of the Secretary to that Government and may appoint an Additional State Relief Commissioner or such other officer or officers to assist the State Relief Commissioner in discharging his functions for the purpose of calamity management.

(v) The State Government may also appoint any officer or officers as District Relief Commissioner(s) at the District level in addition to the District Magistrate of the District and officer(s) so appointed shall be responsible for performing all functions relating to calamity management within his territorial jurisdiction.

(vi) The State Government may empower the State Relief Commissioner and other officers and authorities to exercise such powers and to perform such functions as might be required for more effectively carrying out the objectives of this Act.

(vii) It shall be the duty of the State Government to notify the calamity prone areas for the general information of the public and also for the purpose of implementation of the provisions of the Act or Rules made thereunder.

(viii) The State Government shall draw up a plan for calamity management in advance and ensure that the concerned officials and local inhabitants are given adequate training for the successful execution of the plan.

(ix) The State Government shall declare an area where a calamity has occurred to be a calamity affected area and then it would be the bounded duty of all concerned authorities to take necessary actions required for carrying out the objectives of the Act.

(x) Notwithstanding anything contained in any other law but subject to the provisions of this Act, the State Government, in exercise of its powers and performance of its functions may frame Rules under this Act, and/ or issue directions or orders in writing to any person, officer, or authority and such person, officer, or authority shall be bound to comply with such directions or orders.

6. Duties and Functions of the Central Relief Commissioner

(i) The Central Relief Commissioner shall be placed incharge of and be responsible for calamity management in calamity affected areas and all such operations in such areas shall be carried on under his over-all supervision and control.

(ii) The Central Relief Commissioner shall have the power to issue directions or orders to the State Relief

Commissioners/District Relief Commissioners appointed by the State Government:

(a) to draw up calamity management plans in respect of their territorial jurisdictions for prevention, preparedness, mitigation, response, warning emergency operations, rescue, evacuation, relief, recovery and rehabilitation,

(b) to organise training programmes, public hearing and exercises,

(c) to issue timely warnings to state and local officials and also to the people likely to be affected by any calamity regarding risks and hazards,

(d) to utilize the services or facilities of government organisations, Central or State; Local Bodies, including Panchayat and Gram Sabha,

(e) to seek support/assistance from any Institution, organisation, authority, both Government as well as Non-Government,

(f) to provide public health and safety information including dissemination of such information,

(g) to adopt health and safety measures,

(h) to arrange for distribution Of medicine, food and other consumable supplies and emergency assistance,

(i) to strive earnestly to save lives and to protect properties,

(j) to strive earnestly to protect and improve the natural environment including forest, flora and fauna,

(k) to endeavour earnestly to assure atleast a minimum standard of relief and rehabilitation as may be prescribed in this behalf and while so prescribing, special care be taken for the infirm, the old, children and the women, in particular, and

(l) to ensure that medicines are stored at convenient places so that at times of crisis they could be reached to the needy at a short notice.

7. Powers of Central Relief Commissioner, State Relief Commissioner and District Relief Commissioner

(i) Notwithstanding anything contained in any other Act it shall be lawful for the Central Relief Commissioner/ State Relief Commissioner and District Relief Commissioner to issue such guidelines/instructions or orders or directions to all departments and authorities including the Police, Para-military Forces, Fire Services, Homeguards and Civil Defence as might be considered necessary by him for the purpose of effectively carrying out the objectives of this Act/and it shall be the duty of such persons and authorities to carry out such guidelines, instructions, orders or directions.

(ii) The Central Relief Commissioner or the State Relief Commissioner or the District Relief Commissioner, if he considers it necessary, may require any officer in command of any group of persons belonging to the armed forces render such assistance as might be required and every such officer of the armed forces shall obey such requisition and would extend every possible help and assistance for effective management of the calamities.

(iii) It shall also be lawful for the Central Relief Commissioner or State Relief Commissioner or any of their nominees, duly authorised in this behalf:

(a) to requisition the services of any adult private individual and to assign to him such responsibility, consistent with his age and ability, as may be deemed fit and proper, for the purpose of carrying out the objectives of this Act and translating its provisions into action, and

(b) to requisition men and material from any Government organisation, department, corporations, companies, public sector undertakings, and the like, functioning within his jurisdiction, with a view to operationalise the Act and the persons in charge of such organisations, departments, corporations, companies, public sector undertaking, shall be bound to comply with the requisition made in this behalf.

(iv) Whoever being called upon in writing by the Central Relief Commissioner and State Relief Commissioner/ District Relief Commissioner to comply with such requisition, without reasonable excuse, refuses or neglects to do so, shall be deemed to have committed an offence, punishable u/s 187 of the Indian Penal Code.

(v) It shall be lawful for the Central Relief Commissioner or State Relief Commissioner or District Relief Commissioner or for any other person authorised by general or special orders to enter into or upon any building or land with or without assistants or workmen in order to make any inquiry, inspection, measurement, valuation or survey or to execute any work, which is authorised by the Act, or to see whether the provisions of the Act were complied with.

(vi) It shall be lawful for any person, authorised by or under the Act to make an entry into any place, to open or cause to be opened, any door, gate or other barrier in saving lives and/or properties, if he considers the opening thereof necessary for the purpose of such entry; and, if the owner or occupier is absent, or being present, refuses to open such door, gate or barrier for purposes specified below:

(a) Removal of Debris,

(b) Conduct of search and rescue operations,

(c) Providing Emergency shelter,

(d) Provisioning of food, medicine and other essential needs,

(e) Requisitioning transport from private parties or which is available nearby,

(f) Constructing temporary bridges,

(g) Demolition of unsafe structure which may endanger the public,

(h) Warning of further risk and hazards,

(i) Dissemination of information including do's and don'ts,

(j) Rendering technical advice to the district and to the local Government, and

(k) Reduction of all immediate threats to life and public health and safety.

(vii) (a) It shall be the responsibility of the Central Relief Commissioner or State Relief Commissioner and/ or District Relief Commissioner to make adequate arrangements for evacuation of the inhabitants before the occurrence of calamity and for the purpose, they shall be competent to give appropriate direction for evacuation.

(b) In the event of such direction being disobeyed, it shall be lawful for the Central Relief Commissioner/State Relief Commissioner/ District Relief Commissioner or such authority as may be empowered in his behalf to use such amount of force as may be necessary for effecting the evacuation of inhabitants before the occurrence of calamity.

(c) Wilful violation of such directions shall constitute an offence under the Act.

(viii) It shall be lawful for any of the principal authorities, namely, Government of India, Central Relief Commissioner, National Centre for Calamity Management, State Government, State Relief Commissioner and District Relief Commissioner to use or cause to be used by Doordarshan, Cable TVs, All India Radio, FM Radios for broadcasting news and disseminating information regarding intensity of disaster likely to be caused by any of the calamities.

8. National Centre for Calamity Management

(i) The Government of India shall constitute a National Centre for Calamity Management which would consist of:

(a) Director General of the National Centre for Calamity Management to be appointed by Government of India as the Administrative Head of the National Centre for Calamity Management and he would be an officer not below the rank of the Joint Secretary to the Government of India; and

(b) any such other officer or officers as may be appointed by Government of India to aid and assist the Director General.

(ii) The principal office of the National Centre for Calamity Management would be located in New Delhi as an attached office of the Ministry of Agriculture and would function under the over-all control and supervision of the Ministry of Agriculture. It may have such other branch or branches as might be necessary for the purpose of carrying out different functions and responsibilities,

(iii) The National Centre for Calamity Management shall be the nodal agency for calamity management in respect of the calamities including those specified in Schedule-1 and the management of calamities as provided for in the Act shall be effected through the National Centre for Calamity Management. It would have the powers to take all such measures as it deems necessary and expedient for the purpose of management of calamities including those specified in Schedule-1.

9. Scientific and Technical Advisory Committee

(i) The Government of India, in consultation with the National Centre for Calamity Management, shall constitute a Scientific and Technical Advisory Committee to advise the National Centre for Calamity Management, and it would have such number of technical and other experts as the Government of India, may determine,

(ii) The Committee would cause all relevant data relating to calamity management to be procured and would provide all scientific and technical advice and assistance to the National Centre for Calamity Management.

CHAPTER III

10. National Calamity Contingency Fund

(i) There shall be a National Calamity Contingency Fund in the nature of an imprest which shall remain at the disposal of the President of India to enable advances to be made by him out of this fund for meeting the urgent and unforeseen expenditure for the purpose of calamity management and for more effectively carrying out the objectives of this Act.

(ii) The corpus of this fund would be a sum of Rs. 500 crores which would remain as an imprest money. The corpus may be increased by Government of India from time to time. The annual expenditure on account of calamity management to be incurred out of this fund would be recouped from time to time by levy of surcharge on the receipts to the Public Account of the Union.

CHAPTER IV

Liabilities and Legal Proceedings

11. Offences

(i) Wilful violation of any duty imposed by the Act or Rules made under shall be deemed to be an offence.

(ii) Such offence shall be punishable with imprisonment of one year or with fine of Rs. 5000 or with both.

(iii) Every offence under the Act shall be cognizable and non-bailable within the meaning of the Code of Criminal Procedure, 1973 (2 of 1974).

12. Penalty for Contraventions of the Provisions of the Act and the Rules, Orders and Directions

(i) Whoever fails to comply with or contravenes ,of any of the provisions of this Act or the rules made thereunder or orders or issues directions in this behalf shall in respect of each such failure or contravention be guilty of an offence against this Act.

(ii) Such offence shall be punishable with imprisonment of either description, simple, or rigorous, for a term which may extend to six months or with fine which may extend to Rs. 5000 or with both.

(iii) Notwithstanding anything contained in the court of Criminal Procedure Code, 1973 no court inferior to that of Metropolitan Magistrate or a Judicial Magistrate of First Class, shall try any offence under this Act.

13. Offences Committed by the Government Department/ Agency

(i) Where an offence under this Act has been committed by any department of Government, the Head of the Department or Office shall be deemed to be guilty of the offence and shall be liable to be proceeded against and punished accordingly, provided that, nothing contained in this section shall render such Head liable to punishment if he proves that the offence was committed without his knowledge or that he exercised due diligence to prevent this commission of such offence,

(ii) Notwithstanding anything contained in sub-section (i), where an offence under this Act has been committed by a Department of Government and it is proved that the offence has been committed with the consent or connivance of/or is attributable to any neglect on the part of any officer or official other than that and the Head of the Department or office, such officer or official shall also be deemed to be guilty of that offence and shall be liable to be proceeded against and punished accordingly.

14. Civil Liability for Misuse of Funds

(i) Any official/functionary entrusted with or engaged in any relief and/or rescue operation, if found responsible, directly or indirectly, for loss of public money or damage to public property shall be liable for recovery of funds which shall be to the tune of 150 per cent of the total loss/damage caused.

(ii) An amount to the tune of 150 per cent of the embezzled/misappropriated amount shall be recovered and a penalty in cash shall be imposed on such official/functionary without prejudice to any other legal proceedings or criminal prosecution that may be launched against him.

(iii) The Competent Authority for imposing such penalty shall be as prescribed for loss of public money and damage to public property.

15. Previous Sanction of the Government

(i) No prosecution shall be instituted against any person other than a public servant in respect of any offence under the Act without previous sanction of the Central Relief Commissioner, State Relief Commissioner or District Relief Commissioner as the case may be.

(ii) When any public servant not removable from his office save by or with the sanction of the Government is accused of any offence alleged to have been committed by him while acting or purporting to act in the discharge of his official duty under the Act, no court shall take cognizance of such offence except with the previous sanction:

(a) In the case of a public servant who is employed or, as the case may be, was at the time of commission of the alleged offence employed, in connection with the affairs of the Union, of the Central Government; and

(b) In the case of a public servant who is employed or, as the case may be, was at the time of commission of the alleged offence employed, in connection with the affairs of the State, of the State Government.

CHAPTER V
Miscellaneous

16. Protection of Action taken in Good Faith

No suit, prosecution or other legal proceeding shall lie against any person for anything which is in good faith done or intended to be done under the Act.

17. Bar of Jurisdiction

No Civil Court shall have jurisdiction to entertain any suit or proceeding in respect of anything done, action taken or order or direction issued by the State Government or any other authority or officer in pursuance of any power conferred by or in relation to its or his functions under the Act.

18. Effect of Other Laws

(i) Subject to the provisions of sub-section (2), the provisions of the Act and the Rules or orders made thereunder shall have effect, notwithstanding anything inconsistence therewith contained in any enactment other than the Act.

(ii) Where any act or omission constitutes an offence punishable under the Act and also under any other Act, then the offender found guilty of such offence shall be liable to be punished under the other Act and not under the Act.

19. Power to make Rules

(i) The Government of India may make rules to carry out the purposes and objects of this Act.

(ii) All Rules made by the Government of India under this Act shall be published in the official gazette and on such publication, shall have effect as if the Rules were enacted in this Act.

(iii) Every Rule made by the Government of India under this Act shall be laid, as soon as may be after it is made, before Parliament.

List of Calamities

I. Water and Climate Related Calamities

1. Floods and Drainage Management
2. Cyclones
3. Tornadoes and Hurricanes
4. Hailstorm
5. Cloud Burst
6. Thunder and Lightning
7. Snow Avalanches
8. Heat Wave and Cold Wave
9. Sea Erosion
10. Droughts

II. Geologically Related Calamities

1. Earthquakes
2. Landslides and Mudflows
3. Dam Bursts
4. Mine Fires

III. Chemical, Industrial and Nuclear Related Disasters

1. Chemical and Industrial Disasters
2. Nuclear Disasters

IV. Accident-Related Disasters

1. Urban Fires
2. Village Fires
3. Forest Fires
4. Electrical Disasters and Fires
5. Serial Bomb Blasts
6. Oil Spill
7. Festival-Related Disasters
8. Air, Road and Rail Accidents
9. Boat Capsizing
10. Mine Flooding
11. Major Building Collapse

V. Biologically-Related Disasters

1. Biological Disasters and Epidemics
2. Pest Attacks
3. Cattle Epidemics
4. Food Poisoning

FIVE

GOVERNANCE AND MANAGEMENT

Disaster is a calamity which is suddenly thrust either by nature or by man himself on himself. It blows out, dismantles and smashes all the 'orders of life' haywire. It may occur in any walk of life and at any moment of time. It has a potentiality of putting a man non-plussed. It obviously causes immense loss to mankind. In the twentieth century, if anything has browbeaten mankind so often, it is 'disaster'— disaster of every kind. The more the mankind has progressed and developed, the more it has become vulnerable to the blows of disaster. Disaster keeps on striking in all parts of the world, with almost a 'disciplined regularity'. It may be a sudden outbreak of war at one place. Or, it may be an earthquake at some other place. It may be flood, hurricane, nuclear leakage at some place, or a big fire suddenly flashing and flaming in blocks of apartments at some other place. One may think of any misfortune which suddenly hits human population. And it all has a 'disaster' potential.

But then how to meet the challenges of disaster? It is going to be a towering exercise to the man of the 21st century. To meet the challenges of disaster, we need to evolve some 'universal' and some 'specific' tools which may effectively handle the situation of disaster. Unless we do that, we shall not be able to save the world from great catastrophes to which mankind now seems more vulnerable to, in the years to come. Obviously, disaster management is going to be a vital discipline of study in the next century.

Keeping this proposition in view this study is an attempt to study the dimensions of governance disaster; as the 'governance disaster' in near future, is going to be the most dangerous threat to the largest number of people; spanning from east to west and from north to south of the globe. The style, technique, policies, implementation and execution of such policies have quite often in the past triggered off several incidents of disaster. The governments all over the world have at times initiated such policies which invariably led to a chain of great catastrophes in their respective countries. The nature of such policy implementation in different countries have been quite diverse. From 'apartheid' to 'social justice'—their implementations and executions have sordidly resulted into great social clashes, counter-clashes and even upheavals of great magnitude. Even the developmental policy executions have sometimes resulted in great protests and rebellions by people in several countries. We may, for example, see the questions of policy implementation in the field of environmental pollution, ecological sustenance, etc. However, such cases of policy implementations cannot always be attributed to defective policy formulations at the topmost level. Sometimes even good and socially imperative policies, when implemented or executed, have resulted into disastrous consequences.

Government of India planned a grand project named as Narmada Valley Development Project (NVDP) to the tune of 3 billion pound investment. This project plans for 30 big dams, 135 medium sized ones and 3,000 small dams in Narmada valley. However, the entire project is hanging in balance. The execution of this project is likely to render at least 1,00,000 people homeless. The 40 megawatt Maheshwar dam alone was going to displace at least 2,200 families in 61 villages and destroy thousands of acres of cotton, chillies and wheat *(The Hindustan Times,* 16 January, 1998, Patna, p. 9).

In protest of this project a massive movement has been launched known as Narmada Bachao Andolan (NBA). Only recently in 1997, hundreds of villagers protesting the construction of dams across the Narmada in Madhya Pradesh, took control of the site, forcing the government to suspend the construction work. Sensing the sensitivity of the whole issue, World Bank pulled out of the controversial project five years ago.

Narmada Bachao Andolan protagonists want this project to be completely stopped. They justify their movement on the ground of environment protection as well as humanitarian causes. As a result, a massive developmental exercise of government seems to have been shelved, at least for a while.

Narmada Bachao Andolan which has emerged as a people's protest against the execution of governmental plans is a significant example of governance disaster.

Economic and financial handling of state affairs is one of the most crucial and vulnerable spots where governance can doom disasters for people. There are many governments in the world which have pushed their state to a point of near disaster, if not total disaster. But near disaster situation can very well inaugurate a situation of disasters. Even fifty years of independence of India has not been able to acquire a position of economic power in the world in spite of such huge natural resources and manpower potential, for which it has only itself to blame for. There are many countries in the world which have become economic powers even within forty years of their total destruction.

Only recently in late 1997 and early 1998 the Indian rupee value started falling against dollar to a level where it had never arrived in the past. Governance and quality of governance has lot to offer in this connection, the explanations of economic theories notwithstanding. If the downslide of Indian rupee is not halted at the earliest possible, its balance of payment in relation to other countries may create unprecedented problems for Indian economy. The falling Indian rupee may lead the Indian economy to another governance disaster.

However, to understand the gravity of this downslide of Indian rupee, we may examine the mechanism of exchange rate which determines the value of rupee vis-a-vis dollar.

In a floating exchange-rate regime the rates are neither fixed, nor administered. They are determined by the forces of demand and supply. Demand and supply forces are in turn influenced by a host of ordinary variables, such as inflation rate, rate of interest, balance of current account, etc., and extraordinary variables, such as political upheavals, war, etc. Any change in these variables may lead to changes in the supply and demand schedules and in turn to changes in the exchange rate.

By the mid-1970s, when adjustable peg system was given a good-bye in favour of floating exchange rate regime, various theories were developed explaining changes in exchange rate in the new environment. One such theory was developed by PR. Allen and RB. Kenen. The proponents of this approach, known as the balance of payments approach, feel that the differentials in money supply, income growth and in rate of interest between two countries influence the balance of payments and thereby the exchange rate. The first two influence the current account, while the rate of interest influences the capital account through effecting the flow of investment. A favourable balance of payments helps appreciate the domestic currency.

Another school of thought led by J.A. Frenkel is known as monetary approach. Frenkel believes that the three variables as discussed above influence the demand for, and the supply of money and thereby the exchange rate. An increase in money supply causes the domestic currency to depreciate. Similarly, a rise in rate of interest lowers the demand for money which causes further depreciation in domestic currency. On the contrary, a rise in income encourages demand for money and helps appreciate the domestic currency. On the last two counts, the monetary approach thus runs contrary to the balance of payments approach.

The monetary approach was amended by R. Dornbusch who presented a detailed explanation of interest rate impact and who emphasized on the differential inflation rate. In the views of Dornbusch, changes in interest rate influence the exchange rate in two ways. One is that a high interest rate helps enlarge the loanable funds in the money market, as a result of which the domestic currency depreciates. But at the same time, a high interest rate encourages the foreign investment inflow into the country which acts positively on the external value of domestic currency. The Fisher Effect explains further that it is the real interest rate differential that matters.

Again, as far as inflation rate differential is concerned, it is also very important in determining the exchange rate. The explanation is based on the Purchasing Power Theory and the theory of one price. It means that the currency of a country with higher inflation rate loses its purchasing power and hence depreciates vis-a-vis foreign currency. It is because of this the pre-inflation exchange rate cannot be sustained.

Again, there are economists who believe that it is not the supply and demand for money alone that determines the exchange rate. But it is the entire portfolio of financial assets that has an impact on the exchange rate. Mckinnon, the leading proponent of this school of thought argues that growth in budgetary deficits leads to growth in domestic bonds which leads to monetisation of debt and an increase in money supply. Current account surpluses cause an increase in holding of foreign bonds. In both the cases, domestic currency will tend to depreciate. If domestic interest rates go higher, demand for foreign bonds and thereby demand for foreign currency will be lower. Domestic currency will appreciate. Thus changes in the preference for money, domestic and foreign bonds influence the exchange rate.

In a forward market, the size of premium or discount depends mainly on the current expectations of future events. Suppose if the dollar is expected to depreciate, the holders of the dollar will start selling it forward. The forward sale will help depress the forward rate of dollar. The explanation of forward differential finds an important place in the theory of interest rate parity. This theory states that the currency of a country with lower interest rate should be at a forward premium in relation to the currency of a country with higher interest rate. More precisely, the forward differential should approximately equal the interest rate differential for each maturity.

Rupee is on managed float. Any variation in its value is natural. The RBI can intervene in the foreign exchange market in order to stabilize its value. The recent fall in the value of rupee is nothing new. In October, 1995, there had occurred a drastic fall and so was in February, 1996. This time too, rupee has experienced a substantial depreciation which goes to about 10 per cent. The value of rupee, which was Rs. 36.1 per dollar on October 24, 1997 dropped to Rs. 39.50 per dollar by the 1st of December. Such a scenario involves primarily three questions. One is, what should be the size and frequency of RBI's intervention. The other is, what are the possible causes for the drastic fall. Last is whether the package introduced by the RBI should prove efficacious.

The RBI sells dollar in the foreign exchange market as a result of which supply of dollar increases vis-a-vis rupee. Rupee tends to appreciate. On the other hand, purchase of dollars by the RBI helps rupee to depreciate. This is the intervention by the RBI. But the question is whether intervention should be a routine affair or it should be very rarely used leaving in normal cases the exchange rate to represent the macroeconomic fundamentals. Arguments for both the possibilities are there. However, in the Indian case, the RBI feels that it should not be frequent. At the time of the recent fall of rupee, it was said that the fall was long overdue in view of maintaining export performance in the wake of the depreciation of some South-East Asian currencies.

At a seminar on the occasion of IMF-World Bank meeting in Hong Kong in September 1997, it was stated that "competitive devaluation would soon become a policy issue... the question will arise, sooner or later, as to how India will retain competitiveness if South-East Asian currencies have depreciated so sharply." Rangarajan's policy of least intervention is not devoid of realities, especially in view of the fact that the South-East Asian countries are India's main competitor as far as agricultural exports and export of textiles are concerned. Both taken together account for almost one-half of India's total export earnings. If depreciation of rupee is not checked at least to a reasonable extent, Indian exports will fare better.

But such a thinking is not beyond doubts. It is because rupee has depreciated by about 10 per cent vis-a-vis 45 per cent depreciation of Thai Baht; 32 per cent depreciation of Malaysian Ringitt; and 28 per cent depreciation of Indonesian Rupiah. On the contrary, India's import bill will inflate as many imports are price-inelastic. Some of the petro-products like diesel are indexed to international prices and so, a fall in Indian rupee would mean higher prices of petro-products. Costlier imports will not only affect the current account balance but also push the domestic prices. Depreciated rupee will enhance the servicing cost of external borrowings. Budgetary deficit will be hit this way. Rupee depreciation will erode the earnings of the foreign institutional investors from the capital market in India and enhance their exchange risk. This is perhaps the reason that their net investment in Indian capital market dropped from Rs. 345 crores during 2-24 October, 1997 to Rs. (-)199 crores during 24 October, to 4 December, 1997, that is when rupee depreciated.

If RBI goes for aggressive intervention to arrest any depreciation in the value of rupee and if it fails to do it, foreign exchange reserves will be badly hit. In fact, during the recent debacle, this actually happened.

In recent times, a lot of issues with regard to governance have been boiling in the minds of policy-makers. One such issue is the call of "bandhs". Bandhs have in recent times caused a lot of disasters, related with governance. On many important occasions, against certain decisions of the government, call for bandhs have been given by several opposition political parties and other interest groups. These bandh calls have literally paralysed government functioning. As a result any call of bandhs in essential services were declared illegal.

But recently even general calls of 'bandhs' have been declared illegal and unconstitutional in India by a ruling of Supreme Court of India. It has sparked a debate of immense magnitude. How far the bandh calls are responsible for disasters? Are the bandh calls results of governance disasters? Are the bandh calls genuine? Will they really help the cause of people?

Is the illegal declaration of bandhs called by political parties, trade unions and other organizations a 'cruel slap' on people's democratic rights or a crucial step to restore the fundamental rights of individuals? The verdict confirming a Kerala High Court order has already launched a debate.

There is considerable opinion that bandhs, ensuring total closure of all activity in a city or across a state, is a normal way of protest. Some feel the protests could be conveyed through partial closures, although 'mass movements' were acceptable to arouse public awareness. Talk has also started to look for 'alternative' methods of protest.

The 'bandh' was used by veteran Communist leader S.S. Dang in the early sixties to organize protests that had mass participation. The All India Trade Union Congress (AITUC) that he led did a lot of preparatory work to arouse sympathy for its actions. The practice was initially followed by political parties and trade unions so that bandhs were successful and not hated. Down the years, the groundwork was neglected and an element of coercion introduced.

It is widely believed that as a form of protest the bandh had evolved during the freedom struggle itself and the nation's top leaders gave numerous calls to people to suspend all work to convey how serious they were.

Analysing the judgement, Communist Party of India (CPI) general secretary A.B. Bardhan says that the Supreme Court order denies the 'basic right' of the people to voice their grievances and demands through agitational means. The bandh was one of the agitational methods that was devised by the Indian working people in the course of their movement.

Mr Bardhan says, "I may understand if they expect certain regulations to be followed. But a blanket ban, that too confirmed by the Supreme Court, is a serious infringement of democratic rights". Hundreds of bandhs had been organized in the country and one would not say that anything untoward had happened. If it was a question of inconvenience caused, then one could even argue that a procession also caused inconvenience.

"Is it not a fact that the movement of VVIPs also causes inconvenience to the ordinary people? Are we therefore for stopping the movement of VVIPs?" asks Mr Bardhan. He feels the Supreme Court failed to take into account that people had a right to voice their grievances. Freedoms guaranteed under the Constitution could be taken away by the judgement. Its impact could operate against the weaker sections and for the doubtful conveniences of the more affluent.

AITUC deputy general secretary H. Mahadevan says the trade unions were not merely worried about their demands. The issue was not just legal but had social aspects. How could social change be effected without protest, he asks. The bandh was just a form of protest. "Change without protest is not possible. Prayers will not bring about change", he says.

A trade union leader who himself organized bandhs. Mr. Mahadevan says bandhs always exempted essential services like water, milk supplies, fire and medical services. "We are part of the society. We don't want to behave irresponsibly", he says.

The Supreme Court judgement does not go into social situations which could arise suddenly, "Anyway, we are not cowed by the judgement. With rich experience in the field, we will not be found wanting in alternative methods of protest", he says. Solidarity actions were often organized to express support on various issues. A fundamental right to protest, and that too supported by ILO conventions, could not be given up easily.

Striking a different note, Bharatiya Mazdoor Sangh (BMS) leader R.K. Bakhi says his union had at no stage taken part in any Bharat Bandh or a state-level bandh. Even though the union was strongly opposed to the new economic policies, it did not take part in a bandh. "We are for industrial bandhs and not for total bandhs", he says.

The union feels that the new economic policies could increase the American stranglehold over the Indian economy and would organise a "mass movement" in June next year. The union would go to villages and mobilise the people against the policies in the same manner as Mahatma Gandhi used to do.

The judgement has upset the Left movement. Communist Party of India (Marxist) politburo member Prakash Karat says that by upholding the Kerala High Court verdict, the Supreme Court had entered an area which was in the domain of "political activities". The judiciary, he says, should not be "decreeing what is the acceptable form of political or public protest action."

The bandh was not an instrument of protest to be used casually. It was always resorted to when a wider and higher form of protest was required to express popular grievances. The judgement, according to Mr Karat, was predisposed to the viewpoint of the propertied classes and those who were not victims of the present socio-economic system. It sought to enforce a directive which was neither feasible nor advisable in a democratic system.

The very word 'bandh' evokes images of closed shops, patients dying for want of medical care and empty streets with remains of burnt vehicles. Little wonder then that the recent Supreme Court ruling upholding the Kerala High Court judgement declaring that bandhs are a violation of the Fundamental Rights has won laurels from several senior politicians and legal experts. The distinction made by the apex court between voluntary participation and the use of coercion to make the protest successful has been lauded by the general public.

This form of protest was initiated in India by Mahatma Gandhi against the Rowlatt Act in 1918. The target of his protest was an alien regime. In the present context, a bandh paralyses everyday life and the sufferer is the common man and the loser the nation.

As an instrument of protest against British imperialism, the bandh proved its efficacy. With life, business and industry coming to a standstill, the worst hit was the ruling class. Today, apart from hardship for the daily wagers who constitute a huge chunk of the floating population in the metropolises, it spawns violence and loss of life and property. Equally serious is the damage to industry and the national economy in terms of productivity and the man-days lost.

Bandhs completely jeopardize the functioning of business, industry and normal life. The Supreme Court has heeded the voice of the public and done the right thing. Those calling for a bandh must realise that they as citizens, have to work. They have no right to bring this to a halt.

But as a means for ventilating grievances, bandhs have lost their mass appeal. The participation in such events are generally confined to party cadres. The politics of agitation is, in fact, an anachronism in the urban ambience dominated by the service sector. Not surprisingly, therefore, political parties are hard pressed these day to even mobilize crowds for public meetings. Consequently, the organizations calling for bandhs end up resorting to violence to make their protest appear successful.

A bandh is a visible form of protest, it is a clear and constant reminder about the issue against which the protest has been organized. As such it is a very effective means of protest, explains civil liberarian, Prashant Bhushan. But with the political parties giving bandh calls for all the wrong reasons, he says. This form of protest has become trivialized.

There is also the tendency for the ruling party to collaborate with the organization calling for a bandh, if it serves its purpose, and opposing it if it does not. Bandh calls on issues lacking mass involvement are destined to fall.

If any decision is against the interests of a political party, a bandh call is given. The decision may not necessarily be against the interest of the people, yet they are sucked into the protest.

Bandhs have thus a lot to contribute to governance disaster. Likewise, governance disasters have a lot to contribute to such bandh calls too.

Governance disasters can also be seen in the way law and order of the state is handled. In developing countries, rising unemployment, spiralling prices, poor quality of life, political immaturity of leadership all combine to create a situation where governance becomes so bad that it often results in disasters. As a result crime rates go alarmingly higher and higher.

In recent times, we can take the case of Andhra Pradesh. Crime rate has sharply increased here which is a testimony of governance disasters.

The banned People's War Group (PWG), the most militant of all the extremist groups operating in the State, began in the year '97 with a major offensive on January 10 blasting the Karakagudem police station in Khammam district killing 16 policemen, the largest number of casualties in an extremist attack against the police. Eighty Naxalites belonging to four *dalams* (armed squads) had surrounded the police station and carried out the attack in the early hours in a meticulously planned operation.

While the extremists killed 165 people, including 47 policemen, the number of murders committed in 1997 stood at 245 including the slaying of 51 policemen (one deputy superintendent of police, one circle inspector, four subinspectors and 39 constables). The extremists had carried out landmine attacks against policemen on six occasions.

The number of extremists killed in encounters was 146 in 176 cases of exchange of fire while 132 Naxalites were killed in 135 encounters during the year.

With the PWG setting out a violent agenda aimed at converting the Telangana and Dandakaranya regions (comprising parts of Andhra Pradesh, Maharashtra, Madhya Pradesh and Orissa) into guerrilla zones, the attacks on public and private properties as also on political representatives registered a sharp increase. The State Government was forced to renew the ban on PWG and to ask the Centre to deploy additional Central paramilitary forces in the Naxal-dominated regions.

Bidding adieu to its poll promise to implement total prohibition in the State, the ruling Telugu Desam Government relaxed the dry law by permitting the sale, manufacture and consumption of Indian-made Foreign Liquor (IMFL) through an amendment to Andhra Pradesh Prohibition Act, amid protest from opposition members in the Assembly and women's groups outside.

Chief Minister Chandrababu Naidu justified the move on the grounds that it had become difficult to enforce dry law in toto in the State with none of the neighbouring states having prohibition. Besides it was leading to the emergence of gangs of bootleggers and mafias indulging in illicit liquor trade.

Other states are not far behind. Let us take the case of Bihar. Apart from general and sporadic crimes spreading in the length and breadth of Bihar, the organized group crime has taken a very ugly turn. They all demonstrate in themselves different forms of governance disasters.

A chronology of events given in the following Table is illustrative of this fact.

Governance disasters have not only taken its toll in developing countries like India, they have also taken a very heavy toll in developed countries. They cannot only be seen in the area of economic performance, law and order, crime, insurgency, etc., but also in the area of polity itself take, for example, elections. What is the price, a country like India has to pay if elections occur every now and then on account of governance mismanagement. They spell out great disasters for the people— as it is the people who ultimately bear the entire cost of such untimely elections. India has had to hold the third successive election in 1999, in the past three years (13 Lok Sabha) when the BJP government was voted out of power after 13 months of rule.

CRIMES IN BIHAR DURING 1984-97 SHOWING GOVERNANCE OF DISASTERS

Year	*Incident*	*Casualty*	*Group Involved*
1984	Danwar-Bihta (Bhojpur)	29	CPI-ML and landlords
1986	Arwal (Patna)	24	Police killed 24 party unity cadres
1987	Dalelchak-Baghoura (Aurangabad)	54	MCG kills landlords
1991	Tiskhora (Patna)	15	CPI-ML activists killed by Kisan Sangh.
1991	Deo Sahiara (Bhojpur)	15	CPI-ML kills landlords
1992	Bara (Gaya)	34	MCC kills landowners
1996	Bathanitola (Bhojpur)	22	Ranbir Sena kills CPI-ML activists.
1997	Haibaspur (Patna)	10	Ranbir Sena kills Dalits
1997	Jalpura (Patna)	11	PU kills landowners

Estimates suggest that in 1996 general elections for Lok Sabha (11th Lok Sabha) Election Commission itself spent Rs. 500 crores. Compared to this last ten general elections in India put together have cost the tax payers about Rs. 607.22 crores. While the first poll cost the country Rs. 10.45 crores, the expenditure on the conduct of elections in 1991 crossed Rs. 300 crores. And by 1996 it touched a whopping Rs. 508.68 crores. In the 1998 elections it is likely to cost the tax payers around Rs. 800 crores.

Apart from these election expenditures let us calculate the price which the country might have paid with frequent changes of government at the centre. After 1st December, 1989 when Rajiv Gandhi was voted, out India has till date six prime ministers. Out of these six prime ministers only Narasimha Rao lasted for about five years. Among the rest none could exceed 350 days in office. V.P. Singh lasted for 341 days, Chandra Shekhar lasted for 224 days, K.D. Devegowda lasted for 325 days. I.K. Gujral also did not last for a year. Atal Behari Vajpayee came in as Prime Minister in the 12th Lok Sabha. His government was voted out of power after it had completed 13 months of governance after great difficulty in April 1999.

The cost of these changes are nothing less than disastrous for people of India.

We would therefore, conclude that governance disasters are in fact much more serious issue today than anything else. It must be seen in right perspective to arrive at anything meaningful for the people and the polity.

GUIDELINES FOR HAZARD ASSESSMENT AND VULNERABILITY ANALYSIS

I. Hazard Assessment

A process of analysis which attempts to specify the "hazard occurrence probability" of an event of a given proportion occurring in a certain area within a stated time period (type/intensity/space/time).

The process of identifying and assessing the relative properties and direct effects of hazards with reference to time is based on the collection of historical and scientific data able to be presented in scales, maps or other means of comparison for analysis. The accuracy and degree of sophistication possible or desirable will depend on the extent of perceived risk and the detail of available information, determined by the human, financial, technical and temporal resources available.

A. *Types of Hazards*

1. Earthquake
2. Landslide
3. Tsunami
4. Volcanic eruption
5. Tropical cyclone (typhoon, hurricane)

6. Flood
7. Drought
8. Environmental degradation (pollution, desertification, etc.)
9. Bushfire (wildfire)
10. Civil conflict
11. Population displacement
12. Epidemic, biological
13. Technological hazard (industrial accident)

B. *Physical Characteristics of Hazard Occurrence*

1. Identity — knowledge of hazard, its development and behaviour
2. Nature — types of forces associated with the hazard
3. Intensity — capacity, or potential of destructive forces, effects
4. Extent — geographical distribution, range of impact
5. Scope — community, sectoral extent, range(s) of impact
6. Predictability — consequence of physical, temporal properties
7. Manageability — consequence of primary causes, properties

C. *Temporal Characteristics of Hazard Occurrence*

1. Frequency — how often the event occurs
2. Duration — expected time of lasting impact
3. Speed of onset — rapidity of arrival of impact
4. Forewarning — time between identification/warning and impact

D. *Hazard Assessment Considerations*

1. History
2. Probability of various intensities
3. Maximum credible threat

4. Necessity to consider secondary hazards, or 'knock-on' effects of primary forces or main triggering event (e.g., earthquake causes dam burst/landslide causes flash/impounded flood, causes building collapse, causes population displacement, etc.).
5. The more rare hazards are in a given area, the less historical or statistical information there is to work with. Therefore, they present a less confident opportunity for prediction or common awareness and they can be a greater liability.

E. *Elements at Risk to the Effects of Hazards*

(Direct consequences of the forces of hazards): Those elements, people, property or environment, processes or systems affected by the forces of a hazard if it occurs:

1. People, loss of life
2. Personal health, injury or disease
3. Damage, destruction of property
4. Damage, destruction of infrastructure, public service systems
5. Damage, destruction of environment
6. Damage, destruction of crops
7. Disruption, loss of production
8. Disruption, loss of livelihood
9. Disruption, loss of essential services
10. Disruption, loss of national infrastructure
11. Disruption to governmental process, systems
12. Loss to national, local economies
13. Disruption, loss of community or lifestyle
14. Sociological and psychological consequences

II. Vulnerability Analysis

A process which results in an understanding of the types and levels of exposure of persons, property, and the environment to the effects of identified hazards at a particular time.

Vulnerability = People + Condition + Place + Time + Event

The process to identify physical, social and economic conditions susceptible to the effects of hazards of a given intensity by focusing on the types of risk to which they are exposed. Different elements vary significantly in their susceptibility to damage of disruption and vulnerability also differs according to intensity of the hazard.

A. *Types of Vulnerability*

1. *Physical Vulnerability,* pertaining to mattters of location, proximity, structural and infrastructural conditions, frequently including agricultural assets as representing physical 'plant'.
   (a) Building—considering their use, site, design, shape, proximate locations, materials used, state of maintenance, construction techniques and quality.
   (b) Infrastructure—structurally-based systems and related processes necessary for the social and economic functioning of a society or a community, which in terms of their essentiality are sometimes referred to as 'lifelines'.
      1. Transportation systems and component elements
      2. Telecommunication system (external and internal)
      3. Public utilities services (water, electricity, drainage)
      4. Essential public or community services and related facilities (health, public administration, emergency or security services and facilities, essential economic structures, critical civil protection systems or measures, etc.)
   (c) Agricultrual—primarily considering physical assets related, but opportunity loss potential of essential natural resources, crops, trees, livestock, fisheries, also should be recognised.
2. *Economic Vulnerability,* determined by evaluating the direct loss potential of economic assets and processes, indirect loss potential, and consequent secondary effects, generally derived from previous historical data applied to current

conditions affected by a variety of disaster scenarios. As the direct disaster assistance, seldom exceeds a small fraction of total assets loss, it is in terms of net opportunity cost that economic vulnerability must be measured. Any complete assessment of economic vulnerability must be linked to studies of physical and social vulnerability.

(a) Direct loss potential:
   1. Damage, destruction of buildings, plants, facilities, raw material, products
   2. Replacement costs
   3. Loss of employment
   4. Crop losses
   5. Damage to means of production

(b) Indirect loss potential:
   1. Impact of lost production
   2. Impact of lost employment
   3. Destructions of savings
   4. Loss of markets
   5. Loss of opportunity
   6. Loss of vital services
   7. Loss to consequential income-earning activities

(c) Secondary effects:
   1. Inflation
   2. Indebtedness
   3. Income disparities
   4. Labour migration
   5. Reorientation of capital allocation
   6. Frustration of developmental investment
   7. Economic isolation of affected areas

3. *Social Vulnerability,* determined by the perception of risk and the ability of people to take measure to reduce that risk. Social vulnerability is more difficult to measure than either physical or economic vulnerability, but efforts can be made to identify those elements of society or social behaviour which may reflect a greater risk of adverse affect:

   (a) Critical indicators of perceived risk, ability of response:
      1. Poverty, limitation of resources, reserves or options,

2. Degree of public awareness about the immediate social and physical environments as they relate to hazards and effects,
3. Prior personal experience of specific risk, consequence,

(b) Demographic considerations:

1. Magnitudes, total population,
2. Concentration densities,
3. Demographic distinctions, vulnerable groups of socially disadvantaged people or those requiring special attention:
   (a) children,
   (b) disabled or physically/mentally impaired people,
   (c) single parent families,
   (d) elderly people,
   (e) women, particularly if pregnant or lactating,
   (f) remotely located, isolated groups of people, and
   (g) seasonal, temporary or migrant populations.
4. Socio-political or cultural attributes affecting social vulnerability
   (a) Educational and literacy levels,
   (b) Leadership, extent of coherent and effective governance,
   (c) Political viability, integrity, public confidence,
   (d) Extent of self-reliance, community organisation capabilities,
   (e) informed, practiced, local or traditional coping mechanisms, and
   (f) Nature of belief systems, people's view of themselves and their own abilities.

B. *Capabilities*

When conducting vulnerability analysis, a special note should be taken of positive attributes able to be identified that may contribute to an enhanced ability to prevent or mitigate the effects of a disaster, or which may strengthen a community's ability to respond effectively to the hazard.

C. Vulnerability Analysis Considerations

1. Need to focus on degrees of loss, damage,
2. Focus attention on important elements, concentrate analytical resources on critical or significant items:
   (a) people, concentrated populations,
   (b) lifelines,
   (c) economic activity, resources,
   (d) areas of developmental importance, and
   (e) production facilities.
3. Essential requirement to consider relationships of factors that determine social and economic systems and processes, over time.

III. Risk

Risk is the expected loss from a given hazardous event for a given element of vulnerability over a specified time period, it is a function of:

- the probability of a hazard of a particular magnitude occurring,
- the elements susceptible to potential loss or damage (`at risk'),
- the nature of vulnerability of those elements, and
- a specified future time period.

A. Risk Management

Risk Management, is the process of analysis which leads to the estimation of the magnitude of a given risk and the determination of how important such a risk is to matters of 'our' concern. It includes an evaluation of all the elements that are relevant to an understanding of existing or contemplated hazards and their effects on a specific environment. When this evaluation is considered in social or political terms, it enables the determination of appropriate hazard prevention, or vulnerability reduction, or mitigation strategies.

1. Risk Assessment

The scientific quantification of risk determined from data and an understanding of the processes involved determines the magnitude of the risk.

2. Risk Evaluation

The social, economic and political judgements of the importance of various risks faced by those exposed to them determines the accepted importance of the risk.

3. Conditional Elements

(a) Importance of amount and type of information and a careful understanding of the nature of the hazard and its associated forces. Prevailing ignorance constitutes a major risk factor.

(b) There is a need to balance rigorous scientific or rational analysis against other "belief factors" of social or personal importance:

1. people respond to risks which they perceive, which may be affected by media exposure, previous experience, or judgemental bias. Perceptions may be altered by vividness or frequency of exposure, dread or imagination, and
2. variation of voluntary and involuntary exposure and presumed ability of effective response (prevention and controllability).

(c) Relative costs and benefits associated with specific options of risk reduction:

1. affordable risks, literal costs and benefits,
2. acceptable risks, personal, social or political choices, and
3. degree of risk over time, relative probability of risk.

B. Policy Options for Risk Reduction

1. Decision-making—Essential to have political commitment:

   (a) priority needs of attention,
   (b) time and resource allocation, and
   (c) decide relative effects of intervention.

2. Importance of Information:
   (a) for policy determination, and
   (b) for public knowledge.
3. Hazard Prevention:
   (a) man-made hazards offer much potential for prevention, and
   (b) natural hazards offer less potential for prevention.
4. Vulnerability Reduction.
5. Mitigation of Effects:
   (a) structural measures of mitigation, and
   (b) non-structural measures of mitigation.

SIX

IMMEDIATE PLANNING

India is one of those countries, which has the unique distinction of being prone to several natural disasters. About two-thirds of the country comes under the arid, semi-arid and dry sub-humid conditions and is prone to recurrent drought. The coastal region is prone to cyclones between June and October. Around 56% of the geographical area of the country is susceptible to seismic disturbances of varying intensities. Over 40 million hectares of land area in the country experiences periodic floods. The hilly region is prone to landslides and the Himalayan region to avalanches. Fire hazards inflict serious damage to life and property in rural habitations and urban slum pockets in the summer months. Amongst all these disasters earthquakes, landslides, floods and cyclones affect housing areas in significant magnitudes.

Immediately after a disaster communities face several problems. In a specifically short span of time a community which was hitherto prosperous is rendered homeless and its economic assets wiped out or damaged beyond repair. It is faced with current and future crisis of magnitudes, which have both short-term and long-term implications on survival and recovery.

Secondly, disasters like earthquakes do not have warning systems; thus no preparedness measures can be taken. In the case of other disasters like floods even though problem areas are identified, economic and livelihood conditions prevent communities from protecting themselves. Once disaster strikes, the existing administrative setup is required to take up immediate relief operations of a magnitude which it is not equipped to handle. In cases where the administration fails there is chaos leading to further loss of lives and property.

In practically all situations, housing is the major physical asset possessed by the community and it is this asset which faces the maximum damage. An asset, which has taken generations to build up, is physically damaged and rendered unusable overnight. Not only is the housing stock damaged but community buildings, road networks and all other infrastructure facilities, which are the backbone of any community, are also destroyed.

A community, which is rendered poor and homeless, is forced to take on the task of reconstruction when it is fighting for its very survival. It is at this time that the community requires material, manpower and financial resources of a magnitude, which are well beyond all planned allocations. Procurement and placing in position these resources by itself leads to management problems which both the community and administration is not equipped to handle. The need of the hour is to enable people to be housed temporarily in a short span of time so that some semblance of normalcy returns to family and community life.

While there are the problems that the community faces immediately after a natural disaster there are another set of long-term problems which come into being by the very nature of the rehabilitation programs which follow. There is a failure on part of organizations to comprehend the magnitude of the complexity involved in providing housing which is viewed as a product and not a process. The typical rehabilitation program not only excludes the victims from participation in decision-making, but also ignores the local building materials and labour skills possessed by the community. It relies upon non-existent skills and ignores the issue of post-delivery maintenance, which the shelter would generate.

This system of delivery is followed up by an erroneous system of program evaluation, which is quantitative rather than qualitative. A program is declared successful if a certain number of shelters are provided within a stipulated span of time for a certain percentage of beneficiaries. The acceptability of new housing stock, capacity of the stock to respond to future growth, its suitability to family and community lifestyles is mostly ignored.

Against this backdrop of problems it would be appropriate to discuss the central issues which must be understood before formulation of short-term and long-term goals for disaster mitigation. Firstly, it must be realized that disasters have a crippling effect on the economy of the region or settlement. They not only undermine development efforts and create unnatural demands on scares resources, but pull back development by destroying initiatives. The direct effect is damage to property, infrastructure and productive assets leading to imposition of huge economic and social burden on society. The indirect effect is decline in production, loss of income due to unemployment, indebtedness of the poor and increased costs of goods and services.

Disasters also create a differential impact, which is based on the socio-economic status and access to productive resources of any community. Thus, vulnerability of the people to disaster increases with poverty level. The rural and urban poor and the disadvantaged groups per force live in the most disaster prone areas and are least equipped in terms of resources to cope with the disruption. This vulnerability is furthered by environmental degradation, undertaking of development activities ignoring disaster concerns under various economic pressures and certain patterns of consumption which has the cumulative effect of aggravating their vulnerability. Thus, the very approach to development needs a shift in emphasis to include the concept of sustainable development in the background of reduced vulnerability. This implies that planning measures such as land-use planning, introduction of technology and resource management must be driven by the vulnerability analysis of the communities in question.

Unfortunately as things stand today, planned efforts in the hands of planning experts executed by the administrators are top down efforts. These efforts do not take into account, the existing community interrelationships between social and economic groups and existing semiotic relationships of people with people and people with land. With the present status of government as provider, community initiatives have been crippled to a great extent. As a consequence there is erosion of the resilience of the community to face disasters.

Furthermore, traditional planning organizations lack training and capability in the special area of disaster and its management.

Government and community-based organizations involved in this area do not work in tandem. At times of disaster the lines of control get blurred within organizations themselves and between sister concerns. This leads to poor management for disaster mitigation at the first instance and subsequently for rehabilitation and other long-term measures.

If we examine the significant issues in our perspective planning exercises at the national and state level one finds that disaster concerns are given the least priority. Planning measures are preoccupied with traditional socio-economic concerns. The fact that formulation of policies which will lead to long-term disaster reduction will by itself pay rich dividend in the long-run is not realized. Planning is at best concerned with short-term goals in tune with political concerns and visibility.

Against the backdrop of these factors let us examine those specific issues which must be addressed with respect to housing and disaster mitigation. At the settlement level land use patterns have other major considerations. For example, vulnerability to disaster of developed areas may be given lower priority to another issue like a good workplace home relationship or housing affordability. As a consequence, the poor to house themselves develop low-lying areas thereby placing themselves in a high-risk area. In hill areas, flat lands are used for cultivation there is a tendency to build on slopes to conserve a sustainable productive use of land. Proximity to sea is essential for fishing communities. High densities of development in urban areas which are also consequence of land values may be detrimental to the population as the primary and secondary damages to such areas are much higher.

From the above it is obvious that the poor live in disaster prone areas because of circumstances that are beyond their control. So it is unrealistic to imagine that they would make any major change to their housing condition with respect to location, building materials, etc. Thus, a more obvious application of pre-disaster mitigation principles is towards new settlements. Unfortunately, even here, housing for the poor would predominantly remain an informal sector activity. Thus, applications of principles generated by vulnerability analysis with respect to siting, building design, nature and type of materials to be used would be quite irrelevant for this section of society; the market forces would ensure that the benefits of this research accrue to the upper strata of society.

At the meso level when one examines the existing housing stock one finds that 21% of the stock is over 40 years old and 10% is over 60 years old. Most of these units are partly or highly dilapidated. People themselves construct the bulk of the housing in the country. Building materials and construction techniques traditionally used for housing have been arrived at by use of local materials through a process of trial and error over generations of crafted buildings. Housing forms have been highly responsive to local climatic conditions, material availability and experience structural performances under natural circumstances. Due to poor affordability these buildings are not engineered to resist extreme natural forces.

This leads to the following constraints for vulnerability analysis and recommendatory measures:

* Variations due to level of maintenance which a complex product of material use and its age.
* Variation due to many diverse combinations which would need many diverse solutions for retrofitting.
* Variations in the scale, dimension and nature of the attack and the lack of exact knowledge of how all these above mentioned factors would affect the nature of the damage.
* What is the right level of risk which one can accept as a trade-off for affordability when housing is traditionally a people's activity using local skills and materials.

Thus, any attempt at making broad recommendations is by itself fraught with difficulties. What would be required is to work with specific communities at a local level, which is the antithesis of the present system of top down planning efforts in the country.

When we look at the global level we realize that there is a better understanding of material properties under dynamic loading, engineering design, methods and performance specifications which have enabled assessment and design for risk easier. However, all this database is related to urban structures, which use modern building materials like steel, reinforced concrete and glass. Considerable research efforts are required to generate performance specifications and criteria for validation for use of traditional materials and non-engineered construction to serve needs of developing countries. To this is added the Indian complexity of great bio-climatic and geological diversity with 50-60% of land area being susceptible to various disasters.

Though it is recognized that disaster mitigation measures are end targets to be achieved considerations must be given to affordability, as some measure is better than none. There is a need to clearly understand the importance of cost benefit analysis for new housing *vis-a-vis* retrofitting. Further, there is a need to establish difference standards for community buildings, which are products of community effort, and at times of disaster prove to be community assets.

Another significant issue, which is often ignored at times of devising relief and rehabilitation measures, has to do with the externalities of the input. These differ from case to case and therefore need careful monitoring. Firstly, the coping abilities of the disaster survivors has to be understood with respect to:

* The existing strengths and weaknesses of social mechanisms within surviving communities;
* Significance and priority given to disaster by the community itself and the priority given to the housing component once the disaster has taken place; and
* Understanding the consequences of cash flows within the community and its effect on the building material and skilled labour market, once a housing rehabilitation program is generated within the region.

Secondly, the role of the outside agencies has to be understood with respect to:

* Nature of their role in the rehabilitation program as initiator, provider or supporter; and
* Their accountability to the community or to the funding agency or to both.

Against the background of the preceding discussion let us examine the existing policies of the government. The report of the National Commission of Urbanization 1988, a treatise on the spatio-economic planning efforts in India for the last few decades does not mention the aspect of disaster as an issue for consideration. Further, despite the fact that 50-60% of the land in our country falls under the effect of one or several disasters, no consideration of this aspect has been taken when land-use planning policies and objectives are stated. The section on housing is also silent on this issue.

The National Housing Policy took 6 years in the making. Finally approved by parliament in August 1994 in the middle of the International Decade for Natural Disaster Reduction (1991-2000) it did not discuss this issue. It is only mentioned in passing in two areas of the policy.

Firstly, as a component of rural housing where it has been recommended that there should be a rehabilitation of households affected by natural calamities in terms of assistance for reconstruction and access to services, within the National Scheme of Calamity Relief. Secondly, there is a mention under special programs for disadvantaged groups where the victims of natural calamities are clubbed with households de-housed by development projects. The only objective in any case is to accord priority to the promotion of access to shelter. Neither of the two mentions attack the problems and issues in a direct and focussed manner despite the fact that this has become an area of key concern in international forums.

However, it was realized that the problem of disaster mitigation and relief is one of the stupendous magnitudes and involves coordination of a large number of agencies concerned with different aspects. The Planning Commissions set up a Task Force in 1988 on Housing in Disaster Prone Areas. The terms of reference of work were:

* Study types of damages which occur to houses in each disaster.
* Review work evolved by R & D institutions with design, construction of new houses for these areas.

* Review work regarding retrofitting of existing houses.
* Guidelines for sitting and relocation with view that it would lead to framing suitable building regulations.
* Suggests specific areas of research and developments.

In keeping with the terms of reference the recommendations were grouped in three categories of technical measures, sitting and control measures and also identified areas of required search. The group had recognized the importance and urgency of the problem of evolving appropriate, economical solutions for housing in disaster prone areas. A need for a well planned strategy along following lines was recommended:

* Identification and implementation of short-term and long-term steps for developing disaster resistance houses.
* Developing knowledge on subjects based on traditional materials, building demonstration houses with them by incorporating strengthening measures.
* Preparation of manuals of type designs and details of strengthening measures to guide various housing agencies and private house builders.
* In-service training of personnel, engineers and architects in the private field through short-term courses seminars and symposia with dual purpose of propagating technologies and strategies on relief and disaster mitigation measures.
* Promotional activities via print and audio-visual media.
* Formulation of IS Codes of Practice, incorporation of appropriate standards in building bye-laws, zonal plans and master plans on various aspects pertaining to planning, design and construction.
* Including the subject on housing and building in disaster prone areas in curriculum of engineering colleges and architectural schools.

Against this backdrop of general measures let us examine the existing practices for housing development in disaster prone areas. Despite the nature and magnitude of the potential risk no actual work has been undertaken to revise building bye-laws to confirm to codes of building practices in most areas. IS codes have been developed and existing codes revised from time to time to incorporate alternative construction systems and ongoing research in building materials. However, most of these are not incorporated in housing, which remains the private activity of the house owners in most parts of the countries. The reasons for the same are:

* Most codes focus on the construction of new houses. Suggested remedies increase the cost by 5-10% and are hence avoided due to the question of priorities. Moreover, the common man has no means of knowing about them.
* Codes do not attempt to discuss retrofitting which is the need of the hour in most disaster prone areas.
* There is no sufficient awareness amongst the professionals and the common public about the importance of taking up these measures.
* Master plans for city levels and regional development plans also do not evolve land use patterns based on any vulnerability analysis and give considerations to long-term aspects of disaster mitigation through adoption of appropriate siting and planning as this is a low priority area.

In India, the primary responsibility for management of natural disaster vests with the state governments. The Central government supplements their efforts in dealing with disaster response. There is an institutional arrangement at the national, state, district, and sub-district levels to deal with the emergency situations. A National Contingency Action Plan exists for ensuring emergency assistance in the wake of natural disasters in the national, state and district levels. The State Governments have Relief Manuals and Codes, which lay down the procedures and powers for emergency management and provision of relief.

The national organizational arrangements consist of a cabinet committee on Natural Disaster Management. The group is chaired by the Cabinet Secretary. A Central Relief Commissioner in the Ministry of Agriculture effects disaster relief coordination. Each state government has a Relief Commissioner and State Cabinet level coordination committee. At the district level, the District Collector presides over the Relief Committee, which consists of people's representatives. A Calamity Relief Fund is allocated to each state on an annual basis, 75 per cent of which is contributed by the Central Government. The Indian Meteorological department makes long-term forecasts regarding rainfall. The National Remote Sensing Agency reports on crop status used for planning for drought management and the Central Water Commission has a flood forecasting system.

It is obvious from this hierarchical set up that all institutional arrangements in India are geared towards only disaster response. In this too the approach is top down wherein all major decisions are taken at a point far removed from the actual region where the disaster has struck. The recent calamity at Gujarat has shown that due to poor management skills at the local level, rescue and relief operations were jeopardised and rescue agencies were left idling. There is no doubt that there is a need to strengthen disaster response by better management skills, higher levels of co-ordination and involvement of all external agencies. However, this aspect is but only one side of the coin. There is a strong need to shift focus away from response action to preparedness both in the long-term and short term.

In this regard the targets of the International Decade of Natural Disaster Reduction could be used to sum up the required direction that Government and Community-based organizations should take:

* A comprehensive assessment of risks from natural hazards.
* Mitigation assessment and integration of the same into the planning process.
* Building community awareness and preparedness as part of an on-going exercise.
* Access to warning systems and dissemination of warnings.

Unless the focus of planned effort shifts from disaster relief to include disaster mitigation as a central issue for planning of settlements, much of our so-called development efforts would be self-destructive.

CONCEPTS OF HAZARDS AND VULNERABILITY ANALYSIS

I. Introduction

- A. Definitions—hazard, vulnerability, risk, analysis
- B. Nature of Hazards
- C. Hazard Assessment Process
- D. Nature of Vulnerability (and Capabilities)
- E. Vulnerability Analysis

A. Definitions

Hazard

An event or occurrence that has the potential for causing injury to life or damage to property or the environment. The magnitude of the phenomenon, the probability of its occurrence and the extent and severity of the impact can vary. In many cases, these effects can be anticipated and estimated.

Vulnerability

A set of prevailing or consequential conditions composed of physical, socio-economic and/or political factors which increase a community's susceptibility to calamity or which adversely affect its ability to respond to events. The community and its members may or may not be willing participants in contributing to, or tolerating the conditions. Taken together, they create a dynamic mix of variables, each of which results from a continuous process. Vulnerabilities can be physical, social, or attitudinal and can be primary or secondary in nature.

If there are positive factors, that increase ability to respond to needs effectively or which reduce susceptibility, they are considered to be capabilities.

Risk

A probability that injury to life or damage to property and the environment will occur. The extent to which risk is either increased or diminished is the result of the interaction of a multitude of causation chains of events.

Hazard Assessment, Vulnerability Analysis, Risk Analysis

Structured analytical procedures to identify hazards and to estimate the probability of their occurrence and the consequences in light of conditions. Taken together with a similar structured analysis of actual or potential vulnerabilities these estimations are then to be compared with a standard or criterion in order to decide whether or not action is desirable, to reduce the probabilities or to protect the people, property, or environment. Realistically, it is necessary also to consider to what extent perceived constraints of time, resources, or effect may impede the application of desirable counter-measures indicated.

B. Nature and Conditions of Hazards

I. Example Cyclone Hazards

1. Primary:
   - (a) Wind
   - (b) Water
     - (i) Rain
     - (ii) Flood
       - (a) Marine
       - (b) Riverine
       - (c) 'Run-off
       - (d) Low-lying
     - (iii) Wave and tidal
     - (iv) Storm surge
   - (c) Land
     - (i) Slips, slides
     - (ii) Erosion
     - (iii) Alteration of river course
     - (iv) Marine encroachment
2. Multiple (or Sequential) Hazards:
   - (a) Multiple examples

(b) Cascade examples

3. Secondary:
   - (a) Health Risks
   - (b) Economic Loss
   - (c) Loss of Shelter, Infrastructure
   - (d) Destruction of Food Supply
   - (e) Destruction of Water Supply
   - (f) Erosion, Destruction of Land, Natural Resources
   - (g) Destruction of Community

II. Characterisation of Hazards

1. Frequency
2. Duration
3. Speed of onset
4. Scope
5. Intensity
6. Predictability
7. Forewarning time
8. Controllability

III. Factors Affecting Magnitude of the Physical Effects of Hazards

1. Geographical pattern of severity
2. Number, spatial distribution and density of population
3. Vulnerability of people, things to a given force
4. Effect of local conditions in modifying severity of effects

C. Hazard Assessment Process

I. The Hazard Assessment Process

1. Hazards—Community—Environment—Consequences —Policies
2. Sequence of assessment:
   - (a) Identification of hazards
   - (b) Collection of information
     - (i) About the hazard
     - (ii) About the community
     - (iii) About the environment
   - (c) Analysis of information

(d) Application of the analysis to policy, planning, management

3. Assessment Process:
   (a) Overview:
      (i) History
      (ii) Probability
      (iii) Vulnerability
      (iv) Maximum threat to protect against
   (b) Factor Analysis:
      (i) Frequency
      (ii) Duration
      (iii) Speed of onset
      (iv) Scope
      (v) Intensity
      (vi) Predictability
      (vii) Forewarning
      (viii) Controllability
   (c) Cross-Hazard Analysis:
      1. Management requirements that are common to two or more hazards:
         (a) Awareness programme
         (b) Information and communications
         (c) Operations (procedures, centres)
         (d) Evacuation or rescue (procedures, service functions)
         (e) Coordination
         (f) Resources
         (g) Time sequencing
      2. Requirements specific to individual hazards.
4. Conceptual Model of Hazard Analysis:
   (a) History
   (b) Technological analysis
   (c) Pre-requisite to vulnerability analysis

D. Nature and Conditions of Vulnerability

I. Types of Vulnerability

1. *Physical (material):*
   (a) Geographical, geophysical (location and exposure)

(b) Poverty—Poor suffer more, fewer resources, no reserves, on influence, little political power of influence

Overall, limited means and fewer options (if any)

If not a Consequence of Ignorance, the Vulnerability to Natural Hazards is Essentially Determined by Conditions of Poverty.

(c) Capital Resources—Cash, property, land, personal capital goods, reserves (and the nature of their allocation)

(d) Basis of livelihood, economic activities, options, multiples

(e) Occupational tools, equipment, goods (land, boat ownership)

(f) Skills, labour

(g) Environmental (locale, situational, prevailing practice)

(h) Climatic

(i) Infrastructural (access, protection)

(j) Strength, health (food+nutrition, clean water, etc.)

(k) Domestic (shelter, access to food, water)

2. *Social (organizational)*

(a) Community organization, its cohesiveness, commitment. Extent of social, ethnic, economic, political, religious divisions.

(b) Leadership, the governance of a community, how decisions are taken.

What internal conflicts? How they are addressed?

(c) Resource possession and control, degree of access, application to common or individual benefit.

(d) Information, where, when, and how the community gets it and how it contributes to common knowledge and decisions.

3. *Attitudinal (motivational, cultural)*

(a) How people view themselves (and are encouraged to view themselves) particularly in terms of capacities. Perception of limitations and capabilities to affect their own environment.

(b) Traditional belief systems, degree of indigenous, historical coping mechanisms.

II. *Characterizations of Vulnerability*

1. Location of population groups in relation to hazard.
2. Population densities, rate and distribution of growth.
3. Special population groups (aged, women, disabled, children).
4. Location, value, access to economic and material resources.
5. Location, value, 'capacities' of vital facilities.

III. Recurrent *Elements Contributing* to *Vulnerability*

1. *Rural Areas*
   (a) unequal access to land
   (b) inability to produce a surplus
   (c) absence of other income earning opportunities
   (d) no access to credit
   (e) forced migration
   (f) ecological damage, degradation
   (g) reduction of natural or essential local resources
2. *Urban Areas*
   (a) low income settlements sited or able to squat only in vulnerable areas
   (b) subsistence income levels
   (c) inadequate personal, social, infrastructural, or transport services
   (d) population in-migration, compressing risks.

IV. Why do People Live in Conditions of Vulnerability?

1. Ignorance of the vulnerability or limited perception of risk:
   (a) *Antidote:* education, communication, awareness.
2. Limited interest, authority, ability to change it:
   (a) *Antidote:* attitude, motivations, capabilities.
3. Poor, ineffectual leadership to alter conditions:
   (a) *Antidote:* political or community alteration.

4. Few, if any, alternate options (physically, socially, economically, politically)—no choice:
   (a) *Antidote:* empowerment (generally economic or political).

E. Vulnerability Analysis

I. Process of Risk Analysis

1. Identify the nature, extent, and risk of threat.
2. Determine the existence and degree of vulnerabilities.
3. Identify the capabilities and resources available.
4. Determine acceptable levels of risk, cost-benefit considerations.
5. Set priorities relative to time, resource allocation, effectiveness of results.
6. Develop methods to protect people and key resources and reduce overall losses.
7. Design effective and appropriate management systems to implement and control.

II. Factors Determining the Magnitude of Physical Vulnerability

1. Geographical pattern of the severity of the hazard(s):
   (a) Pattern of highest wind, direction, relative timings, and
   (b) Location, extent, depth, direction, timing, tidal circumstances to storm surge.
2. The number, density, spatial distribution, special characterization of population groups exposed to the effects of the various hazards.
3. The degree of vulnerability of the elements at risk to a given force, (e.g., wind, water, sea, land) or to a combination of these forces. Consideration of primary and secondary or consequential effects.
4. The effect of local conditions, capabilities, in modifying the severity of effects:
   (a) natural topographic features
   (b) degree of awareness and foreknowledge
   (c) state of preparedness abilities
   (d) mitigation practice (non-structural and structural)

III. The Vulnerability Analysis Process

1. Key elements:
    - (a) Persons—Place-Time-Event
    - (b) Risk—probability of threat actually occurring
    - (c) Rates—risk over time
2. Conceptual Model:
    - (a) Overview
        1. Historical
        2. Community experience
    - (b) Nature and extent of hazards
    - (c) Nature and extent of vulnerabilities
    - (d) Determination of relative risks and benefits
    - (e) Map areas of risk ANALYSIS/RESPONSE
    - (f) Planning
    - (g) Nature of intervention
    - (h) Education
    - (i) Preparedness
    - (j) Mitigation
    - (k) Response
    - (l) Management structures
3. Factors:
    - (a) Data (information)—for a purpose:
        1. Availability
        2. Quantity
        3. Quality
        4. Structure
    - (b) Designated group responsible:
        1. Understanding of purpose
        2. Authority
        3. Needs
        4. Knowledge
        5. Skills
        6. Technical access
    - (c) Resources:
        1. Time
        2. Money

IV. Strategies for Improved Application of Analysis

1. Include analysis of natural hazard risk as part of ongoing natural resource evaluation and development strategy formulation.
2. Identify and formulate mitigation measures for development investment projects.
3. Make information on natural hazards and community vulnerability more widely available, more accessible to emergency response and development planning departments.
4. Train planning technicians and decision-makers in hazard assessment, vulnerability analysis, and disaster mitigation appreciation and techniques.

V. Special Considerations for Further Emphasis

1. Review risk perceptions of different economic groupings, (e.g., farmers, fishermen, small business community, labourers, etc.).
2. Coastal zone storm surge risk assessment.
3. Special emphasis on 'lifeline systems' vulnerability analysis.
4. Energy sector vulnerability in relation to natural hazards.
5. Flood hazard assessment and early flood alert systems as part of integrated development (or agricultural) projects.
6. Include hazard assessment and vulnerability reduction measures as a part of provincial capitals/ towns' urban development plans.
7. Include landslide hazards and vulnerability assessments in metropolitan areas and on critical transportation routes (viz., Baguio conditions).
8. Use of geographical information systems in national, sub-national, and metropolitan level analysis of natural hazards, resources, populations, critical facilities and infrastructure.

SOME BETTER KNOWN DAMAGING EARTHQUAKES IN INDIA

Year	Area	Date	(I.S.T.) Time hr:m:s	Latitude degrees North	Longitude degrees East	Magnitude M tnt.	Max. MM	Deaths
1	2	3	4	5	6	7	8	9
1819	Gujarat (Kutch)	Jan. 16	Mid Night	-	-	8.0	XI	Many Thousand
1833	Bihar	Aug. 26	-	27.5	86.5	7.7	XI	Hundreds
1897	Assam (Shillong)	Jun. 12	16:36:00	25.9	91.0	8.7	XII	1600
1900	Kerala (Palghat)	Feb. 8	-	10.7	76.7	6.0	-	
1905	Himachal Pradesh (Kangra)	Apr. 4	06:20:00	32.5	76.5	8.0	XI	20000
1930	Assam (Dhubri)	Jul. 3	02:33:34	25.8	90.2	7.1	IX	Many*
1934	Bihar-Nepal	Jan. 15	14:13:26	26.6	86.8	8.3	XI	14000
1941	Andamans	Jun. 26	-	12.4	92.5	8.0	X	Many
1943	Assam (NE)	Oct. 23	22:53:17	26.8	94.0	7.2	X	
1950	Assam (NE)	Aug. 15	19:39:28	28.7	96.6	8.6	XII	1500
1956	Gujarat (Anjar)	Jul. 21	21:02:36	23.3	70.0	7.0	VIII	Hundreds
1956	Uttar Pradesh (Bullandshahar)	Oct. 10	28.1	77.7	6.7	VIII	Many	
1958	Uttar Pradesh (Kapkote)	Dec. 28	-	30.0	80.0	6.3	VIII	Many
1960	Delhi	Aug. 27	21:28:59	28.3	77.4	6.0	VII	
1963	Kashmir (Badgam)	Sep. 2	07:04 :.32	33.9	74.7	5.5	VII	Hundreds

(Contd.)

(Contd.)

1	2	3	4	5	6	7	8	9
1966	Western Nepal	Jun. 27	-	29.5	81.0	6.3	VIII	
1966	Uttar Pradesh (Moradabad)	Aug. 15	-	28.0	79.0	5.3	VII	
1967	Nicobar	Jul. 2	-	9.0	93.4	6.2	-	
1967	Maharashtra (Koyna)	Dec. 11	04:21:19	17.4	73.7	6.5	VIII	200
1970	Andhra Pradesh (Bhadrachalam)	Apr. 13	-	17.6	80.6	6.5	VII	
1970	Gujarat (Broach)	Mar. 23	07:23:03	21.7	72.9	5.7	VII	
1975	Himachal Pradesh	Jan. 19	-	32.5	78.4	6.5	VIII	
1988	Bihar-Nepal	Aug. 21	04:39:10	26.76	86.62	6.6	VIII	1003
1991	Uttar Pradesh (Uttarkashi)	Oct. 20	02:53:00	30.75	78.86	6.6	VIII	715
1993	Maharashtra (Killari)	Sep. 30	03:55:47	18.07	76.62	6.3	VIII	7928
1997	Jabalpur	May 22	04:22:31	23.1	80.1	8.0	VII+	38

*Many will mean less than a hundred.

Source: Report (Part-I) of Expert Group set up by Ministry of Urban Development, 1998.

OBSERVED NUMBER OF CYCLONIC STORMS CROSSING THE INDIAN COASTS, 1891-1990

Degree Latitude	*Arabian Sea Coast*		*Bay of Bengal Coast*	
	All C.S.	*S.C.S. only*	*All C.S.*	*S.C.S. only*
8-9	1	1	2	2
9-10	1	1	4	3
10-11	2	1	13	4
11-12	2	2	7	4
12-13	—	—	15	8
13-14	2	1	11	4
14-15	—	—	10	7
15-16	—	—	11	4
16-17	—	—	18	4
17-18	1	1	7	2
18-19	3	1	12	4
19-20	1	1	23	3
20-21	6	3	34	8
21-22	8	4	95*	35*
22-23	3	0	X	X
23-24	3	2	X	X
Total	33	18	262	92

* These are upto Long. 90 E, hence, the number crossing Indian Coast upto about 89 E will be less.

X : No sea coast here

C.S. = Cyclonic storm

S.C.S. = Severe Cyclonic Storm

Source: Report (Part I) of Expert Group set up by Ministry of Urban Development, 1998.

Cyclone Data 1891-1990, IMD, G.O.I.

Along the west coast, the Gujarat and Maharashtra coasts are more vulnerable compared to the southern part.

The EI-Nino effect on weather is seriously being studied by Indian scientists and the outcomes of these studies will help in better communication of early warnings as well as preparedness planning.

Flood Occurences

The country receives an annual precipitation of 400 million hectare meter. Of the annual rainfall, 75 per cent is received during four months of monsoon (June-September) and, as a result, almost all the rivers carry heavy discharge during this period. The problems of sediment deposition, drainage congestion and synchronization of river floods compound the flood hazard. The area liable to floods is 40 million hectares; the average area affected by floods annually is about 8 million hectares. The average annual total damage to crops, houses and public utilities during the period 1953-97 was about Rs. 972 crores, while the maximum damage was Rs. 4630 crores in the floods of 1988.

Research & Development, Education & Training

Research, education and training in earthquake engineering were started by University of Roorkee through School of Research and Training in Earthquake Engineering in 1960. Through this initiative, national capacity has been built for design and construction of earthquake resistant structures from small to tall buildings, all types of bridges and dams, conventional to atomic power plants and petro-chemical industrial structure, etc. Indian Standard codes of practice on earthquake safe design and construction were initially developed in the sixties, later revised and updated from time to time. A Master of Earthquake engineering degree program exists since 1965 and hundreds of short training programs were organized for engineering teachers and professionals. This type of activity has expanded in several institutions, such as HTs, Universities and research institutions to cover floods, cyclones as well as landslides. Sophisticated testing, measuring and computing facilities including shake tables and wind tunnels are available in a number of institutions.

Initiatives Taken during the Decade

The Yokohama message emanating from the IDNDR midterm review Conference held at Yokohama in May 1994 underlined the need for an emphatic shift in the strategy for disaster mitigation.

STATEMENT SHOWING FLOOD DAMAGE FROM 1961 TO 1997

Sl. No.	Year	Area Affected in Million Hectare	Population Affected in Millions	Damage to Crops		Damage of Houses		Cattle Lost Nos.	Human Lives Lost Nos.	Damage to Public Utilities in Rs. Crores*	Total Damages Crops. Houses and Public Utilities in Rs. Crores* (Col. 6+8+11)
				Area in M. Hec.	Value in Rs. Crores*	Nos.	Value in Rs. Crores*				
1	2	3	4	5	6	7	8	9	10	11	12
1.	1981	6.120	32.490	3.270	524.560	912557	159.630	82248	1376	512.314	1196.504
2.	1982	8.870	56.010	5.000	589.400	2397365	383.869	246750	1573	671.607	1644.876
3.	1983	9.020	61.030	3.290	1285.850	2397365	332.327	153095	2378	873.429	2491.606
4.	1984	10.710	54.550	5.190	906.090	1763603	181.308	141314	1661	818.164	1905.562
5.	1985	8.380	59.590	4.650	1425.370	2449878	583.855	43008	1804	2050.043	4059.268
6.	1986	8.310	55.500	4.580	1231.580	2049277	534.410	60450	1200	1982.535	3748.525
7.	1987	8.890	48.340	4.940	1154.640	2919380	464.490	128638	1835	950.590	2569.720
8.	1988	16.290	59.550	10.150	2519.640	2276533	741.600	150996	4252	1377.800	4630.040
9.	1989	8.060	34.150	3.010	956.740	782340	149.820	75176	1718	1298.770	2405.330
10.	1990	9.303	40259	3.179	695.610	1019930	213.733	134154	1855	455.266	1708.920
11.	1991	6.169	33.844	2.511	573.795	1125254	179.388	41065	1145	685.618	1438.801

(Contd.)

Table (*Contd.*)

1	2	3	4	5	6	7	8	9	10	11	12
12.	1992	2.092	19.090	1.427	654.918	560969	221.884	76804	1367	1170.806	2047.608
13.	1993	4.632	22.901	3.129	169.3	470951	124.57	11990	930	48.088	341.958
14.	1994	2.752	21.024	1.896	888.619	601379	165.205	21698	1511	739.641	1793.465
15.	1995	6.111	38.831	3.359	351.552	1195114	152.595	70371	2209	67.710	571.857
16.	1996	7.420	39.393	3.365	404.287	406718	95.601	60215	1306	861.619	2204.777
17.	1997	3.855	26.548	1.838	449.743	399334	145.578	27178	929	971.615	1566.936

* 1 crore =10 million. Rupee value given are for the year concerned.

Source: Central Water Commission, Ministry of Water Resources, Government of India.

"Disaster prevention, mitigation, preparedness and relief are four elements which contribute to and gain from the implementation of sustainable development policies. These elements, alongwith environmental protection and sustainable development, are closely interrelated. Therefore, nations should incorporate them in their development plans and ensure efficient follow up measures at the community, national, subregional, regional and international levels."

"Disaster prevention, mitigation and preparedness are better than disaster response in achieving the goals and objectives of the Decade. Disaster response alone is not sufficient, as it yields only temporary results at a very high cost. We have followed this limited approach for too long. This has been further demonstrated by the recent focus on response to complex emergencies which, although compelling should not divert from pursuing a comprehensive approach. Prevention contributes to lasting improvement in safety and is essential to integrated disaster management."

In the light of this message and to meet the objectives stated in the IDNDR, a number of important initiatives were taken by Government as well as Non-Government Organizations. The initiatives taken and also the activities following the initiatives and the results achieved thereby are summarized in the following paragraphs:

Human Resource Development

The Department of Agriculture and Cooperation, MOA, initiated a Central Sector Scheme in 1993 including human resource development, research, consultancy services and documentation of various natural disasters. Under the scheme a National Centre for Disaster Management (NCDM) was established at the Indian Institute of Public Administration (IIPA) at New Delhi and 15 States of India set up Faculties in disaster management in different institutions of the States.

A National Advisory Group is initiated by leading organizations to establish the agenda for measuring and managing vulnerability and taking up policy issues. The output may be integrated into curriculum of the ATIs.

In addition, investments are being made to build capacity of NGOs and CBOs for working with the community as well as with the government.

The research and development work, education and training in the institutes of higher learning like Earthquake Engg., Earth Sciences, Hydrology Deptt. of University of Roorkee, the Central Building Research Institute, Jadavpur University, HTs at Kanpur and Bombay and SERC, Chennai, have been further expanded and developed and good number of M.E. and Ph.D. thesis written during the Decade on the topics related to earthquakes, floods and cyclone disaster. The research work also continued at CBRI, CRRI and University of Roorkee on landslide hazard zoning and mapping, etc.

Role of Voluntary Sector

The Decade has been of great stimulation to the Voluntary sector and NGOs in India. A number of NGOs and private industrial houses have initiated various activities. Some of the leading NGOs like OXFAM (India) Trust, CASA, CARE-India, Ramakrishna Mission, DMI, Dasholi Gram Swarajya Mandal, etc. have been active in responding to almost every disaster with timely and effective relief operations.

CARE-India, CASA, DMI, etc., have developed an extensive network of the community amateurs for disaster preparedness programmes. DMI is promoting building food, water shelter and work security with the local community through action planning and participatory methods. The OXFAM (India) Trust with its partners have initiated activities of relief that can be achieved by the agencies over the years. Dasholi Gram Swarajya Mandal has integrated the natural forest resource management with disaster mitigation in the hill areas of U.P. The JAC has organized eight annual conventions on Disaster Management in different parts of the country. JAC was also instrumental in the development of Global Forum for NGOs. CAPART has started playing an important role in supporting the NGO activities in post-disaster rehabilitation activities.

Suggestions for the Next Decade

For rapid progress towards appreciable reduction in the disastrous impact of natural hazards, the policy of the governments may include the following:

* To invest on Global Observations and Early Warning Systems, and to give a boost to the science of observation and measurement on which the real progress will depend.
* To enhance the scientific content of prediction methodologies and reliability of forecasts.
* To map the hazards on a large scale, and line the maps intimately with the process of Development Planning.
* To foster closer partnerships with financial and legal institutions, insurance companies, community-based organizations and industry.
* To create an all India Institutional Network, to involve in Disaster Preparedness, Mitigation Management and Prevention.
* To invest more on public awareness, education, training and human resources development in the area of Disaster Mitigation.

MAJOR ISSUES IN DISASTER MANAGEMENT

(i) Failure to comprehend the magnitude of damage and complexities in providing relief of organizing rehabilitation.

(ii) Tendency to be clinical and partial in approach rather than being holistic. Occurrence of disaster affects not only the part where it occurs, but it has ramified influences in the rest of the society. Ignoring these ramifications may lead to serious imbalances.

(iii) It is generally ignored that different types of disasters require different types of response. Even a similar type of disaster in a different setting, or at a different time, requires different type of response. In both the situations, generally cultural context is lost sight of and tailor made solutions are offered which fail to adequately meet the specific needs. Due attention should be paid to traditional technologies and cultural coping mechanisms.

(iv) There is invariably a failure to understand disaster in the broader context of development. Development may not cause disaster but can certainly aggravate its impact if it is not environmentally sustainable. Similarly, a well thought out developmental strategy might work to minimize the impact of natural disasters.

(v) Confusion and crisis are caused by lack of cooperation and interface between organization— both governmental and non-governmental involving relief at all levels. Attention needs to be paid to forge closer links between the administration and different sectors of civil society.

(vi) There is generally a lack of sophistication in designing post-disaster developmental strategies, particularly, the cultural factor is ignored and the local community participation is not fully ensured. In designing-post disaster strategies the role of social science must be recognized.

(vii) There exist inadequate criteria for programme evaluation of post-disaster developmental activities. This is another area where social science intervention could be of considerable help.

Need of Involving Local Self-Government

As of now the field task of disaster management has been entrusted to the district collector. He is already too busy and district being vast, cannot be handled by one centre. It would be better if Local Self-Government, i.e. Urban and Rural Government is involved. 73rd and 74th amendments provide for a planning forum wherein the disaster management would be included. This would result into the following benefits:

(1) A large and well trained workforce would be available in advance to handle tasks of such emergency nature.

(2) It would facilitate the involvement of elected members of urban and rural governments and also ensure people's participation—*a sine-qua-non* for disaster management.

(3) This would lessen the burden of Deputy Commissioner resulting in efficiency and economy.

Emergency Planning

As stated earlier, the emergency planning and implementation falls in the domain of the State governments. The various States have contingent plans for emergencies related to hydrological hazards, namely, drought and flood situations. Considerable experience has been gained in managing such disasters on account of their recurrence year after year. However, in the case of the rapid onslaught disasters like earthquakes, which occur without any prior warning, the State and District administrations are found in a state of unpreparedness. Fortunately, the cyclonic storms do now permit reasonable prior forecast and warning, so that evacuative actions are being taken to save the people. Local Government can help in emergency planning.

Public Information and Awareness

There are four steps to be taken by L.S.G.:

(i) to prepare and distribute suitable information materials such as simple maps, illustrated brochures, video and T.V. Programmes, etc.,

(ii) to hold specific training for the community under high risk,

(iii) to hold public simulation exercises, and

(iv) to anlayse the results and improve the plan.

National Commission on Urbanization (NCU) has suggested urban planning to make the city functional and help in smooth handling of disaster plan. To quote NCU: Experience has shown that our planning system, where in the preparation of master plans is the principal activity of urban development, is a static concept, whereas in today's context urban planning in India must be seen as a dynamic, adaptive, interactive and continuous process of anticipating, planning and managing social and economic change brought about by the economic development of the country. Master plans, with their rigid landuse, zoning and development controls, have proved extremely poor instruments for regulating the process of urban growth. The core problems of urban planning are not only spatial but functional as well ... If urban planning is to make a positive contribution to our national development, it cannot continue in its present sterile form. It must shift from its present emphasis of landuse planning to guiding the very complex, interrelated processes of socio-economic change.

Before we make a city beautiful, we have to make it functional. This means that people can live, trade, produce, move around, be entertained in the city in the least costly and in the most efficient manner, so that their income levels keeps rising. If a city provides only for the rich and lets the poor fend for themselves, no amount of two-dimensional landuse planning can make the city beautiful. Not all the parks in Delhi and its city forest can hide the horrendous slums and squatter colonies of the city. It is only when the slum dweller begins to earn enough to look after himself better that the city can improve. Therefore, unless our city plans provide the space and create the environment in which people can prosper, the city plans will fail. It is only when the city plans provide for upgradation of the services so that in the matter of water, sewerage, sanitation and access, there is greater equity throughout the city, that the plans will succeed. The proper implementation of the city plan, therefore, is built into the type of plan, which is prepared. The sooner our planners move away from the western concept of a properly zoned city, which looks beautiful and begin to find the human scale where people can begin to live little better than before that our plan will be implemented and our cities managed well.

A National Conference on Funding Disaster Prevention and Mitigation (Dec. 19-20, 2000) was organized by Disaster Management Division, National Institute of Rural Development, Rajendranagar, Hyderabad.

United Nations decided to designate the 1990's as the International Decade for Natural Disaster Reduction (IDNDR). As a result, IDNDR has been set up under UN.

A critical analysis of organizations involved in disaster management reveal the following problems. These are based on study, discussion and management tools.

(I) Nodal Agency may not be with Ministry of Agriculture but should be directly under the Cabinet Secretariat headed by Prime Minister to provide seriousness and priority to this neglected area.

(II) State Government Organisations for disaster management are defunct. This activity should be directly entrusted to Chief Minister and Chief Secretary should directly deal with this issue. It was evident in Gujarat.

(III) District administration, which is considered to be focal point for disaster management, leaves much to be desired. Deputy Commissioner is too busy and very junior officers lacking maturity, expertise and experience are being appointed to this post. The key responsibility should be given to Divisional Commissioners who are comparatively free and possess the necessary maturity and experience.

(IV) Divisional Commissioners should exercise control over the machinery at district and lower levels to ensure disaster management

(V) Organisations at all levels should remain alert round the clock and not only at the occurrence of some disaster.

(VI) NGO's should be identified for this task and training may be imparted to them to deal with disaster situation.

(VII) A good Disaster Management Information System should be developed which can provide forward and backward linkages as well as send information downwards and upwards.

(VIII) List of articles required should be prepared so that these can be procured from the right sources immediately.

(IX) All the steps to manage disaster should be taken

systematically and not in a hurry causing more harm than benefit.

(X) A good chain of delivery should be established so that deliveries of goods and services reach the right places and right persons promptly and economically.

(XI) All these procedures should be kept away from politics.

(XII) Multilateral and bilateral assistance should be channelised through established channels.

(XIII) Transparency and responsiveness should be ensured during all operations.

(XIV) Persons possessing genuine interest, expertise and willingness may be associated at the time of occurrence of disaster as it is a difficult and a challenging job.

(XV) Organisations dealing with disaster management should be flexible as the magnitude and density of disaster is uncertain.

(XVI) Authority should be decentralized to make the lower levels functional.

(XVII) Regular reporting should be done to assess program and difficulties encountered.

Suggestions for Consideration and Analysis

- Effective implementation of plan without loss of time after ascertaining needs of affected people.
- Aspects of effective management of earthquake and other disasters.
- Dedicated and qualified leadership based on team work.
- Effective communication, co-ordiantion and control of relief and rehabilitation operations.
- Information to speed up operations through internet.
- Use of inventory control to optimise its use.
- Participation of People.

SEVEN

INFRASTRUCTURE

After formulation of the plan, an organization is designed to implement the plan. According to Dimock and Dimock, "Organization is the systematic bringing together of interdependent parts to from a unified whole through which authority, coordination and control may be exercised to achieve a given purpose... Organization is both structure and human relations."

According to Mooney, "Organization is the forum of every human association for the attainment of common purpose."

An organization is a structure created to fulfil a purpose. It is made up of resources, structure and technology, which is composed of people who run and manage it. There can be different kinds of organizations—government, private, voluntary, cooperative, etc. Modern civilization is nothing but a complex of organizations to meet the varied and diverse needs of the people. Some organizations cut across the barriers of nation states, like United Nations or World Health Organization. Organizations provide the medium through which the efforts of the people in them are coordinated and output is increased.

Herbert A. Simon has concluded that organization affects the people who work for it in five different ways:

(i) The organization divides work among its members, by giving each employee a particular task; it limits and concentrates its attention on that task.

(ii) The organization establishes standard practices; by working out detailed procedures, it relieves employees of the need to determine such procedure, each time they use crossways.

(iii) The organization transmits authoritative decisions by despatching such decisions downwards, upwards and crossways;

(iv) The organization provides a communication system; and

(v) The organization trains and indoctrinates its members by providing for the 'internationalization' of influence relating to knowledge, skills and loyalties; training enables employees to make decisions as the organization would like them to be made.

Let us now mention some more definitions given by experts in the field of organization. Some stress on its structural importance, while others lay stress on its social and interpersonal importance.

Joseph L. Massie defines organization "as the structure and process by which cooperative group of human beings allocates its tasks among its members, identifies relationships and integrates its activities towards common objectives."

Amitai Etzioni states, "Organizations are social units (or human groupings) deliberately constructed and reconstructed to seek specific goals."

W. Richard Scott: "Organizations are defined as collectivities that have been established for the pursuit of relatively specific objectives on a more or less continuous basis."

Robert V. Presthus defines organization as "a system of structural interpersonal relations . . . individuals are differentiated in terms of authority, status and role with the result that personal interaction is prescribed . . . Anticipated reactions tend to occur, while ambiguity and spontaneity are decreased."

It is clear from all these definitions that a suitable organization needs to be developed wherein, like a human body, most of problems are internally and automatically solved. This requires talent, experience and interest in developing an organization. Religious organizations, like the Ramakrishna Misson etc., have been carefully developed with devotion and perfection. These ideas of organization building need to be incorporated in Government organizations.

P.R. Dubhasi has rightly said that organization building is extremely important in the field of public administration. No administrative performance is possible without a suitable organization. Building an organization is, therefore, the starting point of any administrative performance.

ADMINISTRATOR'S ROLE IN ORGANIZATION BUILDING

The purpose of administration should be role congruence of the organization and its members. Role is the point where the organization and the individual meet. Role means the pattern of actions expected of a person in activities involving others. Role analysis aims to decode the organization's expectation from the individual and the individual's expectations from his association with the organization; and brings into focus where these can meet so as to ensure better performance and effectiveness. When expectations of role are materially different or opposite, a person tends to be in role conflict. This generates psychological reactions—low self-actualization, low self-esteem, job tensions, job disenchantment/alienation and job dissatisfaction. Role anlaysis may be used to define a role more clearly to pave the way for effectiveness. The purpose of role analysis exercise is to help the role occupant to clarify his role to reduce role ambiguity so that he may become more effective.

Organizational effectiveness follows from the effectiveness of the individuals in their respective roles. Our efforts should be to maximize the effectiveness of each individual in his role so that we can maximize the contribution of each individual. The ultimate goal of role analysis should be to ensure integration of the goals of management, employees and the organization.

India is a large country and has had more than its share of major natural hazards like drought, floods, earthquakes and cyclones throughout its history of civilization. Naturally, the country developed its own practices and strategies for coping with the various natural calamities. Since independence in 1947, India has developed a nationwide relief administration where a lead role for the State governments is envisaged.

Management of Disasters in India

The basic responsibility for management of disasters is that of the State Government concerned. The role of the National government is supportive, in terms of supplementation of physical and financial resources and complementary measures in sectors like transport, and interstate movement of food grains. The national government also sets out the policy climate and draws lessons from disasters. The lessons learned are communicated to States and national initiatives are made possible. The Union Department of Agriculture and Cooperation (DAC) is the nodal Department. An Additional Secretary in the DAC is designated as the Central Relief Commissioner. He provides the focal point for interaction with the State Governments, and other Departments and agencies of the Union Government and for the implementation of the decision of the Union Government. Now, as a national initiative, the representatives of the communities and the NGOs are invited in the operational and policy processes so as to achieve greater impact of mitigation and preparedness measures. For example, CARE (India) coordinates the Government of India NGO Committee and Disaster Mitigation Institute is invited to join in dissemination of information and awareness programmes and different task forces constituted for disaster management related activities.

The Department of Agriculture and Cooperation in the Agriculture Ministry is the nodal Department for all matters concerning natural disasters relief at the Centre. In the DAC, the Relief Commissioner functions as the nodal officer to coordinate relief operations for all natural disasters.

The Central Relief Commissioner receives information relating to forecast/warning of the natural calamity from the Director-General, India Meterological Department (IMD) or from the Central Water Commission on a continuing basis. Besides, he also monitors the developments taking place and provides the necessary feedback, through the Agriculture Secretary to the Agriculture Minister, Prime Minister and the Cabinet.

Cabinet Committee

The Cabinet may set up a committee for effective implementation of relief measures in the wake of natural disaster. The Secretary in the Ministry of Agriculture acts as the Secretary of this committee. In the absence of such a committee, all the matters related to the relief shall be reported to the cabinet secretary.

National Crisis Management Committee (NCMC)

Under the chairmanship of the cabinet secretary, the NCMC has been constituted in the cabinet secretariat. The other members of this committee include the Secretary to Prime Minister, Secretaries in the Ministries of Home Affairs, Defence, Research and Analysis Wing and Agriculture and Cooperation along with Director Intelligence Bureau and an officer of cabinet secretariat. The NCMC gives direction to the crisis management group as deemed necessary.

Crisis Management Group (CMC)

A group under the chairmanship of the Central Relief Commissioner comprising the senior officers from the various ministries and other concerned departments formed to review every year—contingency plans formulated by the Central Ministeries/Departments; to review the measures required for dealing with a natural disaster, to coordinate the activities of the Central Ministries and the State Governments in relation to disaster preparedness and relief and to obtain information from the nodal officers on measures relating to the above. The Joint Secretary (NDM) and Additional Central Relief Commissioner is the convenor of CMC. The CMC meets every six months.

At the State level, the State Relief Commissioner (or Secretary, Department of Revenue) supervises and controls relief operations through Collectors or Deputy Commissioners, who are the main functionaries to coordinate the relief operation at district level.

State

As pointed out earlier, the Central Government only supplements the efforts of the State Governments. The State Governments are autonomous in organizing relief operations in the event of natural disaster and in the long-term preparedness/ rehabilitation measures.

The States have Relief Commissioners who are in charge of the relief measures in the wake of natural disasters in their respective States. In the absence of the Relief Commissioner, the Chief Secretary or an Officer nominated by him is in overall charge of the Relief operations in the concerned State.

The Chief Secretary is the head of the State Administration. The State Headquarters has, in addition, a number of secretaries, heads of the various Departments handling specific subjects under the overall supervision and coordination of the Chief Secretary. At the level of the State Government, natural disasters are usually the responsibility of the Revenue Department or the Relief Department. While important policy decisions are taken at the State Headquarters by the Cabinet of the State headed by the Chief Minister, day-to-day decisions involving policy matters are taken or exercised by the Secretary in the Department.

State Crisis Management Group

There is a State Crisis Management Group (SCMG) under the Chairmanship of Chief Secretary/Relief Commissioner of Chief Secretary/Relief Revenue/Relief, Home. Civil Supplies, Power, Irrigation, Water Supply, Panchayat (local self-government), Agriculture Forests, Rural Development, Health, Planning, Public Works and Finance.

District

States are further divided into districts, each headed by the District Collector (also known as the District Magistrate or Deputy Commissioner). It is the District Collector who is the focal point at the District level of directing, supervising and monitoring relief measures for disaster and for the preparation of District level plans.

Earthquake Occurences

India has large part of its land area liable to wide range of probable maximum seismic intensities where shallow earthquakes of magnitudes of 5.0 or more on Richter scale, have been known to occur in the historical past or recorded in the last about 100 years. IMD has prepared a catalogue of all such known earthquakes which is continually updated. The largest earthquake magnitude in India has been 8.7 which has its origin in the Shillong Plateau in 1897. This and the 1950 quake in Sadiya region have been so intense that the rivers changed their courses, ground elevations got changed permanently and stones were thrown upward.

Cyclone Occurences

Over the warm water (sea surface temperature greater than 260°C or 270°C) in the tropical ocean, little away from the equator within the belt of 30°N and 30°S, the occurrence of tropical cyclone is almost a world-wide phenomenon. However, their characteristics like frequency, intensity and coastal impact vary from region to region. But these have been the deadliest when crossing the coast bordering the north Bay of Bengal (coastal areas of Andhra Pradesh, Orissa, West Bengal and Bangladesh), mainly because of the serious storm surge problem in this area.

On the average, about 5-6 tropical cyclones form in the Bay of Bengal and the Arabian Sea every year, out of which 2 or 3 may be severe. More cyclones form in the Bay of Bengal than in the Arabian Sea. The ratio is 4:1. There are two definite seasons of tropical cyclones in the North Indian Ocean. One is from May to June and the other is from mid-September to mid-December. May, June October and November are known for severe storms.

EIGHT

REHABILITATION

Anthropology the Science of Man in its totality has to deal with disaster management at the start of the new millennium and has to equip itself with management skills.

In tribal India, and also in other parts of the world, we frequently find drought, flood, epidemic, mysterious diseases leading to de-population, migration and other allied problems.

The concept of tribe has drawn wide range of attention varying from anthropologists, administrators, policy makers, historians, members of judiciary, politicians, journalists, members of international bodies like UNESCO, Human Rights Commission, UNO, etc. But here we are using the term strictly in Anthropological terminology.

Generally speaking, by the term tribe we mean a group of people living at a particular place from time immemorial.

Anthropologically the tribe is a system of social organisation which includes several local groups, villages, bands, districts of lineages and normally includes a common territory, a common language and a common culture. The elements constituting the tribe may or may not be coordinated by formal or centralized political power, ideally the term 'tribe' implies large elements of solidarity based on strongly shared primary sentiments. Such solidarity becomes contractual in nature as the tribal organisation become more formally organised. The point at which these characteristics become pronounced is perhaps a convenient place to distinguish between the tribe and the nation. In general, anthropologists agree on the criteria by which a tribe may be described viz common territory, a tradition of common descent, common language, common culture, common name, political system, simple economy, religion and belief, primitive law and non-educational system.

Power is the ability to do something, with strength, force, vigour, energy, ability to control or influence others, ability to impose one's will. Thereby, empowerment means inducing all these characteristics in an individual, social phenomenon, community, tribe, caste, racial ethnic group, etc., through planned systematic manner which may be termed as planning for the development of the people of a particular country, region, tribe, caste, etc. Thus, empowerment is an ability to control or influence or make the people willing for the development which may be economic, social, cultural or political.

Empowerment means putting the external force in an individual, tribe, caste, country, etc., to make him powerful. It is a process. It cannot be done in a day. It takes place systematically and scientifically. It is an experiment. If the chemical substances are mixed in proper order, then it is bound to be successful otherwise it will fail. Here comes the role of anthropologists and bureaucratic experts who have sufficient knowledge of social administration inputs like chemical substance. He knows in which or what cultural/social system how much typological variant chemical substances are required.

The various forms of power act and interact on each other so significantly, that if the study of power was confined to a single aspect, such as, political, economic or social power, much would be lost in the understanding of the overall dynamics of the system.

It is perhaps in social systems that the concept of power is most important. One of the great problems in constructing a general theory of power is the taxonomic difficulties. The very word power is used in variety of ways. In social system and human behaviour, there is a larger concept of power: to what extent and how we can get what we want? Within this there is a smaller concept of power, somewhat beloved by anthropologist, which is our capacity to get other people to do things that contribute to what we want. There are three broad categories of power—threat power, economic power and integrative power.

These are closely related to another tripartite division—the power to destroy, the power to produce and exchange and the power to integrate, that is, the power to create such relationships as love, respect, friendship, legitimacy, and so on. Threat power is particularly the concern of political scientists, economic power of economists and the integrative power is the concern of anthropologists although it has not been studied very explicitly.

It is the integrative power that is the most dominant and significant form of power, in the sense that, neither threat power nor economic power can achieve very much in the absence of legitimacy, which is one of the more important aspects of integrative power. Without legitimacy, both threat and riches are 'naked'. The great fallacy specially of political thinking in regard to power, is to elevate threat power to the position of dominance which it does not really possess. Failure to understand this is an enormous source of error in human decisions, both at the individual level of those who control organisations, and at the group level which gets reflected in social control.

The work that comes closest to this argument is that of an important economist, John Kenneth Galbraith (1983). He too classifies power into three categories which he calls *'condigu'*, 'compensatory' and 'conditioned'. The terminology strikes me a little awkward but does correspond roughly to my threat, economic and integrative categories. Galbraith's book, as is to be expected, is full of useful insights, but does not develop the systematic structure that has been one of the principal concerns, particularly in regard to the dynamic aspects of the system.

Thus, it is clear that empowerment is the most elusive term. When additional input is provided to make a man powerful, it is known as empowering an individual, so is the case with a social phenomenon, social group, caste, tribe, man, woman, state, nation, etc. Empowerment means providing systematic developmental inputs to the target group. It is achieved through a continuous, systematic and scientific process. It is a part of the planning process for the development of mankind. While planning for the development of the target group, the desired development is expected through empowerment inputs.

Empowerment can be cultural, ethnic, educational, economic, political, health related, etc. It can be of many more types depending upon the requirement and suitability of the target group for whom the whole exercise of 'developmental planning' is done.

Now comes the question of empowering the tribals. Here we are using the term tribals strictly in anthropological terminology. For some, it may correspond to ethnic group or racial group but we will include them to the extent they fall within our term of reference.

It is true that differential development has taken place at the global level among the tribes. Therefore, the necessity of this Commission has arisen in order to integrate them through the process of an empowerment which is the emerging need of 21st century of anthropology.

Disaster Management

The term disaster may be defined as an unexpected happening causing a huge loss of life and property. It may be both natural as well as man made in the sense that in some parts of the country, floods are coming due to the construction of check dams and embankments on the rivers. Disaster may come in the forms of earthquakes, cyclones, floods, drought, fire, etc., and ruin the life and property of the people. Anthropology is mainly concerned with how to prevent, predict and mitigate major disasters. So far, scientific and technological development the prevention of earthquakes, cyclones, floods, droughts, fires, etc. may be prevented and predicted to some extent, but there is no doubt that proper planning and effective management can reduce the effects and hazards of disasters, since it is not the earthquake itself but the defective buildings which cause loss of life and property.

To prevent disaster, there should be pre-planning of all the available resources, communication facilities, manpower, etc. Experience has shown that before starting the rescue work administration has to clean the roads and bridges which are badly damaged. For this not only an inventory of local resource should be prepared but also bypasses and alternative routes should be identified in the plan itself. Since disaster is a state subject, the state government is responsible for rescue, relief and rehabilitation. However, at the national level ministry of agriculture, Government of India, is the nodal agency and there is one Crisis Management Committee in which all departments are represented along with Planning Commission. Recently the Finance Commission recommended for sharing of relief between the centre and state on 50:50 basis. Further there should be an emergency plan for each and every district in which response mechanism should be clearly spelt out. For instance, what, how and when the relief is to be given, is to be specified. The allocation of work—who will do what; and clarification of organisation into: public, NGOs, army or civil administration should be properly undertaken otherwise the natural disaster results into chaos, anarchy and destruction due to confounded confusion. The price to pay for the demands imposed by mankind on our environment, extravagant to the point of profligacy, is increasing with time. It is the poorest who suffer the most, but all of us are caught up in the same syndrome. Humankind inherit but one earth, which they conspire against while destroying the gifts of nature by reducing the water-table, deforestation and pollution to name a few, which results in climatic changes and consequences measured in terms of human suffering which are likely to be acute.

The common view of disaster is due for a radical change. Though triggered of by natural events such as floods and earthquakes, disasters are increasingly man made. Some disasters (floods, droughts, famines) are caused more by environmental and resource mismanagement than by too much or too little rainfall. The impact of other disasters which are triggered by acts of nature (earthquake, volcano, hurricane) are magnified by unwise human actions. Disasters are social and political events which can be and often are prevented. In the Third World, where the poor are forced to over use their land and live on dangerous grounds, disasters are taking a rising toll. By emphasizing mitigation instead of development, current disaster relief is often inadequate to the task it sets itself.

We can only tackle the root causes if disaster prevention and response are designed so as to incorporate both developmental and environmental strategies. We must get at the root causes and reverse the trends of increasing poverty and environmental degradation before it is too late. A sustainable eco-system must be our aim, as one in which the global family can live in balanced harmony with the whole of nature. The rural poor, who are the principal victims of the three elements which between them make up the major part of the Third World disasters—deforestations, soil erosion and desertification should be central to the work of all disaster agencies. All the trends emphasize that ignorance and grinding poverty accelerate the onslaught of disasters and exacerbate the cruel impact they have, particularly on vulnerable groups of people. The poor, the handicapped, the infant and the aged are the first to lose their basic right to food, shelter and health. They need and deserve our help. The social development of people and their communities in disaster prone areas has been grossly ignored by governments and agencies alike. Such appalling human conditions can best be fought through the weapons of self-reliance, literacy, preventive health care and equitable pricing structures for rural food producers, that is, helping people to respond to their own basic needs, within their environment.

The common view of natural disaster is due for a radical change. A new term may even be needed, such as 'nature disaster' to distinguish calamities associated with the forces of nature from such tribulations as war and factory explosions. Today humans are playing too large a role in natural disasters for us to go on calling them natural.

So a distinction must be made between the "trigger events" too little rain, too much rain, earthshocks, hurricanes—which may be natural and the associated disasters which may be largely man made. Scientists, politicians, decision makers and the general public have been very slow to make the basic distinction between the trigger and the disaster.

Most of the scientific effort and money devoted to natural disasters has been spent on studying climatological and geological triggers—over which humans have very little control—rather than on studying the wide range of human actions—over which humans do have some control—which bring more disasters upon people every year.

Contemporary natural disasters research has become the single greatest impediment to improvement in both the understanding of natural calamities and the strategies to alleviate them.

Researchers have concentrated on the physical aspects of disasters rather than the social and political aspects, governments have been lured into putting their trust in grand physical prevention and mitigation measures.

Despite the death, destruction and after affects of major natural disasters, they have received surprisingly little scientific attention. Science has not even had much success defining what it means by the term 'disaster'. Dictionaries use words such as 'misfortune' or 'calamity' implying, that for them to be a disaster, people must suffer. Thus, a cyclone or an earthquake is not a disaster unless it kills people or damages their property. This seems obvious but it is not since 1966 the UN Educational, Scientific and Cultural Organisation (UNESCO) has listed each year's natural disasters earthquakes, Sunami (large ocean waves) storm surges and volcanic eruptions.

Other experts take almost the opposite view, defining disasters only in terms of their impact upon people. For instance, in order to produce some consistency in disasters, the Natural Hazard Research Group at the University of Colorado (US) came up in 1969 with the following definition of a disaster:

* more than $1 million in damage, or
* more than 100 people dead, or
* more than 100 people injured.

This definition had the effect of separating the disaster event—destruction, death and injuries from the trigger mechanisms— high winds, earth shocks, lack of rain, excess of water, lava and high waves. It also served to emphasize that most of research on disaster by climatologists and geologists is really on the trigger mechanisms. Other definitions of disaster include:

"An event (or series of events) which seriously disrupts normal activities" Cisin and Clark (1962). "An accident on a new large scale" Walker (1973).

Tribals are unable to draw immediate attention of the policy makers, concerned government activists, anthropologists, etc. The ethnographic studies and the applied anthropology fail to cater to the needs of the tribals. Therefore, the anthropology of disaster management becomes a necessary dimension of Anthropology of 21st century: The century of Anthropology.

Anthropology of 21st century: The century of Anthropology has to widen its horizon according to need of the Man of 21st Century. The science celebrating its century has to be careful in selecting priorities of research and other academic pursuits.

The Indian anthropology will have to grow and shape its branches under the influence of world anthropology.

When one compares the number of people killed per disaster against the income of the country involved, one finds a steep rise in mortality with decreasing income. Gunnar Hagman of the Swedish Red Cross finds evidence that most disaster's are found in middle income countries and most property damage is caused in the rich nations. It is presumed that the middle income nations may have the most disaster events because of an aggressive economic development policy which includes over cultivation, deforestation and other forms of environmental degradation. Both Tokyo, Japan and Managua, Nicaragua are prone to earthquakes. But the people of Tokyo are far less vulnerable to injury by earthquake because Tokyo has strictly enforced building codes, zoning regulations and earthquake training and communications system. In Managua, there are still many people living in top heavy, mud brick houses on hillsides. They are vulnerable to such disasters. The idea of anthropology of disaster management raises questions for the various groups interested in disasters.

* *For governments:* Can government be more effective in protecting its people from disasters by working to change patterns.
* *For relief, aid and volunteer agencies active in disasters:* Might it make more sense to invest some effort and

funds in development before a disaster occurs, rather than putting all efforts after the event.

* *For journalists:* Is it enough to merely count the dead and describe the damage? or is it a journalists' job to look behind the scenes of destruction to expose ways in which people, politics and social systems have been responsible for any given disaster.
* *For those responsible for development:* Are they putting too much emphasis on "growth at any price", a policy which may have more and more people on the margins of society dangerously exposed to disasters?

Many people of the world, specially of Third World are more or less permanently affected by disaster processes and hundreds of millions are vulnerable to flood and droughts and to shortages of food, water and fuel wood. As natural disasters and many resource shortages are on the increase, it is obvious that the current development efforts are having little effect in these areas. This may be partly because rural development is rarely the priority it ought to be.

Prevention is urgent as the increasing frequency and severity of disasters are scaling the point of being unmanageable. In large parts of Asia, Africa and Latin America, the ecological base for human existence is being so damaged that it can no longer support the growing population of these regions.

Most disaster problems in the Third World are unsolved development problems. Disaster prevention and mitigation is thus primarily an aspect of development. Disasters can actually become vehicles for change and involve both development and relief agencies in long-term programmes aimed both at development and at disaster prevention and mitigation.

Disasters are not unforeseen events and the technology now exists to identify the hazards that threaten a community and to estimate the areas and the settlements that will be affected. In most places and segments of society where calamities are occurring, the natural events are about as certain as anything within a person's lifetime. The very essence of disaster mitigation is long-term planning, while the very essence of Third World poverty is the struggle of day to day existence. The local people are more concerned with their children's education or lack of it, their health and the scarcity of medicine in the dispensaries and the difficulties of selling their crops at a decent price, which relates to the problems of access to markets in the accessible terrain. So vulnerability to natural hazards has to be recognised within the cultural and economic context of poverty and deprivation. And as with our own society, long-term logical action is frequently overwhelmed by short-term expediency.

Effective disaster mitigation and prevention depends on long-term planning for development towards a more sustainable and less vulnerable society. Some relief agencies are embarking on new types of community based disaster prevention programmes. Improved self-reliance in respect of food and fuel, access to land, employment, better health and nutrition, family planning and education are important components of disaster prevention. Disaster prevention and the elimination of poverty are closely linked as are poverty and environmental degradation. Many relief agencies are beginning to complement their emergency aid with their development programmes and are now working towards gaining knowledge, experience, training personnel and public backing to initiate new ideas into practice, in order to understand and minimize the problems of disasters.

Spread of AIDS : A Man Made Disaster

The anthropology of disaster management deals with both natural disaster as well as disaster created by man. Prevalence of AIDS in Tribal India is an example of recent disaster created by man.

Tragedy stares at India's tribal population in the face, as the virus that causes AIDS moves from red light areas and shady highway *dhabas* to tribal region. Yet amidst the suffering, people still find the strength to forgive, nurture and fight for their doomed families.

Specialists are grappling with the national implications of answers to combat the new threat that the Acquired Immune

Deficiency Syndrome or AIDS cases pose in India. The attack of AIDS on tribals can clearly be visualized.

Officially the figures do not speak of Indian tribal population becoming AIDS newest victims as yet. The government funded National AIDS Control Organisation reports that out of the 2.9 million screened for the disease nationwide 49,327 tested positive for the Human Immuno Deficiency Virus (HIV). Of them 3,161 had progressed to AIDS in which the virus crippled their immune systems and exposes them to diseases like tuberculosis and cancer.

Perhaps the most worrying aspect is the growing evidence in India of what HIV experts call "transmission chains" by which the virus percolates insidiously through social substrata and afflicts low risk individuals like housewives and children. In tribal areas the HIV infected persons very easily injects the disease of AIDS among women. The tribal women who are living close to urban or industrial centres, mines, etc., are quite often sexually exploited; and in some cases the exploiters are HIV positive persons.

Secondly large-scale migration of tribals from tribal region to Punjab, Haryana, Jammu and Kashmir, West Bengal, etc., are also contributing towards the sexual exploitation of the tribal women resulting in infection of AIDS.

Life of the Indian HIV victim ends the moments he tests positive. Illiteracy, social taboos and retrograde customs are just some of the barriers that confront those infected and those working to prevent the spread of the disease. At the beginning of the new millennium, India is projected to suffer one of the world's most rapid expansions of the HIV pandemic.

Rehabilitation and Displacement Perspective of Disaster

An anthropologist who is quite often turned into a social doctor looks at the problems of displacement and rehabilitation. Anthropological, psychological issues which are natural outcomes of displacement resulting in rehabilitation because of which the development projects are the subject matter of disaster management. It discusses anthropo-psychological consequences on the people affected by these projects and attempts to provide a basic framework to understand its anthropological perspective.

It presents basic guidelines, action strategies for effective implementation of projects with a view to minimize advise anthropo-psychological effects on displaced population. It is also presumed that this will help those who are the key participants in planning and implementation of disaster projects.

Current Status of Displacement and Development

Development is an ongoing process which leads to commissioning of various kinds of development projects such as: Construction of new irrigation dams, establishing new factories, mines, road construction, railways and many other projects related to infrastructural growth leading to regional/ national economic development. This often necessitates the government to acquire land which leads to 'involuntary displacement' of people from the original home land.

Development leading to displacement of people from their own land is inevitable. All activities mentioned above, force the otherwise stable, sedentary population to move away from their original places of home and work. It uproots people from their original land and creates psycho-sociological stress leading to many dysfunctional consequences. More often, both social and economic benefits of such developmental projects are not shared equally by displaced population.

The problem of displacement is normally related to economic aspects but truly speaking, it has more of psycho-sociological implications. Though the meagre economic compensation provides temporary relief to evacuees, but it leads to many psycho-sociological and cultural problem of serious nature. The displacement demands a change in the lifestyle of people and forces them to adjust in a totally alien social milieu. This causes a situation of psychological stress. Compulsory and involuntary displacement together with, 'rarely fair' payment of compensation are its two main reasons as a problem (Menezes, 1991). According to him, the current system fails to acknowledge that an 'oustee' is deprived of a historical right of access to a large number of resources, entire way of life and is not given any opportunity to demand an adequate price for this loss. Apart from his private land and cultural historical heritage, an oustee holds several other livelihood generating assets which are not legally acknowledged. Evidences suggest that these psycho-sociological problems are not well considered neither by the planners nor by those who are the key participants in the implementation of such projects. Therefore, the understanding and management of these problems are more important for effective implementation of these projects.

It is reported that accurate figures of displaced population are not available. Conservative estimate, reveal that around 15 million persons have been displaced from the first to sixth five-year plans. The real figure may be as high as 36 million. Despite the severity of the problems associated with displacement, the country lacks a reliable 'Data base' on the exact situation of displaced people (Vyas, 1993). The official sources, by and large, tend to underestimate the number of persons displaced by developmental projects. For example, different sources reveal different figures of the displaced people from construction of Hirakud Dam as shown below. (Government of Orissa Report, 1968; and Patnaik, Das and Mishra, 1987).

DISPLACEMENT FIGURES OF HIRAKUD DAM PROJECT

Source	*Dam*	*No. of People Displaced*	*Land Submerged*
Govt. of Orissa Report (1968)	Hirakud Dam	1.1 lakh people	1,67,376,83 acres
Patnaik, Das and Mishra, (1987)	Hirakud Dam	1.1 lakh to 1.6 Lakh	1,82,592 acres

Displaced Population

The Report of the Commissioner for Scheduled Castes and Scheduled Tribes (1990), points out that when the land is acquired and under the present law, only its property form is considered vital. Questions concerning the very survival of the displaced persons are settled on this basis. Even those, who are identified, are very inadequately compensated. Lack of accurate data on such crucial issues, such as this, is itself an indication of both the Central and State governments degree of concern for the rehabilitation of oustees (Viegas, 1987). This current status of displacement is leading to an alarming situation. How to sustain the historical right which the oustee has been deprived of, is an important issue today.

Rehabilitation and Development

Rehabilitation is more often understood as economic rather than a psycho-sociological phenomenon resulting from displacement. It is normally perceived as a 'planned change effort'. In a strict sense, it implies that, while there is a change the overall effects of the change is to restore the situation to its original condition. In other words, change or no change (Franks, 1991). Though rehabilitation is sought for development but its nature is quite different from other developmental processes. All developmental efforts imply planned change to improve existing conditions, whereas rehabilitation is designed to restore the status quo. This makes it imperative to understand the term rehabilitation in a much wider perspective, and its components which make it different from other developmental processes.

Components of Rehabilitation

Rehabilitation can be described as having the following components[1]:

(i) Antecedent conditions: Displacement and rehabilitation of people are required when certain 'antecedent conditions' exist in the situation. For example, National long-term interest for socio-economic development of the country leading to commissioning of various developmental projects; National calamities, such as, war and political turmoil; Natural disasters, such as, floods, earthquakes, drought and also man made disasters.

(ii) Cognitive state of the individuals involved, i.e., their perception and awareness of the situation, such as:

* Fears and apprehensions about the possible problems to be faced by the affected people.
* Fears and apprehensions about their acceptability by the host population.
* Fears and apprehensions about fulfilment of government promises with respect to providing facilities.
* Attitudes about various 'developmental projects' and about 'government'.

(iii) Affective state of the individuals involved in the situation: Perception of a situation may affect the people in a variety of ways such as, developing anxieties, psychological tension, stress and hostility.

(iv) Manifest behaviour: Psychological effects manifest themselves in variety of behavioural patterns. These range from passive resistance to active resistance, overt aggression and finally agreeing for displacement under stress leading to many other dysfunctional behaviour patterns resulting in poor mental health.

(v) Rehabilitation: Displacement leading to rehabilitation of people through various rehabilitation programmes such as: Allotment of land: houses, monetary compensation, occupation and many other facilities required for resettlement.

(vi) Further demands by people from government: Any rehabilitation results in an aftermath which manifests itself in further demands by people from government.

Rehabilitation Process

Drawing upon the ways in which components of rehabilitation are described, it is apparent that, displacement leading to rehabilitation can be described as a dynamic process having definite sequential stages coming one after the other. Each stage has its own characteristics which influences the process in its own way. Displacement leads to deterioration of the situation in the initial stages and subsequently to restoration of the situation, quite close to status quo.

The Various Stages Depict:

I. Existing Stage, antecedent condition for displacement
II. Perception/Awareness of the situation
III. Affects on Individual
IV. Manifest Behavioural Patterns
V. Rehabilitation Programmes
VI. Further Problems/Demands.

Rehabilitation process comprises the following six stages:

(i) *Latent Stage:* It refers to the "Antecedent condition", for example, commissioning of developmental project leading to displacement and rehabilitation of population. The nature of antecedent condition will determine the ways of handling the situation in terms of "preparedness measures" and "coping strategies" by the government, other agencies, affected people and also by society. These will influence the characteristic pattern of behaviour of individuals at the next stage, which will also accordingly affect the "Preparedness measures and Coping strategies" for the subsequent stages leading to rehabilitation thereby characterized by certain stable aspects of condition, perceptions, affects and behaviour discussed later.

(ii) *Cognitive Stage:* Fears and apprehensions such as:

* Loss of home
* Loss of primary sources of gratification of needs
* Fear of change of basic style of living
* Loss or change in occupation (source of livelihood)
* Fear of adjustment in new jobs
* Loss of social relationships
* Fear of acceptability by the host population
* Lack of confidence in 'Government initiatives' and 'Programmes'.

All the above listed fears and apprehensions are the natural outcomes of displacement and are unavoidable. These must be acknowledged by all concerned. Correct diagnosis of the situation, appropriate 'preparedness measures' and 'coping strategies' to minimize them, can greatly reduce the severity of onset of next stage of the rehabilitation process.

(iii) *Affective Stage:* Perceived fears and threats may or may not affect the people equally under normal circumstances. These come on the surface and show up in various forms, such as, anxiety, tension, stress and may also lead to hostility. Effective handling of 'affective stage' would accordingly affect the state of next stage of the rehabilitation process.

(iv) *Manifest Stage:* Degree of psychological tension/stress will greatly influence the behavioural patterns at the manifest stage. People's passive and active resistance to 'evacuating the home land', and demand for better compensation may lead to aggressive behaviour and mass agitation. Quite often they finally agree for displacement under great stress leading to further deterioration of mental health.

(v) *Rehabilitation Stage:* This stage finally leads to rehabilitating displaced people through various "Rehabilitation Programmes'.

(vi) *Rehabilitation Aftermath:* Howsoever effectively the various stages of rehabilitation process are handled, it will still lead to an 'aftermath' in terms of further demands by the people leading to increased dependency on the government.

Psycho-sociological Consequences of Displacement

It is universally acknowledged that displacement is stressful and sometimes leads to traumatic conditions. In spite of this, the psycho-sociological issues have been neglected in the displacement of people under various projects. Rehabilitation programmes often lack specific components of the aspects of mental health of people. There is no evidence of discussion of the mental health problems and its implications for assessing cost and benefit of development projects.

A broadly defined psycho-sociological perspective can have important implications for designing rehabilitation policies. It allows us to anticipate inevitable problems that result from displacement of population to assess the consequence of particular policies.

A systematic analysis of what happens to individuals who are subjected to displacement from their homeland and require rehabilitation, will help us to provide the ways and means to minimize the adverse impact of involuntary displacement on mental health of people. Fears and apprehensions discussed earlier are usually perceived as potential threats by the affected population. These are natural and constitute the major components of displacement process resulting in dysfunctional behaviour patterns. These must be considered by all concerned involved in the management of the process. It is imperative to have indepth understanding of the consequences and subsequent careful handling, to minimize their adverse impact on mental health of people. This can be studied at two levels: Individual level and Group level.

Impact at Individual Level

Loss or Change in Primary Sources of Satisfaction of Needs:

The major fear associated with displacement is, loss or change in the primary sources of satisfaction of needs. All behaviours are instigated by needs and are directed towards goals that can satisfy these needs. Personality has a system of organized needs such as

(1) Physiological needs, e.g., thirst, hunger, sex, etc.,
(2) Safety needs, e.g., security and order,
(3) Social needs, e.g., need to belong, identification and love,
(4) Esteem needs, e.g., need to achieve, need to control, self-respect, and
(5) Self-actualisation, e.g., need for identity and self-fulfilment (Maslow, 1954).

Physiological needs are largely determined by the innate factors but others are greatly influenced by the nature of the social environment. Human beings are constantly seeking for pleasures, reflected through satisfaction of above mentioned needs in their unique manner through their established sources of livelihood, social relations, social status, kinship ties, etc. Any change or blockage, though temporarily, in the manner of satisfying these needs, will result in varying degrees of tension and stress in different people. Therefore, social environment together with the satisfaction of needs in an acceptable manner, become extremely important. For example, the satisfaction of the security need which constitutes an important need among the hierarchy of needs in Indian culture is greatly affected by the process of displacement. The compulsive change in the basic style of satisfaction of these needs is usually not welcomed by the people and hence often resisted. People may start perceiving themselves as having low self-worth, 'self-respect' and develop 'negative attitude' towards themselves. In an extreme situation, they may also develop identity crisis. All these result in lack of adjustment, leading to psychological stress or shock or trauma. The major factor associated with this is loss or change in the sources of occupation/livelihood leading to varying degrees of occupational redundancy and loss of social relationships.

(a) Change in Occupation/Livelihood

Fear of change of source of livelihood leads to 'Occupational disruption'. This may lead to low to high degree of 'Occupational redundancy". This loss, even if substituted by the new ways of managing earning of livelihood, often leads to a state of mental stress. Loss of agricultural land by the landowners, though made up by 'Economic compensation' and also new occupational opportunities under various 'Rehabilitation programmes' by the government, could not fulfil the psychological loss such as, social status enjoyed through Feudalistic culture, and the village leadership leading to psychological satisfaction. All these sources of satisfaction of needs usually get blocked by the relocation process in the new environment.

Loss of land and property is a blow to the oustees, who are unable to secure an alternative source of livelihood because of lack of education and skill. Evidence suggests that many development projects created new occupational opportunities but the people were unable to get the share in the benefits of the project. The displaced persons, by and large, were forced into daily wage labour, for example, the persons displaced by the Pong Dam, who returned to Himachal Pradesh or decided to migrate to other states, in the hope of comparatively more comfortable life, were forced to become landless migrant labourers. Another example is that of 16,080 tribal families from 170 villages displaced by Ukai-Kakarpur Project on river Tapi in Gujarat. Surveys reported that 42 per cent of all the families, landed or landless were forced to migrate for work for varying periods of time, most of them in the sugar-cane factories (Mankodi and Gangopadhyay, 1983). All these occupational disruptions, especially loss of job/sources of livelihood, lead people to experience feelings of insecurity, defunctness, powerlessness and loss of self-confidence, leading to stress and in extreme cases, to psychological shock. The change in the job is also associated with variety of problems, such as, lack of skill and interest in the new job. Though people are provided training for the new jobs under various Occupational Rehabilitation Programmes, yet they are unable to use their potentials which demotivates them in the new jobs. They also develop feelings of low Self-efficacy (Grist, 1987), Self-esteem (Brockner 1988), Self-management (Manz & Sims, 1980), Self-montoring (Snyder, 1987), and Alienation, leading to a great stressful situation.

(b) *Loss of Social Relationships*

Displacement also forces individuals to change the pattern of social relationships, individuals have to undergo an entire process of resocialization and adjustment in a new social milieu. This leads to loss of existing social relationships. Kinship ties which are important sources of individual's gratification of social needs are in no way less important for an individual's survival. Evidence also suggests that the oustees are sometimes rejected by the parent group. The hostile behaviour of host population further makes the resocialization difficult for the oustees. Having faced rejection by the parent group and unacceptance by the host population, the oustees go through a tremendous psychological trauma and face an identity crisis. This sometimes leads people to go for second displacement, as in the case of Pong dam oustees (*MARG*, 1987).

Compensation Package

Inadequate or inappropriate compensation package also results in psychological tension/stress among the oustees. It has been reported that adequate or inappropriate compensation packages to the oustees have also resulted in lot of psychological stress for the people. The illiterates found it difficult to utilize the compensation amount appropriately. This has led to social evils like alcoholism, gambling and prostitution (Advani, 1990).

Impact at Group Level

Displacement also results in disintegration of family, other social groups and occupational groups. Evidence from Augucha Mines of Hindustan Zinc Ltd., at Bhilwara, Rajasthan suggests that providing occupation to one representative of each evacuee's family by HZL, helped families, but created family tension resulting in breaking of joint family system and difficulties in getting match in their own community for their children (Advani, 1990).

All these psycho-sociological factors discussed above, result in psychological tensions, stress, hostility, sometimes leading to trauma. These get manifested in variety of dysfunctional behaviours leading to mental ill health and sometimes to mental sickness.

Management of Displacement and Rehabilitation Process

In order to achieve the efficacy of various objectives of resettlement and rehabilitation projects, minimizing the adverse effects of displacement must form the primary focus. The success of these projects depends upon, how effectively the displacement is managed and the various rehabilitation programmes are perceived, as appropriate and adequate sources of gratification of needs by the affected population. This makes it imperative to plan, design and implement strategies as 'preparedness measures' and 'rehabilitation programmes', to cope with negative aspects of displacement, at the appropriate stages of the rehabilitation process.

Need for a 'National Policy'

Recognizing the adverse impact on human beings, the sufferings and hardships caused by involuntary settlement, the World Bank Policy states as its first requirement, that "whenever feasible, the involuntary resettlement must be avoided or minimized and alternative developmental solutions must be explored" (Cemea, 1988). Notwithstanding this policy, there have been cases, when projects have been designed and approved without examining such possible alternatives. Lack of provision of psycho-sociological consideration in the Land Acquisition Law 1994 and also Land Acquisition Amendment Act 1984, further weakens the implementation of the Bank Policy. Though rehabilitation has normally been envisaged as a planned change effort, evidences suggest that implementation of each project, called for an ad hoc policy of its own. The Bank Policy can be made effective only, if a well-defined National Policy is designed. Introducing of psycho-sociological perspective in the Land Acquisition Law will also greatly enhance the efficacy of bank policy. Therefore, the need for a well-defined national policy is a first pre-requisite for effective implementation of resettlement and rehabilitation projects.

Strategies for Minimizing Psycho-Sociological Consequences of Resettlement at Various Stages of Rehabilitation Process

(a) Latent Stage

Nature of 'Antecedent condition' determines the ways and means of managing resettlement and rehabilitation process. Preparedness measures and coping strategies, need to focus around the factors leading to displacement and their counter impact on population. The rehabilitation process must be pursued with a developmental objective rather than merely as coping mechanism in the situation. All preparedness measures and coping strategies at each stage of the process, must reflect the achievement of the developmental objective. These must provide if not better, but almost similar physical amenities and sources of livelihood, by restoring quite close to the status quo and then focusing on further development of the people. Therefore, appropriate interventions at Government level, NGOs level, affected population level and other community level, become very important and can make displacement little easier for the people.

(b) Cognitive and Affective Stage

Disastrous psychological effects on people start showing up in the population to be displaced in the form of tension and stress even before the actual onset of displacement. Issue of the evacuation notices to the people for acquiring the land is the beginning of the psychological problems of the people. The degree of stress and tension which the people experience at this stage, because of inherent fears and threats, should be the focus of designing management strategies. Therefore, reduction of this state of tension and stress become extremely important.

Appropriate preparedness measures needed to be designed at this stage are as follows:

Preparedness Measures

Preparedness measures must focus around issues like:

(i) Prepare individuals psychologically to agree for displacement without much resistance.

(ii) Dissemination of timely information about displacement.

(iii) Minimising adverse impact on people.

Conscious efforts at all levels are required to formulate motivational strategies, around perceived potential fears and threats by the people. The following 'Operational Interventions' are needed at this stage:

Operational Interventions

Detailed Microlevel Planning: Detailed Planning in advance, before the onset of displacement, should necessarily form an integral part of the process. The government must procure the data regarding the following aspects about the population to be displaced.

MANAGEMENT OF REHABILITATION PROCESS

Well Defined National Policy	*Latent Stage I*	*Antecedent Condition*
		Acquisition of Land Leading to Displacement
PREPAREDNESS MEASURES OBJECTIVE	COGNITIVE STAGE II	PERCEPTIONS/AWARENESS OF SITUATION
* Preparing individuals of displacement * Dissemination of timely information about displacement * Minimizing adverse impact on people		* Fears and Apprehension About * Possible Problem * Fulfilment of Government promises
OPERATIONAL INTERVENTION * Detailed micro level planning * Communication Strategy * People's Participation		* Acceptability of host population * Attitudes about development projects
ROLE OF GOVT./NGO'S/OTHER AGENCIES COMMUNITY AND HOST POPULATION	AFFECTIVE STAGE III	DEVELOPING * Anxiety * Physiological Tension * Stress * Hostility * Shock/Trauma
MANAGEMENT STRATEGY	MANIFEST STAGE IV DISPLACEMENT	BEHAVIOURAL PATTERNS
* Negotiations with government. Affected people local leaders, other influential people of the area and NGO's * Taking help from: Social research organizations and other agencies for conducting social survey.	REHABILITATION STAGE-V	* Passive Resistance * Active Resistance * Overt Aggression leading to mass agitation * Agreeing of displacement under stress
* Rehabilitating displaced	REHABILITATION STAGE VI	

Data Needed Regarding Displaced Population

(i) Correct estimate of land to be acquired.

(ii) Number of households/families to be displaced.

(iii) Housing pattern of the area.

(iv) Population structure of the place: adults, males, females, children and old people.

(v) Caste structure of the area.
(vi) Educational profile of the people.
(vii) Professional skills available with the people.
(viii) Aptitudes and potentials available with the people.
(ix) Correct estimate of movable and immovable property with the people.
(x) Schools, hospitals, temples, transport and other facilities available to the people in the area.
(xi) Attitude of the host population to know acceptability of the displaced population.

The services of research organizations and other agencies can be of immense help in this regard.

All this data will provide the guidelines to decide the nature of compensation package and facilities to be offered to the people. It will also enable the government to design appropriate communication strategy to create a desirable impact over the people in generating positive outlook about displacement.

Communication Strategy: Communication strategy should have the following objectives:

(a) Developing awareness among individuals about need for displacement.
(b) Providing knowledge about the rehabilitation package and its commitment benefits to people.
(c) Preparing individuals psychologically to cope with the unwanted psychological stress.
(d) Preparing host population for accepting the displaced people.

People's Participation: People's participation should be the core managing technique in designing as well as implementation of communication strategy. All castes, different occupational groups, local leaders and other influential people who are key participants in day-to-day functioning of the affected area, should be represented in the rehabilitation process. Resettlement and rehabilitation plans about site for resettlement of people, housing pattern, compensation packages and other facilities should be drawn in consultation with the core participative group. People's involvement would enable the government to elicit commitment and would make the displacement less uncomfortable for people.

Procuring all this data from the people before the onset of displacement can provide a glimpse of government's sincere intentions and efforts of rehabilitating the people after displacement. This will have a positive impact on people and would considerably reduce the adverse affects of displacement.

(c) Manifest Stage

Careful and timely handling of cognitive and affective stage through appropriate preparedness measures would greatly reduce the psychological tension and stress generating dysfunctional behaviour at the manifest stage. In many cases the government has taken an unduly long time in deciding the compensation package, forcibly evacuated the people and acquired the land. Evidences suggest that people have shown their actual resistance and resorted to mass agitation under certain development projects. Such a situation can be effectively handled through negotiations between government and affected population. All infrastructural facilities such as land, houses, schools, hospitals, etc., should be provided to people before displacement. This would help in minimizing resistance.

(d) Rehabilitation Stage

Rehabilitation programmes necessarily need to be designed according to the felt needs of the affected population. Data about population, procured earlier as preparedness measures, must be appropriately used for designing the programmes.

Rehabilitation programmes should make use of available skills and talents and also focus upon providing new skills and competencies to the affected population, to equip them to face the outer world. Efforts should be made to develop settler's commitment to self-support and sustenance, to avoid onset of settlers dependency syndrome psycho-therapeutic/health programmes in the form of family counselling, stress reducing exercises, community programmes and other socio-occupational programmes should form an essential complement of the rehabilitation package along with adequate compensation package. The perception of compensation package, as adequate and good, is greatly influenced by, how effectively the psychological tension, stress and traumatic situation is handled through these programmes.

(e) Rehabilitation Aftermath

Effective management of earlier stages will greatly reduce the further demands by the people from the government,

Conclusion

The population which is more often displaced by the developmental projects usually belong to lower strata of society, such as Scheduled Castes and.Scheduled Tribes who are more affected as compared to other displaced population. Therefore, as a part of socio-economic development, the Rehabilitation Programme must concern with safeguarding the interests of minority, the affected population, and minimizing the negative impacts of relocations.

In spite of intentions of the government to provide a comfortable rehabilitation to the affected population, no attention has been paid to the psycho-sociological consequences associated with the process. Though rehabilitation projects are often viewed as a planned change effort with developmental objectives, they are rarely implemented in a manner to achieve those objectives. People have been made to evacuate from their land forcefully and have been made to experience psychological shocks, undergo trauma, more often resulting in mental illness. In fact, if these psychological consequences are not effectively handled, perhaps, new resettlement colonies created under the so-called development projects, having objectives of overall development of people, for better quality of life, leading to national development, will turn into mental asylums. It is, therefore, the right time to reflect on this problem and seriously evaluate the extent to which the policies, planning and strategies together, with their implementation by the government, have been inadequate and draw lessons for further action.

All managers, who are responsible for managing rehabilitation of people and concerned community, must appreciate and understand the complex psycho-sociological nature of displacement. Rehabilitation must be addressed as a planned changed effort, having sequential stages requiring detailed advance planning for each stage. Steps are needed to arrest the psychological consequences resulting at each stage. This requires correct diagnosis, designing and implementing appropriate interventions as preparedness measures and coping strategies.

It is believed that the perspective presented and guidelines suggested in this chapter are functional and would be able to solve many of the deficiencies of the current management approach to problems associated with displacement and rehabilitation.

NINE

ROLE OF LOCAL INSTITUTIONS

Ability to reduce social and economic risks from natural and man-made hazards require adoption of a "culture of prevention". It can only be accomplished through global commitment of nations for development of effective disaster reduction policies through partnership for 'safer world' and preparation of societies at the local level who had to face the consequences of disaster.

It is evident that the concept of disaster and environment management will dominate developmental programmes of the nations. The linkage between them is of significance because of their interdependence on each other. Urban population is more vulnerable to natural disasters on account of very high densities and locations on flood plains, coastal areas, seismic belts, etc. During the last century, the world has witnessed a considerable increase in losses due to natural disasters. Globally natural disasters account for 80 per cent of all disaster affected people. Urbanisation is occurring at a very fast rate in areas where risks of natural disasters are greatest. There are 40 out of 50 fastest growing cities in the world which are in earthquake zones. Another reason for larger risks in urban areas is due to destruction of the eco system. Due to high densities and lower availability of land, residents are forced to stay in high-rise buildings, which are highly vulnerable to deaths. People living in illegal squatter settlements in urban areas are also a reason of vulnerability. In India, during 1988-97, disaster affected over 24 million people and killed more than 5000 in each year. Based on this problem in India, where 59 per cent of its area is vulnerable to one or multiple hazards, an approach for any disaster mitigation programme needs to be conceived at the following levels:

(1) Individual;

(2) Community;
(3) Local level;
(4) State level; and
(5) National level.

Disaster occur due to floods, cyclones, earthquakes, etc. It is, therefore, required that all the development programmes in the disaster prone areas will include preparedness for such inevitabilities. This includes construction of disaster relief shelters for cyclones, earthquakes and flood relief. These shelters can also be made in school buildings, community centers, etc. Action is also required to be taken to keep personal belongings in a safe place. It has been seen that human settlements are frequently effected by natural disasters, which take a heavy toll on human lives, destroy buildings and infrastructure and have farreaching economic and social consequences for people at large.

The earthquake which hit Gujarat on 26th January 2001 with a magnitude of 6.9 on the Richter scale, having its epicenter 20 km from Bhuj town in Kutch district took a heavy toll on life and property, both in urban and rural areas. 37.8 million population in 21 districts, 171 Talukas and about 8700 villages, was affected. Death toll was much more than the official figures of 16,459 and over 144,927 persons were injured. Over 228,906 houses collapsed and 397,615 houses damaged. It is estimated that loss to property was to the extent of Rs. 135,000 million.

Lessons from Gujarat Quake

The earthquake, which hit Marathwada region on 30.9.1993 with magnitude of 6.4 Richter scale having its epicenter near Killari village in Latur district left an unprecedented destruction behind. An earthquake measuring 6.1 on the Richter scale hit Jabalpur in Madhya Pradesh, on 22nd May 1997 having its epicenter near Koshamghat village causing widespread damages.

The earthquake that destroyed all types of buildings and rendered lakhs of people homeless and workless in Bhuj district of Gujarat was unparalleled. The toll of human life was not small. The crisis has caused a serious disequilibrium in society, leading to a state of emotional turmoil. Under such circumstances people become cynical in their views and approach to life and work. The rich have migrated to safer places. The others who have lost their houses have also lost the will to work.

Nature of Problems

Problems in rural and urban areas are a little different. In rural areas demands of life are low. Most common problems faced by population during such disasters are:

Damage to houses and other structures; Occurrence of fire; Land slides causing damages and/or blocking of roads; Dislocation of essential services and communication facilities; Panic and rumour problems; Bodies buried under debris; Depression in morale of the effected population; Disruption of law and order; Lack of presence of emergency shelters; Disposal of human bodies, Cattle and animals; Lack of first aid treatment; Family separation requiring re-union; Evacuation in emergency; Rehabilitation of destitute persons; and Spread of diseases and epidemics.

Disaster Solution Issues

Many of these problems can be eliminated or minimized by pre-disaster planning and preparedness. In India, the awareness and pre-disaster initiative has not picked up as yet. If proper arrangements are made, the impact and severity of damage caused by natural disasters could significantly be reduced. China has taken steps and death tolls from floods which occur occasionally, have fallen considerably in that country which is clear from the figures that follow:

Year	*Death Toll*
1931	1,40,000
1954	33,000
1981	3,000

New master plans are required to be drawn up to mitigate the above. The current master plans do not provide financially viable investment packages, which are rather long wish lists (UNCHS, 1994). Most of the master plans take a long time to be drawn up and at the time of their approvals, they are already outdated. It can also be said that master planning has not proved to be 'an effective instrument to create access to adequate housing and other services to the population.' In India, master planning and Town Planning Acts have marginalised the poor and compelled them to live in unauthorised settlements. Urban planning in India is exercised by State Governments through Town and Country Planning Departments, but the devolution of urban planning functions in accordance with the 73rd and 74th Amendment of the Constitution, is yet to be implemented.

It is estimated that in the next 40 years India will overtake China and become the most populous country of the world. New urban areas will have to be developed in adequate numbers to accommodate such a growth of urban population and to provide them basic civic amenities.

This growth threatens to make cities unsustainable because of the following:

(1) The authorities have difficulty in providing basic services and as a result most of the population live in densely populated settlements;

(2) Demand for land in cities has lead to use of unsuitable areas, which are prone to natural hazards;

(3) Fast growing cities contain increasing number of poorly, constructed buildings, which can lead to avoidable deaths. This fact is proved due to destruction by the earthquakes, which occurred in Latur, Uttar Kashi, Jabalpur, and Chamoli and cyclone in Andhra Pradesh and Orissa, Bhopal gas and Dabwali (Haryana) fire tragedy. It caused heavy losses not only to human lives but economic activities were also disrupted;

(4) The concentration of hazardous materials and

industrial complexes are increasing in urban areas, which put urban population at risks because in case of any natural hazard they will cause secondary disasters such as fire, explosions, radiation, etc.; and

(5) Urban development also increases the flood risk by disrupting natural drainage channels.

The urban poor who are most vulnerable to natural hazards live in the crowded areas, as they want to be near to a source of income whether it is fertile food plains or industrial complexes. Hence efforts to mitigate the effects of natural disasters must be made to cover social, economic, environmental and physical aspects. United Nations says that better urban planning can minimise the devastating impact of natural disasters such as the recent earthquakes in Turkey and in India. Klaus Toepfer, Head of the Nairobi-based UN Centre for Human Settlements (Habitat) says:

> "The immediate humanitarian needs are an absolute priority. But what has happened in the towns and cities in Turkey is an important symbol of how devastation, caused by natural disaster, is compounded by the unchecked process of urbanisation. The international community has to make a global effort to ensure that our cities are better governed. The best way to minimise the destruction caused by natural disasters is to ensure that local authorities are trained and equipped to enforce appropriate construction laws. That is essential if we are to secure a safe future for ordinary citizens everywhere."

As the trend towards urbanisation is accelerating, the suffering and devastation by natural disasters including earthquake has been worsening.

Entrusting Work to Specially Trained NGO's

The role of Non-Governmental Organisations (NGOs), by virtue of their proximity to the people and their comparative flexibility in operations can be very useful.. The NGOs can be helpful in the following ways:

(1) To prepare a profile of the community and its neighbourhoods in case of natural disaster including earthquakes;
(2) Assessment of risk and vulnerability;
(3) Identification of individuals and community resources;
(4) Identification of gaps in knowledge or resources that will impede effective emergency response; and
(5) Periodical mock drills to test the plan and to up-date it, are of paramount importance.

(c) Support of Urban Local Bodies

The Local Bodies are required to understand the need for intervention in disaster mitigation in an urban area and it is important to understand the risks involved and likely consequences on human life and property. It is therefore required to note the issues relevant to disaster:

(1) To identify risks and consequences thereof—Risk assessment is the basic information of utmost importance. In the urban areas, there is not much difference between man-made disaster and natural disasters;
(2) Risk assessment to variables are to be identified and assessed having:
    (a) Hazard intensity;
    (b) Vulnerability, i.e. what and who is effected;
(3) To identify vulnerable disasters—since urban areas are vulnerable to disasters its intensity can be reduced by moving people away from hazard locations and protecting them accordingly; and
(4) Vulnerability can be reduced:
    (a) By preparing people; and
    (b) By preparing shelters and infrastructure.
(5) To prepare audio-visual films, which can be shown in the schools, colleges other institutions and to the residents of the area.

For constructing regular buildings, research into the question of foundations, the walls and the super structure is very necessary. All that can take a year or two. Plans for the construction of structures, which are quake-resistant, fire-proof, heat-proof, have pucca flooring, are termite-proof, have electricity connection and are also cost-effective need to be launched soon.

Mr. Jagmohan, Hon'ble Minister for Urban Development, Government of India, has set up an experts' committee, for drafting a bill for regulating the construction business. It would require the developers, builders and architects to get themselves registered. This is the first step in what is promised to be a short process.

Among often forgotten, links between disaster and development are prevention and preparedness measures. Protective measures against the forces of nature are not self-evident. The question, therefore, arises as to how to protect people at large from disaster often at minimal additional costs. It can be done by way of management processes, training programmes, new building techniques, new understandings of how we interact with our environment.

The post-disaster activities are as follows:

(1) Rescue;
(2) Release;
(3) Repair;
(4) Rehabilitation;
(5) Reconstruction; and
(6) Renewals.

The immediate post-disaster activities can be formulated by giving assistance to the people who have suffered a great loss by way of rescue, evacuation and provision of shelter: in shelters already built or by constructing temporary shelters if permanent are not available. Assistance can also be given by moving people to a safer place and by providing them basic amenities for example water, sanitation, food, health care, etc., and at the same time, protecting them from diseases and epidemics.

The local authorities are required to categorise the disasters and also equip themselves for damage assessments. The categorisation can be as follows:

G1 - Slight non-structural damage
G2 - Slight structural damage
G3 - Moderate structural damage
G4 - Severe structural damage,
G5 - Collapse

The damage assessment can be—qualitative and quantitative i.e., fully damaged/partially damaged and marginally damaged. After this assessment and categorisation, the local revenue officials can be appointed as assessment officers. There is a need for capacity building and training, both formal and informal, in assessment of damage and valuation of assets, as they are not normally conversant with the methodology of damage assessment.

Rehabilitation

The critical discussion regarding various aspects of mitigation and control of natural hazards emphasise the following points:

What we can do?

(1) Can train communities from grass root level to-professional and administrators level;
(2) Can adopt villages, townships and cities to demonstrate healthy, safe and environment friendly lifestyle, and
(3) Can extend our hand to fund rehabilitation programmes under schemes of the Government.

What We Need to Do?

(1) Need to set up a techno-legal regime by enacting laws for enforcement of provisions for disaster resistance techniques including by-laws on use of building codes;
(2) Prepare vulnerability atlas in place;
(3) Need to disseminate message of preparedness through training workshops and research and design efforts;
(4) Prepare disaster and community action plans;
(5) Involve community for the purposes of planning to development action plans;
(6) Introduce regulations for disaster prone areas;

(7) Need for urban and regional planners to work closely with engineers and architects; and
(8) Need to carry out resource inventories in conflict prone zones.

Awareness and People's Participation

From the discussion above, Kobe Towns' Mayor says:

> "What is needed for construction are three things; money, technical skills and the understanding of people in the community, most important is the latter."

Therefore, it is required that we must train and educate the community on pre and post-disastrous situations. Community is required to be better informed through awareness and education programmes. At the same time, the community should also work closely with local bodies, NGOs, etc. The community volunteers can play an important role as they are flexible and that official authorities are not.

Training of Professionals

Capacity building for the technical/professionals persons is very material. This should also include refresher courses. Communication channels and warnings are the most vital issues. Local authorities are required to establish the communication system for warning, evacuation and relief measures, etc. Local authorities are required to assist in management of post-disaster audits and can also reveal facts or weakness in present procedures. Last but not the least, resources including trained people should be organised and deployed where they will have the greatest effect. They should also prepare a list containing Do's and Don'ts for the information of general public. These lists should be displayed in all the local schools, offices, libraries, etc. They should also undertake mock exercises to make people aware the steps to be taken in case of any such exigency.

District Planning Cell can be Made More Active

Lastly, as per the 74th Amendment to the Constitution, the district planning committees are required to be constituted, wherein a plan can be formulated keeping in view both the preparedness, i.e. pre-disaster and post-disaster aspects, to meet the exigencies at the time of emergency. The Government should hand over the regional planning aspect as formulated under the 12th Schedule to Panchayati Raj Institutions (PRIs) in view of 73rd and 74th Constitutional Amendment. Funds required for rehabilitation for giving assistance to the victims of natural disasters, i.e. flood cyclone and earthquake should be at the disposal of district planning committees. PRIs should contribute towards rehabilitation efforts of disaster victims through:

(1) Financial assistance in the form of loans;
(2) Training of local artisans and supervisors in appropriate technologies;
(3) By giving technical advice for disaster resistance, construction and repair through pamphlets indicating do's and don'ts in vernacular languages;
(4) Establishment of building centres for production of cost effective building materials besides dissemination of information on appropriate technologies;
(5) Construction of demonstration units using disaster resistant technologies;
(6) Providing consultancy service for appropriate house design for rehabilitation of disaster victims;
(7) To prepare bylaws through necessary legislation ensuring that the designs incorporate the provisions for required safety measures which are safe enough to resist natural disasters, to which that region is prone;
(8) Invoke unsafe buildings clause to make mandatory in existing deficient houses in case of natural calamity; and
(9) Local bodies to pass the plans for new buildings only if the required provisions have been met with.

Building Safety into System

The Centre has taken an initiative to enact a model law for regulating the activities of developers, builders and architects, which would be seen by the sceptic as a weak attempt to reign in the construction industry, which is amongst the least regulated industries in India today. It is, however, a step that should be welcomed, coming as it does in the wake of the Bhuj earthquake, which exposed the hollowness of the tall claims of structural integrity of high-rise buildings. A major problem with the construction business is corruption and the builder-architect-contractor nexus that has eaten into its very foundation. A builder selects an architect not only for his ability to design safe and aesthetic buildings, but also for getting the building plans "approved". The contractor typically cuts corners because he is under pressure to do the quickest and the cheapest job.

Conclusion

The Chief Ministers of various states should indeed take up the recommendation of incorporating the norms suggested by the National Building Code and Bureau of Indian Standards in municipal by-laws and zoning regulations. While Mr. Jagmohan, Minister for Urban Development, GOI, says that the new law would be enacted and enforced in Delhi, other states would be well advised to follow suit. Since most of the building approval is done at the municipal level, the viability of a proper evaluation system for inspection and approval of buildings should be studied. Even if one percent of the cost of the building were to be demarcated for this purpose, it should not be too high a price for safety. There is no denying that given the lack of proper transportation system and the high cost of lands in urban India, high-rise buildings cannot be avoided. What is needed is a proper system of ensuring quality and accountability. This is a small, but important step towards building safety into the system.

The State of Maharashtra has already formulated its State Disaster Mitigation Plan. The other states are following the lead and are in the process of formulating such plans, which will help in identifying remedial measures suited for the region well in advance to avoid taking hasty decisions in panic. The country should learn a lesson from Latur, Uttar Kashi, Jabalpur, Chamoli, Andhra Pradesh and Orissa, Bhopal gas and Dabwali (Haryana) fire tragedy.

As disasters increase, it becomes clear that neither governments nor local communities can themselves continue to assume the rising costs of compensating the citizens for the losses incurred. The only affordable solution lies in mitigation and prevention. Shared information is the beginning of prevention and partnership is crucial for successful application of disaster prevention practices.

From the above emergent shift the focus should be on Prevention, Preparedness and Protection: For pre-disaster mitigation

The post-disaster initiative will include:
Rescue, Relief, Rehabilitation, Reconstruction, Repairs and Renewals.

TEN

NEW DIMENSIONS

Mankind has survived and lived with natural disasters right from the days of the mythical universal deluge. Floods, volcanic eruptions and earthquakes have plagued and devastated humanity since time immemorial. Recurring floods are believed to have contributed, among other factors, to the extinction of the flourishing Indus valley civilization of South Asia in ancient times. You can do nothing about shifting of tectonic plates beneath the oceans causing devastating earthquakes or lava simmering underneath the earth's crust to erupt violently. And if our astronomers are to be believed, our planet is facing the dire prospect of total annihilation by the Haileys comet striking it in less than one and a quarter century from now. The exact year of their dark prediction is 2116. Human endeavour in respect of such natural disasters, which are beyond human control and regulation, is limited to deep study, fact-finding and forewarning by natural scientists concerned. These are beyond the perview of social scientists.

There is another category of disasters facing humanity today which is very much in the agenda of social scientists. This is the category of man-made disasters which calls for earnest attention of researchers in humanities, if mankind has to be saved from much avoidable damage. Some of these are almost as deadly and certainly more frequent than natural disasters. As man approaches the 21st century he is more and more exposed to the threat of man-made disasters almost invariably resulting from mismatch between the ever proliferating technological innovations and man's capacity to handle them. It is not meant to decry technological innovations in production of goods and services or call for a halt to revolutionary changes they entail in the affairs of human beings.

Rapid technological advance is an irreversible process and, if anything, it is only going to accelerate in future. The objective behind any in-depth study of man-made disasters could only be to increase the awareness about the inherent dangers, which is lacking at present and evolve effective damage control policy.

Before talking about the strategy in abstract, some of the well-known and not so well-known flash points of disasters may be identified and dwelt upon. This study deals with two such flash points—environmental disaster, and industrial disaster. Some factual indicators are being provided in respect of environmental disaster to highlight the dangers involved, which is meant to be only illustrative. Facts about the less known kind of industrial disasters have been derived largely from the Bhopal Gas Tragedy of India which was perhaps the worst industrial disaster of history.

Environmental Disaster

Global warming is the most important component of environmental disaster that mankind is facing today. Unprecedented increase in world population, coupled with even faster increase in economic activities is threatening to disrupt the finely balanced eco-system which sustains life on earth. In 1900 the world population was about 1.6 billion which rose to 2.5 billion by 1950. But during 40 years from 1950 to 1990, the world population more than doubled. What is more, world economic activity increased more than four times in the same period. The need to support more people and rapid technological advance to enable them to live better have been steadily eroding the fine ecological balance. Hyper industrialization is leading to abnormal rise in the level of CO_2 emissions—CFC's (Chlorofluro-carbons), acidified forests, polluted rivers, etc. This has such a disturbing effect on the eco-system that more of sun's radiant energy or heat gets trapped within the earth's atmosphere, as inside the glass of a green house. This results in warming up of not only the atmospheric gases but of everything else on earth.

At the same time, chemical emissions like CFC's are adding up to the harmful effects of solar radiation in another way. The Ozone layer, situated about 20 kilometres above the earth's surface, protects the earth from the harmful effects of sun's rays. Chemicals like CFC's widely in use in refrigeration, air-conditioning, etc., cause depletion of the Ozone layer, resulting in what has come to be known as 'Ozone hole'. The wider the 'Ozone hole', the greater the danger of sun's rays directly penetrating the earth's atmosphere unfiltered by the protective shield of ozone, resulting in serious consequences for global population.

Galloping population and even faster pace of industrialization are thus slowly but steadily leading to a rise in earth's temperature through greenhouse effect and ozone depletion. This could prove to be disastrous for large chunks of inhabitants of our planet. It is estimated that average increase in global temperature in course of the last one hundred years was only to the extent of 0.3° celcius to 0.7° celcius. As against this insignificant rise, it is estimated that double the CO_2 emission levels, consequent upon accelerated population growth and industrialization, will produce an average temperature increase of between 1.5°celcius to 4.5°celcius by the middle of the 21st Century. One of the consequences of this abnormal increase in global warming could be perceptible rise in earth's sea levels. This would be inescapable because a warmer liquid has more volume than an equivalent mass of cold liquid.

In concrete terms, any significant rise in sea level during the 21st Century may spell disaster in many countries of the Third World. For instance, a one-metre rise in sea-level would submerge about 11.5 per cent of the land of Bangladesh containing a population of about 8.5 millions. Similar would be the fate of large populations residing on low-lying deltas in Egypt and China. A two-metre rise in sea-level would completely swallow up the Maldive islands, inhabited by about two hundred thousand people, as well as many atolls in the Pacific ocean.

Although the potential damage caused by global warming may be less severe in developed world, it cannot escape the disastrous consequences altogether. Low-lying regions of Louisiana, New Jersey, the Netherlands, etc., would remain vulnerable to varying degrees of devastations through rise in sea-levels. In the USA alone, a rise of one metre in the sea-level would devour up to eight thousand square miles of wetlands and ten thousand square miles of dryland. The vintage city of Venice and many other towns and habitations located near water's edge would be seriously threatened.

Industrial Disaster

While there is growing awareness about the threat of environmental disaster looming large over the world, not much is known about the ever increasing dangers of industrial disasters. As the process and pace of industrialization goes on accelerating the world over, with poor countries emulating and vying with their richer counterparts in the race towards greater and yet greater industrialization, the threat of industrial disasters is ever widening across the board. Major and minor industrial disasters are taking place regularly across the world but these are not so well-known. Everybody is interested in blanking these off the public gaze, the corporations, governments and the entire network of institutions and people involved in the concerned industries, for their own reasons. In any case, the common people tend to dismiss industrial disasters as no more than accidents or normal hazards associated with any trade or industry. But taken together, they constitute a serious threat to human life with grim prospect of multiplying as the process of industrialization intensifies in the approaching century.

A few samples of industrial accidents taking considerable toll of human lives across the world are given below:

In 1942, a coal dust explosion at Honkaiko colliery in China left 1572 dead on the spot.

In 1947, a Fertilizer ship explosion off Texas city in USA killed 561 persons.

In 1956, 1100 died in a dynamite truck explosion in Cali, Columbia.

In 1975, 433 miners perished in a coal mine disaster in Chasnala colliery in India.

In 1979, an accident in the biological and chemical warfare plant at Novosibirsk in erstwhile Soviet Union took 300 lives.

In November 1984, natural gas explosion at Pomex plant in

Mexico city left at least 452 dead and 4258 injured; 31,000 residents of the area had to be evacuated.

The industrial disaster that dwarfed all others in the scale of devastation occurred at the city of Bhopal in central India in early December 1984. The event which has left many in the city permanently disabled, apart from thousands who were directly consumed by it, was summed by a leading fortnightly, *India Today* dated 31 December, 1984 as follows:

"The night of December 2/3, a night that Bhopal and its 800,000 citizens can never forget. A Monday of macabre death, a killer cloud of gas that silently settled on an unsuspecting city and converted a pleasant, mild winter's night into a nightmare of misery, panic, sickness and, for at least 2500 people, babies and children, fathers and mothers, siblings and grandparents, a slow, painful, unnecessary snuffing out of life. That it was the worst ever industrial accident in history, taking an unprecedented and still unaccounted death toll and leaving no fewer than 50,000 affected, was quickly dwarfed by the tidal wave of human suffering that spread quickly across the city like the poison cloud that caused it.

"Methyl isocyanite (MIC) a product that few in Bhopal knew even existed, which Union Carbide, its makers describe in the manuals as 'an extraordinarily hazardous chemical,' a poison against which 'stringent precautions must be observed to eliminate any possibility of human contact', yet it was this lethal substance, a highly volatile chemical that is used by Union Carbide to manufacture pesticide that vaporised silently into Bhopal's night air".

The tragedy was caused by both systems and human failures. The systems that failed were (a) vent gas scrubber, (b) flare tower, (c) water curtain, (d) refrigeration system and (e) spare tank. Even if some of the systems failed, the plant staff could have adopted the laid down measures to render most of the MIC escaping into the air harmless, which they failed to do. As a result, more than a hundred thousand people living in the vicinity of the factory were exposed to MIC in varying degrees. Around sixteen thousand animals perished immediately.

As the poison gas leaked out of the chemical plant, gradually bringing under its sway a 40 square kilometre area, men, women and children started dying of asphyxiation. The immediate body count put the figure of the dead at 3000, even as more dead bodies were being discovered everyday even a week after the disaster. Even according to the conservative official estimates, no less than one-fourth of the city's population of about eight hundred thousand was affected by the deadly effect of the gas leak. Many were completely blinded, many had their eye-sight and hearing partially impaired and still others were maimed one way or the other. The scars of the disaster are still there on the face of Bhopal in the shape of numerous hapless inhabitants who have become handicapped for life in the prime of their youth. Bhopal has become a symbol of the magnitude and omnious dimensions of industrial disasters the world over.

Yet another disaster of grave magnitude occurred in Chernobyl nuclear plant in the erstwhile Soviet Union in 1986. There have been less serious accidents at nuclear plants in other countries which have generally been kept under the curtain of secrecy by the countries concerned for strategic reasons. But Chernobyl was too big a nuclear disaster to be hidden from world view. Hundreds perished instantly, though the exact tally would never be known, and thousands were maimed by radio activity. Huge expanses of land were rendered infertile for decades. As one observer put it, the poisonous wastes it left behind would have a life time far larger than any human culture has survived.

The range, sweep, scale and frequency of man-made disasters constitute a grim prospect for human well-being in the coming century. It is necessary for social scientists to give serious thought to the problems posed by man-made disasters. By all accounts, there is going to be no let up in the pace of population increase, technological advance and industrialization in the foreseeable future. With the poor and developing countries racing headlong to catch up with the developed ones, there is every possibility of industrialization increasing at a faster pace rather than slowing down, in the process, augmenting the range, ferocity and frequency of disasters. In the event, the only way out is to evolve a suitable strategy to contain and minimize the risks involved.

Human Audit

This would involve reorienting our attitude towards technological advance and industrialization. These are engines of development and essential for economic betterment of people particularly in the poor and developing countries. But in the race for economic development, latent risks of potential disasters cannot and should not be ignored. A bold new approach to the issue is called for. There should be a human audit of technological innovations and modes of industrialization before going ahead with these engines of growth. For instance, the desirability of launching upon chemical and nuclear projects should be examined with reference to the threat they pose to human life in the light of Bhopal and Chernobyl disasters. Human ingenuity is capable of evolving alternative modes of industrialization and tapping new energy sources which are safer or less prone to disaster.

As discussed earlier, hurtling to industrialisation through the carbon route is fraught with possibilities of environmental degradation, leading to global warming and attendant dangers to human life. The human cost involved must be weighed before rushing through such a course of economic development in developed and developing countries. Any such human audit would point to an alternative course, that is, a non-carbon path to industrialization in less developed countries which are seeking to industrialize fast and improve the economic conditions of their people. The developed countries too should evolve and increasingly take to such alternative modes of economic activity, not only to cut down the damage already done, but also to provide a model for the less developed. They are certainly in a better position to do that, being in the vanguard of technological advancement.

PROGRESS IN THE INTERNATIONAL DECADE FOR NATURAL DISASTER REDUCTION

Natural Hazard including earthquakes, tsunamis, volcanic eruptions, landslides, avalanches, tropical cyclones and other windstorms, floods, wildfire, drought, and locust infestations—occur throughout much of the world. Disasters stemming from these hazards kill more than one million people each decade, leave countless others destitute, and cause huge economic losses. Among the myriad of disastrous events in the last few years, each of the largest—a typhoon in Bangladesh and an earthquake in China—has claimed hundreds of thousands of lives. The toll from disasters is particularly severe and tragic in developing countries. In recent years, they have suffered 90 per cent of the deaths and have often had their development goals set back years and even decades. With population growth and urbanisation and with disaster-vulnerable development, the risk of still greater tragedies is increasing. Now is the time to confront this issue head-on.

These are the introductory words in a report presented by the Secretary-General of the United Nations-as a background document, when the UN General Assembly decided to designate the 1990s as the International Decade for Natural Disaster Reduction (IDNDR).

The Munich Re-insurance has estimated that economic losses due to natural disasters have increased three-fold from the 1960s to the 1990s, and in the first few years of the 1990s are running at about $50 billion per year. The majority of these enormous economic losses are incurred in industrially developed parts of the world, but the relative impact is much greater on countries with lower per capita incomes. For countries with the lowest GNP, disaster mortality is several times higher than for middle income countries.

In their important book, *The Environment as Hazard*, Burton, Kates and White describe how deaths and sufferings due to natural disasters are closely related to poverty. "Ninety-five per cent of disaster-related deaths occur among two-thirds of the world's population that occupy developing countries".

Two fundamental observations formed the impetus to the IDNDR. First, the extent of loss of lives, physical damage and economic costs caused by disasters; their overall impact has often become an unbearable burden both on the stricken locations and on the socio-economic development process of vulnerable countries. Second, the availability in today's world of a wealth of scientific knowledge and technological know-how, already used in other sectors, that could be transferred and applied to the reduction of the overall impact of disasters on society. As a key result of the preparatory work for the Decade, these essential considerations found broad recognition and were endorsed by the United Nations in the decision to launch the IDNDR.

Objectives and Goals for IDNDR

When the UN General Assembly adopted resolution 44 / 236 in 1989 and formally decided on the IDNDR, the following objectives and goals were established:

1. The objective of the decade is to reduce through concerted international action, especially in developing countries, the loss of life, property damage and social and economic disruption caused by natural disasters, such as earthquakes, windstorms, tsunamis, floods, landslides, volcanic eruptions, wildfire, grasshopper and locust infestations, drought and desertification and other calamities of natural origin.
2. The goals of the Decade are:
   (a) To improve the capacity of each country to mitigate the effects of natural disasters expeditiously and effectively, paying special attention to assisting developing countries in the assessment of disasters damage potential and in the establishment of early warning systems and disaster-resistant structures when and where needed;
   (b) To devise appropriate guidelines and strategies for applying existing scientific and technical knowledge, taking into account the cultural and economic diversity among nations;
   (c) To foster scientific and engineering endeavours aimed at closing critical gaps in knowledge in order to reduce loss of life and property;

(d) To disseminate existing and new technical information related to measures for the assessment, prediction and mitigation of natural disasters; and

(e) To develop measures for the assessment, prediction, prevention and mitigation of natural disasters through programmes of technical assistance and technology transfer, demonstration projects, and education and training, tailored to specific disasters and locations, and to evaluate the effectiveness of those programmes.

The Assembly underlined the fundamental responsibility of the vulnerable countries themselves; in order to initiate coherent disaster-mitigation activities, countries were requested to create multi-sectoral national committees or focal points for IDNDR, which would stimulate and coordinate local initiatives aiming at the objectives of the Decade. The Assembly furthermore called specifically on scientific and technological institutions, as well as industrial corporations, to participate in disaster-reduction activities, recognising very clearly the extent of the benefits, the capabilities and resources of these groups could bring about.

Such a country-centred approach is indeed geared to obtaining maximum advantage from country-level expertise and should be embodied in disaster-reduction policies and actions right from the outset. To date, over 100 National Committees or Focal Points have been established in response to the call by the General Assembly and to promotional activities that focused on the identification of local expertise and knowledge that could be mobilised in a country-level disaster mitigation effort. An important concern is that these national groups include all relevant local expertise in disaster management and prevention, as well as in scientific and technical knowledge; all these components are essential for the successful application of advanced technologies to disaster reduction.

Organisational Arrangements during the IDNDR

Overall advice with respect to the Decade is provided by a Special High-Level Council, and a Scientific and Technical

Committee (STC) on the IDNDR has been established. The role of the Committee is to develop overall programmes to be taken into account in bilateral and multilateral cooperation for the Decade, paying attention to priorities and gaps in technical knowledge identified at the national level, in particular by national committees; to assess and evaluate the activities carried out in the course of the Decade; and to make recommendations on the overall programmes in an annual report to the Secretary-General.

A secretariat responsible for the day-to-day coordination of the Decade has been established and is located in Geneva, Switzerland. Originally, the secretariat worked in close association with the then UNDRO; since the establishment of the Department of Humanitarian Affairs (DHA), the Secretariat reports to DHA.

The organisations of the UN system have participated in the IDNDR from the early phases of programme development through an Inter-Agency Steering Committee and a Working Group. These have provided a forum for inter-agency coordination and information exchange.

Activities and Progress

The first years of IDNDR have been characterised by the formulation of targets and the initiation of projects. The STC has met on four occasions, the last one being in New Delhi in February 1993. "Three Targets of the Decade" to be completed by all countries by the year 2000 have been adopted, namely:

(a) Comprehensive national assessments of risks form natural hazards, with these assessments taken into account in development plans;
(b) Mitigation plans at national and/or local levels, involving long-term prevention and preparedness and community awareness; and
(c) Ready access to global, regional, national and local warning systems and broad dissemination of warnings.

Criteria for various types of IDNDR projects at national, regional and international level have been established as well, with the following classification:

(a) International IDNDR Demonstration Projects: those

projects intended to provide clear examples of activities which fall within the framework programme of the Decade as already endorsed by the Committee. In addition, those projects need a very good operational organisation and recognised implementing bodies.

(b) International and Regional IDNDR Projects: which fall within the framework programme of the Decade and contribute towards achieving one or more of the targets.

(c) National IDNDR Projects: which fall within the framework programme of the Decade and contribute to achieving one or more of the targets, some of which may carry a particular value.

(d) National IDNDR Demonstration Projects: National Committees and Focal Points may wish to designate a limited number of projects in this category, with criteria similar to (a) above, and notify the Secretariat.

A note of special concern made at the last STC session is that the latest available statistics indicate that in 1991, 162,000 people lost their lives, and that US$ 44 billion in economic damage occurred because of 434 major disasters. In 1992, Hurricane Andrew caused economic losses in the United States of over US$ 20 billion, while thanks to effective advance warnings, loss of life was limited.

Projects

At present about 25 projects have been endorsed as International IDNDR Demonstration Projects and there are many more national and regional projects classified as IDNDR projects. A major problem is of course securing financial support for these projects. National and regional projects are normally funded by a Government (National Committee) or Government (National Committees) of the area(s) in which they would be implemented.

It was reported at the fourth STC that:

> While funding for most projects has already been provided, as for example by the European Community Development Fund (PDF), the Netherlands and Germany, UN agencies and non-governmental

international organizations, other initiatives, including some demonstration projects, are however facing problems in obtaining financial support. The STC therefore recommended that information about individual projects should be disseminated through a variety of channels, including *STOP Disasters*, and that the STC should play a more active part in promoting such projects, including contacts with donors.

Guidance on project development to the Secretariat and advice to the STC is provided for by a sub-committee. The terms of reference for this sub-committee specify that it will:

(a) encourage the formulation of IDNDR projects in all four categories, especially at national and regional levels;
(b) review proposed projects and, if needed, suggest modifications;
(c) periodically review and recommend projects to be designated as International Demonstration Projects, taking into account the need to cover the major programme areas of the Decade and the above criteria;
(d) advise on possible avenues for funding or otherwise supporting International Demonstration Projects and, when requested, other Decade projects;
(e) provide guidance to the Secretariat as required on categorization of projects in line with the above criteria; and
(f) keep under review the above guidelines and criteria and recommend changes to the STC as necessary.

Information Strategy

Eleven issues of *STOP DISASTERS*, the *IDNDR* newsletter, have been issued to date. The press run has been gradually increased from 8,000 to 10,000 (December 1992) and plans are presently under consideration to reach a target circulation of 30,000 in line with the recommendation of the Second STC meeting. The newsletter is currently distributed in 178 countries to national IDNDR committees, national agencies involved in disaster management, inter-governmental, nongovernmental organisations, research institutes, financial and banking institutes, insurance companies, etc., which have an interest in the Decade programme. The newsletter is published by the Osservatorio Vesuviano in cooperation with the IDNDR Secretariat.

The 1992 International Day for Natural Disaster Reduction was observed under the theme "Natural Disaster Reduction for Sustainable Development." An encouraging participation in the observation programme was registered both at national and international levels. At the international level a statement was made by Boutros Boutros-Ghali, Secretary-General of the United Nations, on the occasion of the day. Similar messages were also released to the media by the Secretary General of the World Meteorological Organization and the Executive Director of the United Nations Centre for Human Settlements (habitat). At two Press Conferences organised in New York and Geneva in cooperation with the UN/DPI, Jan Eliasson, Under-Secretary-General for Humanitarian Affairs, James P. Bruce, Chairman of the IDNDR Scientific and Technical Committee, and Charles LaMunieree, Director and Deputy to the Under-Secretary-General for Humanitarian Affairs, briefed correspondents on; the growing human and economic losses resulting from natural disasters, the importance of natural disaster reduction for sustainable development and the opportunity which the Decade programme offers for international cooperation in the field of natural disaster reduction.

Information packages containing a set of audio-visual productions prepared by the IDNDR Secretariat and information material from other sources relating to the theme, were compiled and dispatched to national IDNDR committees to supplement their observance programmes. National IDNDR committees displayed an active interest in the Day and used the opportunity for promoting the Decade's objectives and for mobilizing support for disaster reduction activities. An encouraging feedback has been received from national IDNDR committees which organized varied and innovative observance programmes. The 1993 International Day for Natural Disaster

Reduction will be observed under the theme "Stop Disasters Focus on Schools and Hospitals".

An implementation plan of the IDNDR Information Strategy was approved by the fourth STC session. The plan aims to contribute, through the Decade Programme and a participatory approach to the establishment of a long-term communicative relationship between generators, transmitters and users of information, an essential prerequisite for motivating people to adopt or promote disaster reduction measures.

An information campaign which would concentrate on three targets of the Decade on a step-by-step basis was identified to be important to mobilize the efforts of all Decade partners along a clearly defined path which would enable the achievement of tangible results by the end of the Decade, laying a good basis for continuing efforts in set directions.

In each campaign phase, the scientific community, disaster-prone communities, governments in developing and industrialised countries, the media and all other Decade partners would be asked to contribute their share to the achievement of each target which can be planned and also quantified in terms of achievement The focused approach would also facilitate the mobilisation, the prioritisation and channelling of support to a selected number of disaster-prone groups, countries or regions which might seek assistance or collaborative efforts in each case. The phased approach would also ensure that the basic questions as to who is vulnerable to disasters, why and at what level, would be answered at different levels and addressed sequentially, prior to any attempt at transmitting information on disaster reduction measures.

Follow-up on UNCED and Agenda-21

The STC at its fourth session in New Delhi reviewed the outcome of the UNCED in Rio in June 1992 and identified four major follow-up activities that could potentially help to reduce disaster losses:

1. The formation of a Commission for Sustainable Development to monitor progress on Agenda 21;
2. The Framework Convention on Climate Change;

3. Negotiation of a new Convention on Desertification and Drought; and
4. The Conference on Sustainable Development of Small Island States (Barbados, April 1994).

Of special interest to participants at this meeting may be the reference to chapter seven of Agenda 21. This chapter deals with "Promoting Sustainable Human Settlement Development and contains direct reference to "promoting human settlement planning and management in disaster-prone areas".

World Conference on Natural Disaster Reduction, 1994

A World Conference on Natural Disaster Reduction, organised in coordination with the UN Department of Humanitarian Affairs/International Decade for Natural Disaster Reduction and the Government of Japan, will be held in Yokohama from May 23-27,1994. The aims of the conference are to:

(a) review IDNDR accomplishments at national, regional and international levels;
(b) chart an action programme for the future;
(c) exchange information on the implementation of IDNDR programmes and policies; and
(d) increase awareness of the importance of the progress of disaster reduction policies.

Participation in the conference is to include government ministers and high-level officials who will be preparing and presenting national reports on their IDNDR-related activities. Additionally, participants are expected from regional and international organizations, concerned with natural disasters, governmental and non-governmental representatives, and other interested persons. Furthermore, an invitation is extended to all who are involved in Decade activities, including those from the fields of planning, finance, foreign affairs, health, science, engineering, civil defence, private sector, including the insurance industry, the media and emergency preparedness.

There will be a series of Topical Sessions on:

* Cost Benefits of Hazard Mitigation,
* Drought Management,

* Inter-relationships between Technological and Natural Hazards,
* Buildings Hazard-Resistant Structures,
* Warning Systems and Preparedness for Disaster Reduction, and
* Vulnerable Groups and Communities.

The Conference is designed to be neither exclusively technical nor political, but rather to provide an opportunity for policy-makers to exchange ideas and hazard reduction strategies in a unique forum.

The results of the Conference will contribute to the midterm review of the Decade in 1994 by the United Nations Economic and Social Council, as required by the General Assembly.

Concluding Remarks

The objectives, goals and targets for the IDNDR are straightforward. However, natural disasters occur in many different shapes and cause a wide spectrum of impacts. The consequences of a natural disaster depend on many factors, including socio-economic factors, and it has been suggested that man-made influences are the main cause for the growing disaster potential. In particular, unplanned, often informal settlements in disaster-prone regions and rapid urbanization expose man to dangers directly or indirectly related to natural disasters.

However, there is still hope and I would like to conclude with a quote from a recent speech by Jim Brace, Chairman of the IDNDR Scientific and Technical Committee.

Through the decade of the 90s we are determined to reach a higher plateau of global awareness of the suffering and damages due to natural disasters and to put in place the actions, both possible and necessary, to reduce these human and economic losses. But it will take a major effort on the part of all disaster-prone countries—that is all of our countries—to bring this about. The IDNDR provides an opportunity and a framework for international cooperation. For the sake of the people of the world, let us work together to make it happen.

[Courtesy: IDNDR]

YOKOHAMA STRATEGY AND PLAN OF ACTION FOR A SAFER WORLD

Guidelines for Natural Disaster Prevention, Preparedness and Mitigation

World Conference on Natural Disaster Reduction Yokohama, Japan, 23-27 May 1994

United Nations New York and Geneva, 1995

Yokohama Message

We, the States Members of the United Nations and other States, having met at the World Conference on Natural Disaster Reduction, in the city of Yokohama, Japan, from 23 May to 27 May 1994, in partnership with non-governmental organizations, and with the participation of international organizations, the scientific community, business, industry and the media, deliberating within the framework of the International Decade for Natural Disaster Reduction, expressing our deep concern for the continuing human suffering and disruption of development caused by natural disasters, and inspired by the Yokohama Strategy and Plan of Action for a Safer World,

Affirm that:

The impact of natural disasters in terms of human and economic losses has risen in recent years, and society in general has become more vulnerable to natural disasters. Those usually most affected by natural and other disasters are the poor and socially disadvantaged groups in developing countries as they are least equipped to cope with them.

Disaster prevention, mitigation, preparedness and relief are four elements which contribute to and gain from the implementation of sustainable development policies. These elements, along with environmental protection and sustainable development, are closely interrelated. Therefore, nations should incorporate them in their development plans and ensure efficient follow-up measures at the community, national, subregional, regional and international levels.

Disaster prevention, mitigation and preparedness are better

than disaster response in achieving the goals and objective of the Decade. Disaster response alone is not sufficient, as it yields only, temporary results at a very high cost. We have followed this limited approach for too long. This has been further demonstrated by the recent focus on response to complex emergencies which, although compelling, should not divert from pursuing a comprehensive approach. Prevention contributes to lasting improvement in safety and is essential to integrated disaster management.

The world is increasingly interdependent. All countries shall act in a new spirit of partnership to build a safer world based on common interests and shared responsibility to save human lives, since natural disasters do not respect borders. Regional and international cooperation will significantly enhance our ability to achieve real progress in mitigating disasters through the transfer of technology and the sharing of information and joint disaster prevention and mitigation activities. Bilateral and multilateral assistance and financial resources should be mobilized to support these efforts.

The information, knowledge and some of the technology necessary to reduce the effects of natural disasters can be available in many cases at low cost and should be applied. Appropriate technology and data, with the corresponding training, should be made available to all freely and in a timely manner, particularly to developing countries.

Community involvement and their active participation should be encouraged in order to gain greater insight into the individual and collective perception of development and risk, and to have a clear understanding of the cultural and organizational characteristics of each society as well as of its behaviour and interactions with the physical and natural environment. This knowledge is of the utmost importance to determine those things which favour and hinder prevention and mitigation or encourage or limit the preservation of the environment for the development of future generations, and in order to find effective and efficient means to reduce the impact of disasters.

The adopted Yokohama Strategy and related Plan of Action for the rest of the Decade and beyond:

A. Will note that each country has the sovereign responsibility to protect its citizens from natural disasters;

B. Will give priority attention to the developing countries, in particular the least developed, landlocked countries and the small island developing States;

C. Will develop and strengthen national capacities and capabilities and, where appropriate, national legislation for natural and other disaster prevention, mitigation and preparedness, including the mobilization of non-governmental organizations and participation of local communities;

D. Will promote and strengthen sub-regional, regional and international cooperation in activities to prevent, reduce and mitigate natural and other disasters, with particular emphasis on:

   * Human and institutional capacity-building and strengthening;
   * Technology sharing, the collection, the dissemination and the utilization of information; and
   * Mobilization of resources.

The framework of action of the International Decade for Natural Disaster Reduction provides all vulnerable countries in particular the developing countries, with the opportunity to achieve a safer world by the end of this century and beyond. In this regard, the international community and the United Nations system in particular must provide adequate support to the International Decade for Natural Disaster Reduction, and its mechanisms, especially the secretariat of the Decade to enable them to carry out their mandate.

The Yokohama Conference is at a crossroad in human progress. In one direction lie the meagre results of an extraordinary opportunity given to the United Nations and its Member States. In the other direction, the United Nations and the world community can change the course of events by reducing the suffering from natural disasters. Action is urgently needed."

Nations should view the Yokohama Strategy for a Safer World as a call to action individually and in concert with other nations, to implement policies and goals reaffirmed in Yokohama, and to use the International Decade for Natural Disaster Reduction as a catalyst for change.

Yokohama Strategy and Plan of Action

Introduction

The World Conference on Natural Disaster Reduction,

Having met at Yokohama from 23 to 27 May, 1994,

Recognizing the rapidly rising world-wide toll on human and economic losses due to natural disasters,

Recalling the decision of the General Assembly in its resolution 44/236 of 22 December 1989 to launch a far reaching global undertaking for the 1990s to save human lives and reduce the impact of natural disasters,

Recalling also the forward-looking decision of the General Assembly in its resolution 46/182 of 19 December 1991 to adopt an integrated approach for disaster management in all its aspects and to initiate a process towards a global culture of prevention,

Recognizing that sustainable economic growth and sustainable development cannot be achieved in many countries without adequate measures to reduce disaster losses, and that there are close linkages between disaster losses and environmental degradation, as emphasized in Agenda 21,

Reaffirming the Rio Declaration, in particular Principle 18, which stresses the need for the international community to assist States afflicted by natural disasters and other emergencies that are likely to produce sudden harmful effects in the environment of those States,

Reaffirming also the role assigned by the Secretary-General of the United Nations to the Emergency Relief Coordinator, Under-Secretary-General of the Department of Humanitarian Affairs, through the IDNDR secretariat in charge of the Decade, in promoting and directing activities of the IDNDR in conformity with General Assembly resolution 46/182,

Emphasizing the need for the United Nations system to pay special attention to the least developed and land-locked countries and small island developing States, and recalling in this regard that the outcomes of the first Global Conference on the Sustainable Development of Small Island Developing States and the Programme of Action for the Least Developed Countries for the 1990s call for giving priority attention to small island developing States and least developed countries in the activities of the Decade,

Responding to the request of the General Assembly in its resolution 48/188 of 23 December 1993 to:

A. Review the accomplishments of the Decade at national, regional and international levels;
B. Chart a programme of action for the future;
C. Exchange information on the implementation of Decade programmes and policies; and
D. Increase awareness of the importance of disaster reduction policies:

1. Appeals to the world, at the time of reaching the mid-point of the International Decade for Natural Disaster Reduction and in the light of increasing human losses and damage caused by disasters and acting in a new spirit of partnership to build a safer world, based on common interest, sovereign equality and shared responsibility to save human lives, protect human and natural resources, the ecosystem and cultural heritage, to reaffirm its commitment to pursuing, through national, regional and international efforts, the transformation of the International Framework of Action for the Decade into a decisive intersectoral Plan of Action;
2. *Invites* all countries to defend individuals from physical injuries and traumas, protect property and contribute to ensuring progress and stability, generally recognizing that each country bears the primary responsibility for protecting its own people, infrastructure and other national assets

from the impact of natural disasters, and accepting at the same time that, in the context of increasing global interdependence, concerted international cooperation and an enabling international environment are vital for the success of these national efforts; and

3. *Adopts* the following Principles, Strategy and Plan of Action.

I. Principles

1. Risk assessment is a required step for the adoption of adequate and successful disaster reduction policies and measures.
2. Disaster prevention and preparedness are of primary importance in reducing the need for disaster relief.
3. Disaster prevention and preparedness should be considered integral aspects of development policy and planning at national, regional, bilateral, multilateral and international levels.
4. The development and strengthening of capacities to prevent, reduce and mitigate disasters is a top priority area to be addressed during the Decade so as to provide a strong basis for follow-up activities to the Decade.
5. Early warnings of impending disasters and their effective dissemination using telecommunications, including broadcast services, are key factors to successful disaster prevention and preparedness.
6. Preventive measures are most effective when they involve participation at all levels, from the local community through the national government to the regional and international level.
7. Vulnerability can be reduced by the application of proper design and patterns of development focused on target groups, by appropriate education and training of the whole community.
8. The international community accepts the need to share the necessary technology to prevent, reduce and mitigate

disaster, this should be made freely available and in a timely manner as an integral part of technical cooperation.

9. Environmental protection as a component of sustainable development consistent with poverty alleviation is imperative in the prevention and mitigation of natural disasters.
10. Each country bears the primary responsibility for protecting its people, infrastructure, and other national assets from the impact of natural disasters. The international community should demonstrate strong political determination required to mobilize adequate and make efficient use of existing resources, including financial, scientific and technological means, in the field of natural disaster reduction, bearing in mind the needs of the developing countries, particularly the least developed countries.

A. *Basis for the Strategy*

1. Natural disasters continue to strike and increase in magnitude, complexity, frequency and economic impact. Whilst the natural phenomena causing disasters are in most cases beyond human control, vulnerability is generally a result of human activity. Therefore, society must recognize and strengthen traditional methods and explore new ways to live with such risk, and take urgent actions to prevent as well as to reduce the effects of such disasters. The capacities to do so are available.
2. In this context the least developed countries, small island developing States and land-locked countries are the most vulnerable countries, as they are the least equipped to mitigate disasters. Developing countries affected by desertification, drought and other types of natural disasters are also equally vulnerable and insufficiently equipped to mitigate natural disasters.
3. In all countries the poor and socially disadvantaged groups suffer most from natural disasters and are equipped to cope with them. In fact, disasters contribute to social, economic, cultural and political disruption in urban and rural contexts,

each in its specific way. Large-scale urban concentrations are particularly fragile because of their complexity and the accumulation of population and infrastructures in limited areas.

4. Some patterns of consumption, production and development have the potential for increasing the vulnerability to natural disasters, particularly of the poor and socially disadvantaged groups. However, sustainable development can contribute to reduction of this vulnerability, if planned and managed in a way to ameliorate the social and economic conditions of the affected groups and communities.
5. Vulnerable developing countries should be enabled to revive, apply and share traditional methods to reduce the impact of natural disasters, supplemented and reinforced by access to modern scientific and technical knowledge. The existing knowledge and know-how should be studied and efforts should be made to ameliorate, develop and better apply them today.
6. Global social stability has become more fragile and reduction of natural disasters would contribute to reducing this fragility. In the effort towards effective disaster management, the full continuum from relief through rehabilitation, reconstruction and development to prevention must be the concept guiding actions towards the reduction of human and physical losses which remains the ultimate objective.
7. Notwithstanding the full continuum, disaster prevention is better than disaster response and achieving the goals, objectives and targets of the Decade as adopted by the relevant resolutions of the General Assembly would result in greatly reducing disaster losses. This requires maximum participation at community level which can mobilize considerable potential and traditional expertise in the application of the preventive measures.

B. *Assessment of the Status of Disaster Reduction Midway into the Decade*

8. Approaching the mid-point of the International Decade for Natural Disaster Reduction, the World Conference has

identified, on the basis of national reports and technical discussions, the following main accomplishments and failures:

A. Awareness of the potential benefits of disaster reduction is still limited to specialized circles and has not yet been successfully communicated to all sectors of society, in particular policy-makers and the general public. This is due to a lack of attention for the issue, insufficient commitment and resources for promotional activities at all levels;

B. At the same time, however, activities during the first years of the Decade in training, technical applications and research at local, national and international levels and in regional cooperation, have had positive results in some regions in reducing disaster losses;

C. Equally, the creation of the organizational framework called for by the General Assembly, which includes National Decade Committees and Focal Points and, at the international level, the Special High-Level Council, the Scientific and Technical Committee and the Decade secretariat, has laid the basis for intensified preventive and preparedness efforts in the second half of the Decade;

D. These new efforts in the field of disaster reduction have not systematically been part of multilateral and bilateral development policies;

E. Education and training programmes and facilities for people professionally involved and the public at large have not been sufficiently developed with a focus on ways and means to reduce disasters. Also the potential of the information media, industry, scientific community and the private sector at large has not been sufficiently mobilized;

F. It must be noted that not all entities of the United Nations system have contributed to the Decade's implementation to the extent possible and desired by the General Assembly in adopting its resolution 44/

236. In recent years emphasis has again been placed primarily on disaster response both within the United Nations and beyond. This has slowed down the momentum of the Decade's initial phase, based on the consensus of the importance of action before disasters strike;

G. A number of positive results have been achieved during the first five years of the Decade, although unevenly and not in the concerted and systematic way as envisaged by the General Assembly. Only if these achievements are recognized consolidated and accelerated; will the Decade be able to reach its goals and objectives and contribute to the development of a global culture of prevention. In particular, the existing tools which can yield improvements in disaster response, as part of a comprehensive approach towards disaster management, are not always utilized to the full extent of their potential;

H. There is a strong need to strengthen the resilience and self-confidence of local communities to cope with natural disasters through recognition and propagation of their traditional, knowledge, practices and values as part of development activities; and

I. Experience has demonstrated that, although not a part of the mandate of the Decade, the concept of the disaster reduction should be enlarged to cover natural and other disaster situations including environmental and technological disasters (Na-Techs) and their interrelationship which can have a significant impact on social, economic, cultural and environmental systems, in particular in developing countries.

C. Strategy for the *Year 2000 and Beyond*

9. The World Conference, based on adoption of the Principles and the assessment of the progress accomplished during the first half of the Decade, has formulated a Strategy for Disaster Reduction centred on the objective of saving human

lives and protecting property. The Strategy calls for an accelerated implementation of a Plan of Action to be developed from the following points:

A. Development of a global culture of prevention as an essential component of an integrated approach to disaster reduction;
B. Adoption of a policy of self-reliance in each vulnerable country and community comprising capacity-building as well as allocation and efficient 'use of resources;
C. Education and training in disaster prevention, preparedness and mitigation;
D. Development and strengthening of human resources and capabilities and capacity of research and development institutions for disaster reduction and mitigation;
E. Identification and networking of existing centres of excellence so as to enhance disaster prevention, reduction and mitigation activities;
F. Improvement of awareness in vulnerable communities, through a more active and constructive role of the media in respect of disaster reduction;
G. Involvement and active participation of the people in disaster reduction, prevention and preparedness, leading to improved risk management;
H. In the second half of the Decade, emphasis should be given to programmes that promote community-based approaches to vulnerability reduction;
I. Improved risk assessment, broader monitoring and communication forecasts and warnings;
J. Adoption of integrated policies for prevention of, preparedness for, and reponse to, natural disasters and other disaster situations including environmental and technological hazards;
K. Improved coordination and cooperation among ongoing national, regional and international disaster research activities, at universities, regional and subregional organizations and other technical and

scientific institutions, having in mind that links between causes and effects inherent to all types of disaster, should be investigated through interdisciplinary research;

L. Effective national legislation and administrative action, higher priority at the political decision-making level;

M. Placing higher priority on the compilation and exchange of information on natural disaster reduction, especially at regional and sub-regional levels, through the strengthening of existing mechanisms and improved use of communication techniques;

N. Promotion of regional and sub-regional cooperation between countries exposed to the same natural hazards through exchange of information, joint disaster reduction activities and other formal or informal means including the establishment or strengthening of regional and sub-regional centres;

O. Making available the existing technology for broader application to disaster reduction;

P. Integration of the private sector in disaster reduction efforts through promotion of business opportunities;

Q. Promotion of the involvement of non-governmental organizations in natural hazard management, in particular those dealing with environmental and related issues and including indigenous nongovernmental organizations; and

R. Strengthening the capacity of the United Nations system to assist in the reduction of losses from natural and related technological disasters, including coordination and evaluation of activities through the Decade and other mechanisms.

10. Based on the Principles and the Strategy and taking into account information provided to the Conference in the national summary reports presented by a large number of countries and in the scientific and technical presentations, the Conference adopts a Plan of Action for the future, comprising the following specific actions to be implemented

at the community and national levels, the sub-regional and regional levels, and the international level, through bilateral arrangements and international cooperation.

II. Plan of Action

A. *Recommendations for Action*

Activities at the Community and National Levels

11. During the remaining part of the Decade all countries are called upon to:
    - A. Express the political commitment to reduce their vulnerability, through declaration, legislation, policy decisions and action at the highest level, which would require the progressive implementation of disaster assessment and reduction plans at the national and community levels;
    - B. Encourage continued mobilization of domestic resources for disaster reduction activities;
    - C. Develop a risk assessment programme and emergency plans focusing efforts on disaster preparedness, response and mitigation, and design projects for sub-regional, regional and international cooperation, as appropriate;
    - D. Develop documented comprehensive national disaster management plans with emphasis on disaster reduction;
    - E. As appropriate, establish and/or strengthen National Committees for the Decade or clearly identified bodies charged with the promotion and coordination of disaster reduction actions;
    - F. Take measures to upgrade the resistance of important infrastructure and lifelines;
    - G. Give due consideration to the role of local authorities in the enforcement of safety standards and rules and strengthen the institutional capacities for natural disaster management at all levels;
    - H. Consider making use of NGO support for improved disaster reduction at the local level;

I. Incorporate disaster reduction prevention or mitigation in socio-economic development planning based on the assessment of the risk;

J. Consider the possibility of incorporating in their developmental plans the conducting of Environmental Impact Assessments with a view to disaster reduction;

K. Clearly identify specific disaster prevention needs which could use the knowledge or expertise that may be available from other countries or from the United Nations system, for instance, through training programmes designed to enhance human resources;

L. Endeavour to document all disasters;

M. Incorporate cost-effective technologies in reduction programmes, including forecasting and warning systems;

N. Establish and implement educational and information programmes aimed at generating general public awareness, with special emphasis on policy-makers and major groups, in order to ensure support for, and effectiveness of, disaster reduction programmes;

O. Enrol the media as a contributing sector in awareness raising, education and opinion building in order to increase recognition of the potential of disaster reduction to save human lives and protect property;

P. Set targets which specify how many distinct disaster scenarios can reasonably be given systematic attention by the end of the Decade;

Q. Stimulate genuine community involvement and empowerment of women and other socially disadvantaged groups at all stages of disaster management programmes in order to facilitate capacity building, which is an essential precondition for reducing vulnerability of communities to natural disasters;

R. Aim at the application of traditional knowledge, practices and values of local communities for disaster reduction, thereby recognizing these traditional coping mechanisms as a valuable contribution to the empowerment of local communities and the enabling of their spontaneous cooperation in all disaster reduction programmes.

Activities at the Regional and Sub-regional Levels

12. Considering the many common aspects of disaster vulnerability among countries of the same region or sub-region, cooperation among them should be strengthened by implementing the following actions:
   A. Establishing or strengthening of sub-regional or regional centres for disaster reduction and prevention which, in cooperation with international organizations and with a view to enhancing national capabilities, would perform one or more of the following functions:
      * Collecting and disseminating documentation and information to improve public awareness of natural disasters and the potential to reduce their impact;
      * Formulating education and training programmes and technical information exchanges aimed at human resource development; and
      * Supporting and strengthening natural disaster reduction mechanisms;
   B. Given the importance of vulnerability of developing countries, particularly least developed countries, technical, material and financial resources should be made available in support of concerned sub-regional or regional centres to strengthen regional and national capacities to reduce natural disasters;
   C. Improving the communications on natural disasters among the countries of the region in the context of preparedness and early warning systems;
   D. Establishing and/or strengthening early warning mechanisms for disaster reduction;
   E. Commemorating the International Day for Natural Disaster Reduction;

F. Establishing mutual assistance agreements and joint projects for disaster reduction within and between regions;
G. Reviewing periodically in regional political forums the progress made on disaster reduction;
H. Request and enable regional organizations to play an effective role in the implementation of relevant regional plans and programmes on natural disaster reduction;
I. The international community should give highest priority and special support to activities and programmes relating to natural disaster reduction at sub-regional or regional level in order to promote cooperation between countries exposed to the same risks;
J. As decided by the General Assembly, special attention should be given to the least developed countries in support of their activities in the field of natural disaster reduction;
K. Regional arrangements should be carried out in close coordination with and should supplement the national programmes for disaster reduction; and
L. The international community should assist the developing countries in establishing measures to integrate disaster prevention and reduction within the existing machinery and strategies at the national, sub-regional and regional levels for poverty eradication in order to achieve sustainable development.

Activities at the International Level, in particular through Bilateral Arrangements and Multilateral Cooperation

13. In the context of global interdependence and in the spirit of international cooperation, all activities to reduce disasters, in particular those laid down by the International Decade for Natural Disaster Reduction should be encouraged and supported in the following ways:
    A. It is recommended that extra-budgetary resources be provided for implementation of the Decade and,

therefore, that voluntary contributions from Governments, international organizations and other sources, including the private sector, be strongly encouraged. To this end, the Secretary-General is urged to ensure an effective and efficient administration of the Trust Fund for the Decade, established as requested in General Assembly Resolution 44/236;

B. It is recommended that donor countries should increase the priority on disaster prevention, mitigation and preparedness in their assistance programmes and budgets, either on bilateral or multilateral basis, including increasing contributions to and through the Decade Trust Fund, in order to support fully the implementation of the Yokohama Strategy and Plan of Action, particularly in developing countries;

C. Disaster prevention and mitigation should become an integrated component of development projects financed by multilateral financial institutions, including the regional development banks;

D. Integration of natural disaster reduction into development assistance programmes, through effective means, including as suggested in subparagraph 13(b) above;

E. Ensuring the cooperation in the area of research and science technology development related to natural disaster reduction in order to enhance the capacities of the developing countries to reduce their vulnerability in this respect;

F. The Trust Fund for the Decade should give priority in financing the establishment and strengthening of the early warning systems of the disaster prone developing countries particularly of the least developed, land-locked and small island developing States;

G. Ensuring that from the formulation phase development projects be designed in a way to contribute to reducing, and not increasing, vulnerability to disasters;

H. Improving the exchange of information on disaster reduction policies and technologies;

I. Encouraging and supporting ongoing efforts aimed at developing appropriate indicators of vulnerability (indices);

J. Reaffirmation of the roles of the Special High-Level Council and the Scientific and Technical Committee in promoting Decade activities, in particular the awareness of the benefits of disaster reduction;

K. Enhancing the activities of, and cooperation between organizations and programmes of the United Nations system, inter-governmental organizations, non-governmental organizations and the private sector related to disaster reduction, including more efficient use of existing resources;

L. Supporting efforts of Governments at the national and regional levels in the implementation of the priority areas of the Programme of Action for the Least Developed Countries for the 1990s, and the Programme of Action for the Sustainable Development of Small Island Developing States, related to the management of natural and environmental disasters through measures referred to in paragraph 13(b) above;

M. Providing wider support for the existing mechanism for disaster management and reduction of the United Nations system, in order to expand its capacity to give advice and practical assistance, as required, to countries facing natural disasters and other disaster situations including environmental and technological hazards;

N. Providing adequate support for Decade activities, including those of the secretariat of the Decade, in particular with a view to ensuring the timely implementation of the Yokohama Strategy and Plan of Action. In this regard it is time to consider proposals on ways and means to ensure functional security and continuity of the secretariat of the Decade, to the extent possible through the United Nations regular budget;

O. Recognition of the need for adequate coordination of international disaster reduction activities and strengthening of the mechanisms established for this purpose. International coordination should relate, in particular, to the formulation of development projects which provide assistance for disaster reduction and their evaluation;

P. Establishment or improvement, as a priority, of national, regional and international warning systems and more effective dissemination of warnings;

Q. Effective coordination of international disaster management, in particular by the United Nations system, is paramount for an integrated approach to disaster reduction and should, therefore, be strengthened; and

R. Holding of a review conference on natural disaster reduction at the end of the Decade in order to map a strategy for continued disaster reduction activities into the twenty-first century.

B. Proposals to the Conference

Included in an annex, to the report of the World Conference to the General Assembly. See A/CONF. 172/18/ Add.l.

III. Follow-up Action

14. With the aim of ensuring the early and successful implementation of the Yokohama Strategy and Plan of Action, the Conference decides to:

A. Transmit the report of the World Conference containing the Yokohama Strategy and Plan of Action for a Safer World: Guidelines for Natural Disaster Prevention, Preparedness and Mitigation, through the Economic and Social Council, to the General Assembly at its forty-ninth session;

B. Request the General Assembly to consider adopting a resolution endorsing the Yokohama Strategy and making an appeal to all countries to continue working towards the objective of a safer world for the twenty-first century;

C. Transmit the outcome of the World Conference to the mid-term global review conference on the implementation of the Programme of Action for least developed countries to be held in 1995, as decided by the General Assembly in its resolution 48/171, and to the Commission on Sustainable Development in the initial review of the implementation of the Programme of Action for the Sustainable Development of Small Island Developing States, undertaken by the Commission in 1996, in accordance with the Commission's Multi-Year Programme of Work;

D. Reaffirm the crucial importance of a substantial reduction in the loss of lives and in the physical damage caused by disasters by the year 2000 and of continuing the disaster reduction process beyond the end of this century, as appropriate;

E. Request the Secretary-General to ensure that the outcome of the Conference be given as wide as possible dissemination, including transmission of the Yokohama Strategy to relevant international and regional organizations, multilateral financial institutions and the regional development banks;

F. Request also the secretariat of the Decade to communicate the outcome of the Conference to national committees and focal points for the Decade, relevant non-governmental organizations, scientific and technical associations and the private sector, and to facilitate the review of the implementation of the Yokohama Strategy and Plan of Action and further planning by these institutions at the regional level before the year 2000;

G. Request the Secretary-General to submit an annual report to the General Assembly, based on information provided by Governments regional and international organizations, including the multilateral financial institutions and the regional development banks, the United Nations system and the non-governmental organization community on progress made in the implementation of the Yokohama Strategy.

H. Recommend the inclusion of a sub-item entitled "Implementation of outcome of the World Conference on Natural Disaster Reduction" in the provisional agenda of the Assembly under the item entitled "Environment and Sustainable Development"; and

I. Request that the United Nations, through the secretariat of the Decade, to provide Governments, upon request, with technical assistance in the preparation and development of disaster management plans and programmes.

About the International Decade for Natural Disaster Reduction

On entering the twenty-first century, population growth, ecological damage, rapid industrialization and socioeconomic imbalances make the risk of major disasters around the world higher than ever. We need not, however, be fatalistic about the vagaries of nature.

To make people aware of how much they can do to make themselves safer from natural disasters, the United Nations launched the International Decade for Natural Disaster Reduction (IDNDR, 1990-2000). The World Conference on Natural Disaster Reduction (Yokohama, 23-27 May 1994 was an important milestone in IDNDR's awareness-building process.

IDNDR works through IDNDR National Committees and Focal Points which exist in 138 countries. The IDNDR Secretariat, located in Geneva, is part of the UN Department of Humanitarian Affairs. The IDNDR Scientific and Technical Committee is an advisory body with experts in economics, social science, engineering, public health, industry, geology, meteorology, etc. A group of well-known personalities, the Special High-Level Council, promotes global awareness of disaster reduction. A UN inter-agency group works regularly with the IDNDR Secretariat, as well as a contact group of Geneva-based diplomatic missions.

IDNDR publishes a quarterly magazine, *STOP Disasters*, and conducts a promotional campaign on the second Wednesday of each October, designated as the International Day for Natural Disaster Reduction.

BIBLIOGRAPHY

Bhargava, Gopal, *Environmental challenges and ecological disaster: Global perspective*, Mittal, New Delhi, 1992.

Bhatia, B.M., *Famines in India: A Study in some aspects of the economic history of India with special references to food problem 1980-81*, Konar, Delhi 1991.

Dandekar, V.M., *A Survey of famine conditions in the affected Areas of Maharashtra and Mysore*, Gokhale Institute of Politics and Economics, Pune, 1972.

Mcalpin, Michell Burge, *Subject of famine: food crises and economic change in Western India*, 1860-1920 J.F. Princeton University Press, Princeton, 1983.

Moboisee, Roymond, M., *Industrial Security for strikes, riots and disasters*, Charles C. Thomas, Springfield, 1968.

Sharma, R.K., *Role of farm extension in drought management*, Agriculture Economic Research Centre, University of Delhi, 1990.

Singh, K. Suresh, *The Indian Famine 1967: A study in crises and change*: People's Publishing House, New Delhi, 1975.

Uppal, J.N., *Bengal famine of 1943: A man-made tragedy*, Atma Ram, Delhi, 1984.

Reports

National Policy Analysis-Workshop on Natural Disaster Reduction, organised by Administrative Staff College of India, Hyderabad, December 16-20, 1991.

Workshop on Uttarkashi Earthquake, organised by DEQ-UOR, December, 1991.

World Congress on Natural Hazard Reduction, organised by The Institution of Engineers (India), New Delhi, January 10-14, 1992.

Fourth Session of the Scientific and Technical Committee of IDNDR, organised by Ministry of Agriculture, Govt. of India, February 1-5, 1993, New Delhi.

National Seminar on Hydrological Hazards - Prevention and Mitigation, organised by DH-UOR, March, 1993.

Workshop on Natural Disaster Reduction in the South Asia Region, New Delhi, March 30 - April 2, 1994.

Symposium of Earthquake Engineering, organised by DEQ-UOR and ISET, November, 1994.

Seminar on comprehensive Flood Loss Prevention and Management, organised by ESCAP hosted by Govt. of India, 28-29 September, 1994, New Delhi.

International Conference on Wing Engineering, organised by Indian Society for Wing Engineering, Roorkee, at New Delhi, January 9-13, 1995.

Workshop on Himalayan Eco-Development and Natural Disaster Reduction, organised by NCDM, New Delhi, November, 1995.

International Seminar on Mathematical Modelling of Atmospheric and Oceanic Processes, organised by Department of Mathematics, Berhampur University, Berhampur, Orissa, December 18-21, 1995.

International Conference on Disasters and Mitigation, organised by Anna University, Chennai, January 19-22, 1996.

References

Das, C.R.: Infrastructure Needs of the Coal Industry-in Gondwana, *Journal of Indian Institute of Coal Management*, Ranchi.

Della-Giustina, Daniel E.: *Safety and Environmental Management*, N.Y., Van Nostrand Reinhold Publication.

Dutta, S.K.: Prevention of Accidents in Open Cast Mines. In I, Directorate General of Mines Safety (Ranchi Region).

Govt. of India, Ministry of Labour, *Journal of Mines Safety*, Annual Reports and Standard Notes.

Heyel, Card (ed.): *The Encyclopaedia and Management*: N.Y. Van Nstrand Reinhold Co.

Mahajan, Vinay: Mines Safety in India-Past, Present and Future, *Journal of Indian Institute of Coal Management*, Vol. 2, No. 1, March, 1997.

Molak, Vlasta, (ed.): *Fundamentals of Risk Analysis and Risk Management*, N.Y.: Lewis Publishers, 1997.

Mullen, Samuel: *Emergency Planning Guide for Utilities*, Oklahoma: Penn Well Book, 1994.

Proceeding of the 7th National Symposium on Environment - Indian School of Mines, Dhanbad, 5-7 February, 1998.

Ridley, John (ed.): *Safety at Work*, U.K.: Butterworth Heinemann Publication, 1994.

Sarkar, S.K. and Banerjee, G.: Coal Mines Disaster - The Inevitable Recurring Cycle. Paper presented in the Workshop on Disaster Management in Mines and Mining Areas; August 30-31, 1994.

Sharan, R. and Sharma, G.P.: Impact of Coal Mining on Social Ecology: A Tentative Note. In *Socio-Economic Impacts of Environment*, (ed.), B.B. Dhar and N.C. Saxena, Ashish Publishing House, New Delhi: 1993.

Turner, Berry A. and Pidgeon, Nick F.: *Man-made Disaster*: Butterworth Heinemann Publication, London.

Bannerjee, D.N.: *Land Revenue System in Bengal and Bihar*, London.

Hunter, W.W.: *Annals of Rural Bengal*, Reprint-Calcutta.

James, J.F.W.: *Selections from the Correspondence of the Revenue Chiefs of Bihar*, Patna.

John Shore's Letter to the Committee of Revenue, 5 December, 1783.

Geddes, J.C.: *Administrative Experience Recorded in Former Famines*, Oxford, 1875.

Campbell, George: *Accounts of Famine*, Oxford, 1874.

Srivastava, H.S.: *The History of Indian Famines*, Agra 1971.

Lovedy, A.: *History and Economics of Indian Famines*, London, 1914.

Letter from the Resident of the Chief of Patna, 1 June, 1770.

Hussain, Ghulam, *Siyar-ul-Mutakherin*: Translated by Mustafa Haji, Calcutta, 1902.

Shore, Kalicharan: *Famines in Bengal*, Calcutta 1844.

Smith, Adam: *Wealth of Nations*, London, 1917.

Dutt, R.C.: *Economic History of British India*, London, 1956.

INDEX

W

Y

Z

N